Introduction to Electro-Acoustic Music

789.9   S377i

Schrader, Barry
AUTHOR
Introduction to electro-acoustic
TITLE   music

Introduction to Electro-Acoustic Music

Barry Schrader
California Institute of the Arts

Prentice-Hall, Inc., Englewood Cliffs, New Jersey 07632

Library of Congress Cataloging in Publication Data

Schrader, Barry.
    Introduction to electro-acoustic music.

    Bibliography: p. 211
    Includes index.
    1. Electronic music—History and criticism.
2. Concrete music—History and criticism.   3. Computer
music—History and criticism.   I. Title.
ML1092.S35   789.9   81-19252
ISBN   0-13-481515-7   AACR2

To Donald Beikman: for initial questions and continuing answers

Editorial production/supervision by Peter Roberts
Cover design by Wanda Lubelska
Manufacturing buyer: Harry P. Baisley

ISBN 0-13-481515-7

Printed in the United States of America

10   9   8   7   6   5   4   3   2   1

Prentice-Hall International, Inc., *London*
Prentice-Hall of Australia Pty. Limited, *Sydney*
Prentice-Hall of Canada, Ltd., *Toronto*
Prentice-Hall of India Private Limited, *New Delhi*
Prentice-Hall of Japan, Inc., *Tokyo*
Prentice-Hall of Southeast Asia Pte. Ltd., *Singapore*
Whitehall Books Limited, *Wellington, New Zealand*

CONTENTS

123244

PREFACE

Introduction to Electro-Acoustic Music is a book about a kind of music composed since 1945. The book differs from other volumes on "electronic music" in several ways. It is a book about *music* and is the first work to include numerous descriptions of significant compositions available on record.

This book is intended for people who want to learn more about a music that is made differently, and often sounds differently, from instrumental music composed during the same period. The author assumes no technical expertise nor does he dwell on the technology associated with electro-acoustic music. He gives only enough technical information to enable the reader to understand the new tools composers and performers have used in recent years. The author wants you to hear what he hears in electro-acoustic music—to understand the musical ideas and intentions of the creators of this music.

In most rapidly developing art forms artists influence each other—build on, and transform each other's ideas. This process has been accelerated in electro-acoustic music through the use of technology, which itself is changing rapidly. For this reason the author employs an historical approach to his subject. With each new direction taken, the author explains how currents of musical thinking interact with new technology. Did composers try something different because they encountered new machinery? Or did new ideas about music force them to look for, and in some cases actually invent, new instruments?

The passing of time results in an aesthetic distance that has recently shed new light on the literature of electro-acoustic music. Two observations stand out. First, many unmusical works have been, and continue to be produced by individuals who come to the field because of a fascination with the technology alone. The tendency to let the equipment dictate musical ideas is at first hidden by "newness." The passing of time exposes the absence of musical content in these works and we are able to identify those compositions that have musical value which transcends the technology employed.

This realization leads to a second observation, a personal one. Composers continue to produce significant works using the older techniques. Musique Concrète, analog synthesis, and so on, remain as viable a medium for the composer as the human voice and the string quartet. Luciano Berio feels differently. Toward the end of this book he declares "that the electronic tape piece is dead." This is hardly a new idea. In 1970 Steve Reich wrote that "electronic music as such will gradually die and be absorbed into the ongoing music of people singing and playing instruments."

Although the development of sophisticated live-performance instruments for electro-acoustic music is moving quickly, most of the music heard in the Western world is produced in the recording studio and not performed "live." The techniques used in much commercial music are largely the same as those used in tape music. I suspect Reich is correct in one sense: Musical style is increasingly less dependent on technology. We have music: Some of it is performed live and some of it is recorded. This distinction does make a difference but it is no longer the major influence on musical style.

To be able to listen intelligently to electro-acoustic music gives one a deep understanding of the evolving culture of the second half of the twentieth century. The following pages will enable the reader to take this step.

Jon H. Appleton

Dartmouth College
Hanover, New Hampshire

ACKNOWLEDGMENTS

It has been said that writing a book is something like birthing a baby. Assuming the appropriateness of this analogy, this book may be said to have had many midwives, and the following acknowledgments are in order:

To Jon H. Appleton, without whose initial suggestion and continuing encouragement this book would not exist;

To John Payne for technical advice and assistance;

To Helen De Francesco for typing and transcribing;

To Barbara and Leonid Hambro for reading, suggesting, and encouraging;

To Narciso Mones for putting up with stuff and clutter;

To the library faculty and staff of the California Institute of the Arts for service above and beyond the due dates;

To many composers: Luciano Berio, Pauline Oliveros, Morton Subotnick, Jean-Claude Risset, and Gordon Mumma for their time, patience, and consideration in allowing me to interview them; and to Louis and Bebe Barron, Earle Brown, Stephen Mosko, Mel Powell, Vladimir Ussachevsky, and Frits Weiland for reading and criticizing portions of this book as well as providing much valuable information.

Most important, I would like to thank Donald Beikman, to whom this book is dedicated, for his many and excellent comments and suggestions.

I would also like to make the proper acknowledgments for illustrations appearing on the following pages:

Page 12: Structures sérielles de *l'Étude aux chemins de fer* from Pierre Schaeffer, *A la recherche d'une Musique Concrète* (Paris: *Éditions du Seuil*, 1952), p. 33. Used by permission of Georges Borchardt, Inc.

Pages 17, 21, 41, 42, 43, and 44: Gustav Ciamaga, "The Tape Studio," in *The Development and Practice of Electronic Music*, ed. Jon H. Appleton and Ronald C. Perera (Englewood Cliffs, N.J.: Prentice-Hall, Inc., 1975), pp. 94, 95, 96, 100, 104, and 107. Reprinted by permission of Prentice-Hall, Inc.

Page 27: John Cage, *Williams Mix*, page 5. Copyright © 1960 by Henmar Press, Inc. Reprint permission granted by C. F. PETERS CORPORATION, New York.

Page 71: Eleven examples of Oskar Fischinger's *ornamente sound* drawings reprinted by the kind permission of Elfrieda Fischinger and the Fischinger Archives.

Page 87: Karlheinz Stockhausen, *Studie II*, page one of score. Copyright © 1956 by Universal Edition (London) Ltd., London. Used by permission of European American Music Distributors Corp., sole U.S. agent for Universal Edition, London.

Page 110: Page one of *Symfonia* by Boguslaw Schäffer. Copyright © 1968 by Przedstawicielstwo Wydawnictw Polskich, Warsaw, Poland.

Barry Schrader
November, 1981

1

INTRODUCTION

THE TERMINOLOGY
OF ELECTRO-ACOUSTIC MUSIC

The world of electro-acoustic music is larger than many people imagine. There are many regions and subregions, and perhaps as many styles as there are composers in the field. The term *electro-acoustic music* refers to any music that is produced, changed, or reproduced by electronic means.[1] By this definition, as Milton Babbitt has remarked, the playing of a phonograph record could technically fit into the category of electro-acoustic music. The definition of electro-acoustic music is so broad that it serves only to distinguish such music from *acoustic music*, music produced by naturally resonating bodies. While a pipe organ, for example, produces sound acoustically, a Yamaha organ produces sound electronically.

Since electro-acoustic music is such a general designation, several other terms have come into use to refer to specific means of production and particular sound sources used in the composition of electro-acoustic music.

[1] *Electrophonic music* is a seldom-used British term having the same meaning as electro-acoustic music.

Musique concrète refers to any electro-acoustic music that uses acoustic sounds as source material. If one took music played on a piano, which is an acoustic instrument, and recorded and changed certain aspects of the sound by means of a tape recorder, the resulting composition would be classified as *musique concrète*.[2] The term *musique concrète* was coined by Pierre Schaeffer in 1948. His work is discussed in Chapter 2.

Electronic music refers to music in which the source, or original, sound material has been electronically produced. This is usually done with electronic *oscillators* that produce an electrical signal that is changed into a physical vibration by means of amplifiers and loudspeakers. *Synthesizers* are integrated systems for creating electronic music. They contain oscillators for producing electronic signals as well as several other devices for modifying the quality of the sound. Buchla, Moog, and Arp are among the more commonly known makes of synthesizers, although there are many other manufacturers.

Computer music is a type of electronic music in which a computer is used to generate the sound material.[3] In the computer music studio, the composer usually sends information to the computer by means of IBM cards or a computer terminal. The computer then translates this information into binary code that is recorded on a magnetic tape or disk. Through yet another process of translation, the information is recorded on a conventional tape recorder and can be reproduced as sound.

Electro-acoustic music compositions can contain both musique concrète and electronic music material. In this instance, neither term satisfactorily describes such work. In 1952, Vladimir Ussachevsky remedied this problem by creating the term *tape music*, which refers to a composition that uses recorded sound material whether it is acoustic or electronic in origin. Since tape music depends on tape recorders for the recording and reproducing of sound material, tape music composition is almost always done in an electro-acoustic music studio. *Studio composition* is one of the most important developments of twentieth-century musical practice. Studio composition differs from traditional compositional practice in that the composer produces the final result, the *sounding music*, by himself. There is no live performance, in the traditional sense, of a tape composition. When some kind of live performance of electro-acoustic music does occur, the work is an example of *live/electronic music*.

Live/electronic music usually refers to one of three situations. It may designate a performance of electronic music in which all of the music is

---

[2] *Changed* refers to various tape manipulation techniques, such as direction change, speed change, and splicing. These and other tape manipulation techniques are discussed in Part II.

[3] The term *computer music* is sometimes used to describe music composed for instruments with the aid of the computer in making compositional choices. Since this is not strictly electronic music, this designation is not used in this book.

produced live by synthesizers or other electronic instruments. In this situation, no prerecorded sound material would be used. This is often referred to as a *real-time performance*, which means that the composition is performed in the same amount of time that it takes to hear it. This is very different from an electronic music work composed in a studio; such a composition usually takes much more time to create than it does to hear. Another meaning of live/electronic music is the live performance by one or more performers using acoustic instruments or voice, along with a prerecorded tape.[4] Still another definition of live/electronic music could be a combination of acoustic instruments with real-time electronic performance. Since the term *live/electronic music* is so ambiguous, concerts are usually labeled as to their exact presentation, such as "music for live electronics," "music for instruments and tape," and "music for live electronics and instruments." Other combinations are also possible, such as live and prerecorded electronic music, and live instrumental music modified in real-time by prerecorded electronic material.

The terminology of electro-acoustic music originated and developed with the music itself. This has unavoidably resulted in some confusion to the entire field of electro-acoustic music instead of just music using electronically generated sound. Even the Library of Congress catalog seems confused on this issue, sometimes placing a musique concrète composition under the electronic music classification. The chart shown in Figure 1-1, while in no way complete, will serve to put the classifications of electro-acoustic music that have been discussed into proper perspective.

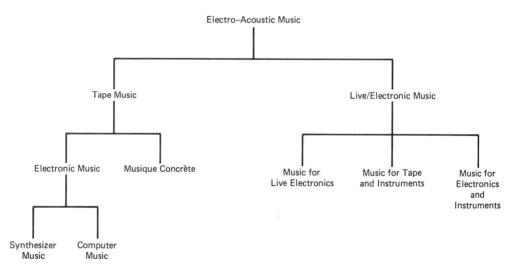

Figure 1-1   Types of Electro-Acoustic Music.

[4] This is sometimes referred to as *live plus electronic music.*

There are several other subclasses of electro-acoustic music. These are discussed in later chapters.

THE PLACE
OF ELECTRO-ACOUSTIC MUSIC

Since the early 1950s, when the first musique concrète and electronic music studios were established, interest in electro-acoustic music has grown rapidly. Today most colleges and universities with music departments have electronic music studios, and a few schools offer majors in electro-acoustic music composition. Many radio and television productions use electronic music, and it is not unusual to find electro-acoustic music in scores composed for major films. Electro-acoustic music has been composed for ballet and theater productions and can often be heard in art galleries and museums accompanying many different kinds of showings. Morton Subotnick composed electronic music specifically for use in elevators.[5]

Why do so many composers work with electro-acoustic music? The answer is that electro-acoustic music presents new resources for the composer to explore. Composers have always been interested in extending their compositional resources. When Cristofori invented the pianoforte in 1709, composers were presented with new compositional possibilities. Because composers such as C.P.E. Bach explored the possibilities of the new instrument and wrote for it, the piano eventually replaced the older harpsichord and clavichord. Every existing musical instrument was new at some time and presented composers with a different technology. Electro-acoustic music systems and instruments are simply the most recent development in the technology of musical sound.

But electro-acoustic music represents more than new instrumental possibilities; it also presents new ways of thinking about music. New timbres can be created by processing acoustic or electronic sound. Timbres can be changed or transformed into totally different sounds. Rhythms too difficult for human performers can be easily realized by electronic means. Sounds can move from speaker to speaker in any manner a composer specifies, thus enlarging the physically spatial aspect of music.

Many composers like the medium of electro-acoustic music because of the control it allows them over their work. A composer working in an electronic music studio is at the same time composer, performer, and recording engineer. It is possible to control all aspects of the music without relying on interpreters. Perhaps more important, the music can be heard as it is being composed; there is no need to wait for months or years in order to

---

[5] Morton Subotnick, *Music for Twelve Elevators*, 1969. This work was commissioned by the Kauffman Construction Co., New York. Unfortunately, the installation was removed after only a few days because the music scared some of the passengers.

hear a performance. This instantaneous feedback allows composers to develop their ideas as well as their compositional maturity.

LISTENING TO ELECTRO-ACOUSTIC MUSIC

Even though the instances of electro-acoustic music are constantly increasing, many people continue to have a stereotyped notion of what it is. The term *electronic music* may bring to their minds associations of "spacey" sounds or science-fiction film sound effects. In the early days of electro-acoustic music this association did not seem uncalled for, since both electronic music and "outer space" represented unknown regions to most people. The electronic music score composed by Louis and Bebe Barron for the 1956 MGM film *Forbidden Planet* popularized this notion, since it was many people's first experience with electronic music. To other individuals, electronic music may be simply "bleeps and bloops" that they have heard as sound effects in some commercial or film. Still others may think of *Switched on Bach* as typifying the sound of electronic music.

To say that a work of music is electronic music does not describe it any more than to say that a work written for orchestra is orchestral music. Both designations describe the means used to produce the sound. If one had heard only one orchestral work, one might suppose that all orchestral music sounded like that work. If that orchestral performance was heard in association only with dancing, one might suppose as well that orchestral music was only suitable as an accompaniment to dance. While these examples may seem rather ridiculous, people with limited conscious experience of electro-acoustic music are often so uninformed.

The fact is that the types and styles of electro-acoustic music are just as varied as are those of orchestral music, if not more so. While the Barrons' score for *Forbidden Planet* is an effective science-fiction film score, and Walter Carlos's *Switched on Bach* is a good transcription of Bach for the Moog Synthesizer, neither of these examples typifies electronic music any more than Ravel's *Bolero* represents all orchestral music.

The listener who begins to explore the world of electro-acoustic music will find a surprising array of music styles. The differences that exist from work to work are due primarily to the different ideas and aesthetics of the composers. This is as true for electro-acoustic music as it is for all contemporary art music.[6] Many listeners experience difficulty in comprehend-

---

[6] Music can be divided into two general categories: folk music and art music. The distinction is made on the basis of the knowledge required to compose the music. The techniques and concepts of art music require special training and usually necessitate formalized education, while those of folk music can be learned by rote and generally demand less technical proficiency. Using this definition, most popular music is folk music, although there are certainly many gray areas that are difficult to label. Although there is a great deal of contemporary popular electronic music, it is not dealt with in this volume. Therefore, when the term "contemporary music" is used in this book, it refers to contemporary art music.

ing a certain composition because they are not familiar with the context of the piece. The context of older or more conventional music seems "natural" to most people because they have experienced it from childhood. To understand music that exists within a different framework requires a conscious learning experience and some effort on the part of the listener. For those who are open to new ideas and are willing to accept new thoughts, the world of electro-acoustic music holds exciting and rewarding discoveries.

PART

I

Musique Concrète and Tape Manipulation Techniques

2
PIERRE SCHAEFFER
AND THE ÉTUDES
OF 1948

THE BEGINNINGS OF MUSIQUE CONCRÈTE

The exact beginnings of musique concrète are difficult to pinpoint. In order for musique concrète to come into existence, it was first necessary to be able to record sound information. By 1930, the phonograph and the optical sound track for film had been invented and developed to the point of practical use. Several composers and film-makers experimented with these recording mediums: In 1928 Walther Ruttmann composed a sound track montage for film without visuals; during 1929 and 1930 Paul Hindemith and Ernst Toch produced several short phonograph studies; and between 1933 and 1937, Arthur Honegger and other composers manipulated sound tracks for their film music. Most of these and other early experiments in the manipulation of recorded sound have been lost or largely forgotten.[1] It is not until 1948 that we begin to have a continuous and recorded history of musique concrète, a history that begins with the works and ideas of Pierre Schaeffer.

[1] For a discussion of these and other early experiments in electro-acoustic music see Otto Luening, "Origins," in *The Development and Practice of Electronic Music,* ed. John H. Appleton and Ronald C. Perera. (Englewood Cliffs, NJ: Prentice-Hall, Inc., 1975), pp. 1-21.

Pierre Schaeffer (b. 1910, Nancy, France) received diplomas from L'École Polytechnique and L'École de Télécommunication de la Radio-Diffusion-Télévision Française and began his professional life as a radio engineer and broadcaster. He had been working with the R.T.F. in Paris when, early in 1948, he conceived the idea of "a concert of locomotives": a musical work based on train sounds.[2] Schaeffer had at his disposal the resources of the R.T.F. studios: phonograph turntables; phonograph disc recording devices; mixers, allowing him to combine two or more audio signals into one; and the considerable library of sound effects records owned by the studio.[3]

THE ÉTUDES OF 1948

Schaeffer spent several months experimenting with the technology available to him. He discovered that he could record sound material on locked-groove discs that repeated instead of spiraling inward like normal phonograph records. These locked-groove discs allowed him to make loops of sound that created repetitive rhythmic patterns.

Using these techniques and sound effects recordings of trains, Schaeffer composed the *Étude aux chemins de fer*, the first piece of musique concrète, in April 1948. This three-minute work contains various train sounds: wheels clacking along the track, steam escaping from the boiler and cylinders, whistles calling out various signals.

Schaeffer decided to call his work musique concrète because of the ways it differed from "traditional" music. Instrumental music, he noted, was "abstract":

> The qualification of "abstract" is used to describe ordinary music because it is first conceived of in the mind, then notated on paper, and finally realized only by instrumental performance. Musique concrète, on the other hand, begins with pre-existing sound elements, which may be music or noise. These elements are then experimentally manipulated and a montage is created. The final composition is a result of these experiments and the ideas contained in the sketches

[2] Pierre Schaeffer, *A la recherche d'une musique concrète* (Paris: Éditions du Seuil, 1952), p. 18. This book contains detailed accounts of Schaeffer's early work with musique concrète as well as his ideas for future application.

[3] Although Vlademar Poulsen had described a magnetic recording device (the Telegraphon) as early as 1898, and the Marconi-Stille recorder had been invented in 1933 and the AEG Magnetophon in 1935, they used cumbersome and inefficient steel tape and were not in common commercial use. Plastic recording tape was developed at the end of the Second World War but was not readily available until the early 1950s. Schaeffer, therefore, had only disc recording and playback facilities in 1948 and did not switch to tape recorders until 1951, a change that caused him some consternation.

for the work. These sketches, however, cannot resemble traditional music notation.[4]

Thus, according to Schaeffer, "traditional" music begins with asbstract ideas that become concrete only in performance, while his "new" music starts with concrete material that is made abstract during experimentation and composition.

By Schaeffer's own admission, traditional music notation is of little or no value in composing musique concrète.[5] Yet he found it necessary and helpful to produce a structural sketch for *Étude aux chemins de fer*. This sketch, shown in Figure 2-1, demonstrates Schaeffer's compositional thinking at the time as well as the inseparable link between the music and the technology.

One of the first things one notes is that the sketch is laid out in series of events. Series I is followed by the same material presented backwards, 1/I. This *retrograde motion* may be evidence of the influence of twelve-tone procedures.[6] Other devices used in the construction of this *Étude* are palindrome constructions (system 6), overlapping (systems 7 and 8), and variations of original material.[7]

Perhaps the most important feature of this sketch is the way it reveals Schaeffer's use of repetition. The locked-groove disc technique was Schaeffer's most important tool: It allowed him to create repetition and, therefore, rhythmic and metric patterns. The Arabic numerals below the lowercase letters on the first system represent meter signatures. Thus fragment a1 is a measure of 4/4, fragment b1, a measure of 3/4, and so on; lowercase e, f, and g are "pinpoints" of sound, although it is not clear how they differ from a 1/4 measure unless a change in tempo occurs. Since these metric measures are repeated to create the larger fragments (AI, BI, etc.) and each fragment is restated in a series retrograde or variation, the basic principle of construction of *Étude aux chemins de fer* is repetition. This constant use of repetition is a result of Schaeffer's technical resources, the sound loop technique being his main device. It is impossible, therefore, to separate the

[4] Schaeffer, *A la recherche d'une musique concrète*, p. 35.

[5] The notation of electro-acoustic music is as much of a problem today as it was in 1948.

[6] It is not within the scope of this book to deal with twelve-tone and serial music. For the reader who is not sufficiently acquainted with these ideas, a good explanation is to be found in Eric Salzman's *Twentieth-Century Music: An Introduction* (Englewood Cliffs, NJ: Prentice-Hall, Inc., 1967), pp. 112-141. Schaeffer does make reference to twelve-tone techniques with regard to the scheme for *Étude aux chemins de fer* in Pierre Schaeffer, "Introduction à la musique concrète," *Polyphonie*, 6 (1950), 50.

[7] The use of the term *system* in this context is the same as that for traditional music scores. See Gardner Read, *Music Notation*, 2nd ed. (New York: Taplinger Press, 1969), pp. 37-38.

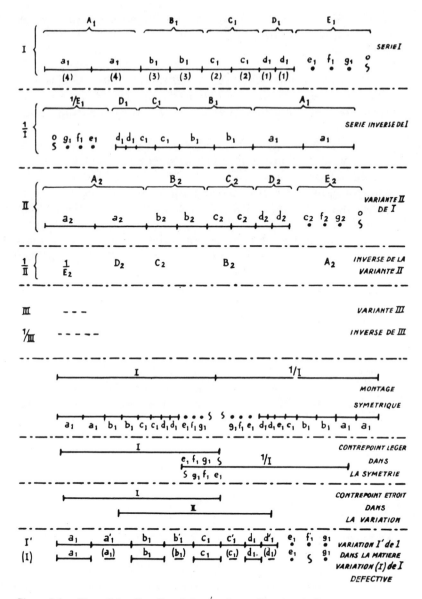

Figure 2.1   Pierre Schaeffer: Sketch for *Étude aux Chemins de Fer.*

locked-groove techique from the composition produced by it. Schaeffer even went so far as to make the act of repetition a basic creative principle: "Repeat the same sound fragment: It is not the same, it has become music."[8]

It is important to note that this interplay between technology and musical thought has occurred throughout the history of music. The music

[8] Schaeffer, *A la recherche d'une musique concrète*, p. 21.

staff was invented to accommodate the needs of organum; but once this was achieved, the new technology of the staff allowed for the development of polyphony, which then made further developments of notation necessary. Schaeffer's ideas about using train sounds as musical material depended upon using the recording technology of the time. This technology partially dictated the compositional procedures, aesthetics, and theories that led to the completed work.

Schaeffer's next work of musique concrète was the *Étude aux tourniquets*. The sound sources for this piece were two "tourniquets" (toy whistling tops), a xylophone, three "zanzis" (African finger pianos), and four small bells. Since all of the sounds are clearly pitched, this etude resembles traditional music more than the *Étude aux chemins de fer*, the result being that of a tiny toy orchestra. The locked-groove repetitions are again prominent, but Schaeffer expanded his technical vocabulary. By playing back recordings at various speeds, he discovered that reproducing a recording at a slower or faster speed not only changed its pitch but also created interesting timbral modifications.

Schaeffer composed three more etudes in 1948: *Étude violette*, *Étude noire* (both for piano sounds), and *Étude aux casseroles*, also called *Étude pathetique*. Of the five etudes, *Étude aux casseroles* contained the largest number of sound sources: saucepan covers twirling on a table top, accordion and harmonica sounds, the chanting of monks, Balinese music, the chugging of canal boats, piano sounds, and sounds of the human voice, including coughing.

On October 5, 1948, the five etudes were broadcast over the French radio under the title "Concert de Bruits." This "concert of noises" was the first public presentation of musique concrète. As might be expected, the audience reaction was mixed. Schaeffer received dozens of letters offering him congratulations, criticisms, and, of course, advice. The *Étude aux casseroles* proved to be the favorite.[9]

THE IMPORTANCE
OF SCHAEFFER'S WORK

It is difficult to assess the originality of Schaeffer's early work. He was aware of the much earlier work of Luigi Russolo and the futurists who presented concerts of "noises."[10] He also knew of John Cage's work with prepared piano. Schaeffer does not note any of the previous experiments in sound manipulation, and it is plausible that he rediscovered the results of previous

[9] Schaeffer, *A la recherche d'une musique concrète*, p. 32.

[10] As early as 1914 Russolo and his followers had presented concerts using such noise instruments as buzzers, exploders, howlers, roarers, and shufflers. For an excellent discussion of the Futurist movement, see Rosa (Trillo) Clough, *Futurism: The Story of a Modern Art Movement: A New Appraisal* (New York: Greenwood Press, 1969).

experiments. But the importance of a work of art does not rest solely on its novelty.

Speaking of *Étude aux chemins de fer*, Lowell Cross makes several valuable observations.

> The significance of *Étude aux chemins de fer* results from the following attributes: 1) the act of composition was accomplished by a technological process, 2) the work could be replayed innumerable times in precisely the same manner, 3) the replaying was not dependent upon a human "performer," and 4) the basic elements were "concrete," thereby offering the listener a mode of audition quite different from that of perceiving "abstract" music.[11]

These attributes, however, are not unique to Schaeffer's work, for they could also apply to the work of his predecessors. There are other facets of Schaeffer's work that are more important.

Schaeffer developed a theory of composition based on available technology. His procedures and aesthetics were linked with his belief that the abstraction of any concrete sound was possible. Sounds could be removed from their usual context and changed by manipulation. This meant that any sound source could be used for musical purposes.

Schaeffer documented his work in *A la recherche d'une musique concrète*. More than a personal record, this book allowed others to study his work and repeated his experiments. Schaeffer also tried to point the way to future developments of musique concrète.

The etudes of 1948 were not isolated experiments. Schaeffer continued to compose musique concrète, developing his ideas and expanding his technology. Earlier attempts at sound manipulation, however novel for their time, seem stillborn by comparison.

Schaeffer's work led to the founding of the first institutionally sponsored musique concrète studio. The R.T.F. Studio, begun in 1951, attracted many composers, such as Pierre Boulez, Pierre Henry, Darius Milhaud, Oliver Messiaen, and Karlheinz Stockhausen.

One of the most interesting facets of Schaeffer's early work is that he successfully utilized methods of sound manipulation similar to the basic *tape manipulation techniques*. There are five basic tape manipulation techniques:

1. tape loops
2. cutting and splicing
3. speed change

[11] Lowell Cross, "Electronic Music, 1948-1953," *Perspectives of New Music*, 7, no. 1 (Fall-Winter), 42.

4. direction change
5. tape delay.

Schaeffer's use of locked-groove discs created effects similar to those of tape loops. In selecting only part of a sound event, such as often occurs in *Étude aux chemins de fer* and *Étude aux casseroles*, Schaeffer effectively altered certain aspects of the event. This is similar to what can be done with certain tape cutting and splicing techniques. He also worked with speed change when he played back a record at different speeds.

The advent of the tape rcorder allowed for greater flexibility in performing these and other manipulations of sound. Tape manipulation techniques offered the composer new and exciting areas for exploration.

DISCOGRAPHY

Schaeffer, Pierre.   *Études.* Philips 6521-021.

FOR FURTHER LISTENING

Schaeffer, Pierre.   *Suite pour 14 instruments.* Philips 6521-021.   Schaeffer composed this work after the *Études of 1948.* This was his first attempt to use his disc techniques to produce an extended composition.

Schaeffer, Pierre and Pierre Henry.   *Symphonie pour un homme seul.* Philips 6521-021.   Written in 1950, this was the first collaboration between Schaeffer and Henry. Its eleven sections make use of Schaeffer's disc techniques on a grand and dramatic scale.

3
TAPE LOOPS

TAPE LOOP TECHNIQUES

Tape loops are made by connecting or *splicing* the ends of a piece of recording tape so that a loop is formed. Usually the loop contains prerecorded sound material. When played back on a tape recorder, the loop can repeat as long as the composer wishes. Tape loops can be of almost any length. The extremes of length are, of course, dictated by the equipment being used, but tape loops can commonly be of from one second to several minutes duration. Figure 3-1 illustrates a short tape loop.

Here a heavy cylindrical object has been placed to the rear center of the *transport* of the tape recorder.[1] This allows the proper tension for the playing of the tape to be maintained. For a longer loop, objects such as microphone stands can be used to maintain tension for points outside the

---

[1] The tape transport is the turntables, motors, and associated tape guides and tension arms. When speaking of a transport that includes head assembly, the term *tape deck* is usually used, although "deck" and "transport" are often used interchangeably. The term *tape recorder* refers to a self-contained unit including preamplifiers, power amplifiers, and, usually, built-in speakers.

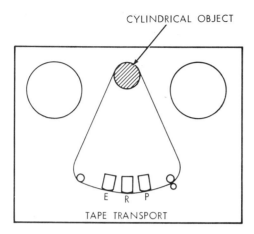

CYLINDRICAL OBJECT

E R P

TAPE TRANSPORT

Figure 3-1 A Short Tape Loop.

space of the tape transport. Very long tape loops are created by using endless loop tape *cartridges* similar to commercial available eight-track tape cartridges.

COMPOSING WITH TAPE LOOPS

The Early Work of Steve Reich

Steve Reich (b. 1936, New York City) has worked extensively with tape loops. In 1964 Reich made a recording at San Francisco's Union Square of a black preacher, Brother Walter, preaching about the Flood. Reich was impressed with the musical quality of Brother Walter's speech and made tape loops of short sections of his sermon, experimenting with various compositional possibilities. He extracted the words "its gonna rain," and made a tape loop of this material. This loop was the basic material for Reich's composition *Its Gonna Rain* (1965). At first, Reich tried to line up two identical tape loops on two tape recorders, keeping some particular relationship between the two loops. The result of this procedure would be to create a kind of canon, or round. Since the two tape recorders did not run at exactly the same speed, one of the loops repeated at a slightly faster rate and shifted out of *phase* with the other loop.

TAPE LOOPS AND PHASE MUSIC

Phase refers to a particular stage in any cyclic event, and, by extension, to a relative relationship between two or more identical cyclic events. Suppose that two identical drums were playing the same repeated rhythmic phrase:

♩ ♩. ♪ ♩ . Were they to begin the phrase at exactly the same time, the combined result of their attack patterns would be identical to the original:

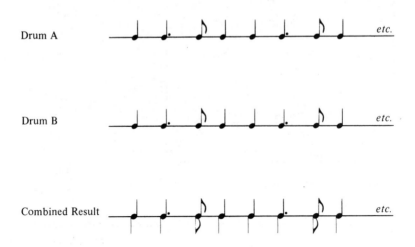

In this case, the two drums could be said to be playing in phase. If drum B were to delay the initiation of the pattern for one quarter note time-value, the combined result of their attack patterns would change:

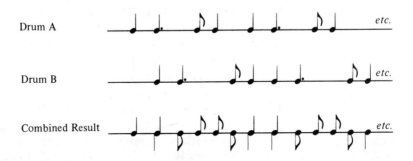

In this instance, the two drums would be said to be out of phase. They are still playing the same repeated rhythmic phrase, but they are playing the same stages of the phrase at different times. It is also possible to measuure the distance that the two drums are out of phase. Since any cyclic event may be divided into 360 degrees, and since there are the equivalent of four quarter note time-values in this rhythmic phrase, drum B may be said to be 90 degrees out of phase with drum A.

While experimenting with his tape loops, Steve Reich discovered that if two identical loops were lined up in unison and allowed to repeat, they would slowly move from being in phase to being all degrees out of phase and eventually back in unison with each other. This was due to the difference in speed of the tape recorders. The length of time required for this 360 degree shift of phase depends upon the relative difference in the speeds of the tape recorders. Using tape loops for the phase shift process allowed Reich to use the phasing technique with any sound material and at any phase rate he wished.

Reich's early work with tape loops demonstrates the close relationship between musical ideas, technical resources, and compositional theory that exists in electro-acoustic music. In order to understand Reich's tape music, it is necessary to understand the possibilities of tape loops as well as the concept of phase relationships. Reich's initial musical thought led to experimentation with tape loops. After working with tape loop techniques, he developed the concept and practice of *phase music.*

Come Out, *by Steve Reich*

In 1966, Reich composed two more musique concrète works using the tape loop phasing technique: *Come Out* and *Melodica.* Like *Its Gonna Rain, Come Out* uses speech as its source material. The voice is that of Daniel Hamm describing a beating he took during the Harlem riots of 1964. Since the police were taking to the hospital only those victims that were visibly bleeding, and since Hamm had no apparent bleeding, he forced open a bruise on his leg so that he too would be taken to the hospital. This situation is the reason for the spoken phrase that begins *Come Out:* "I had to, like, open the bruise up and let some of the bruise blood come out to show them." From this sentence, Reich extracts the phrase "come out to show them," and makes a tape loop of it. Two identical loops of this phrase are then played back simultaneously on two tape recorders. The loops begin in unison and then slowly shift out of phase with each other. This gradual phasing was allowed to go on for several minutes, and the result was recorded on a third tape recorder. This two-voice recording of the phasing of the original loop was itself duplicated. Then these two two-voice recordings were played back simultaneously, again beginning in unison and slowly shifting out of phase. The result of this second stage was again recorded on a third machine, creating a four-voice recording. This procedure was repeated yet another time so that eventually eight voices can be heard.

The result of the phasing process in *Come Out* is quite fascinating. As the phase of the two original loops begins to shift, a gradually increasing reverberation is heard. As the phase shifts further, the relationships become canonic, creating constantly changing rhythms. The rhythmic activity becomes more complicated when more voices become apparent. As the number of voices increases, so does the sound mass; timbres slowly evolve and disappear; pitch relationships are gradually formed and dissolved. The overall effect of *Come Out* is one of slow and constant change and development, always increasing in complexity, always being transient and yet without transitions.

While it is true that *Come Out* is phase music, it is also *process music*. This term is often used to describe a work, such as *Come Out*, in which the compositional process is inseparable from the actual composition. As Reich puts it, "What I'm interested in is a compositional process and a sounding music that are one and the same thing."[2] In *Come Out*, the listener is able to hear the unfolding of the process that, except for the selection of the original material, determines all aspects of the work.

DISCOGRAPHY

Reich, Steve.   *Come Out*. Odyssey 32 16 0160.

FOR FURTHER LISTENING

Reich, Steve.   *Its Gonna Rain*. Columbia MS-7265.   There are two versions of this tape-loop phasing piece, making use of shorter and longer loops. Composed prior to *Come Out*, *Its Gonna Rain* displays some fascinating results of the tape loop phasing process.

[2] Steve Reich, *Writings about Music* (Halifax: The Press of the Nova Scotia College of Art and Design, 1974), p. 10.

4

CUTTING
AND SPLICING

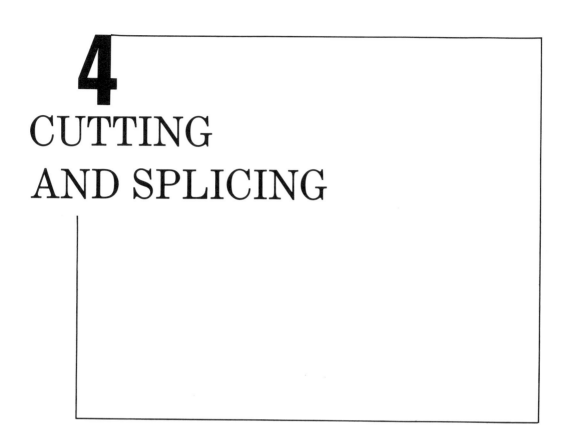

CUTTING AND SPLICING TECHNIQUES

Cutting and splicing are the most commonly used tape manipulation techniques. These procedures involve the cutting of a tape at a desired point and then joining one or both ends of this piece of tape to another piece of tape. By this method, the tape is said to be *edited*.

In the electro-acoustic music studio, the acts of cutting and splicing generally involve three pieces of equipment: a single-edged razor blade, a *splicing block*, and *splicing tape*. Figure 4-1 illustrates the top and side view of a conventional splicing block.

TOP   SIDE

Figure 4-1 Slicing Block.

Usually, the block is made of aluminum and is about six inches long, one inch wide, and three-eighths inches high. The top of the block has a groove the width of the tape. This groove secures the tape during the cutting operation. The block also has two cutting slots, one at 45 degrees and the other at 90 degrees, that guide the razor blade during cutting.

In the act of splicing, a piece of tape is placed into the groove of the splicing block. The point at which the tape is to be cut is lined up with the desired cutting slot and a razor blade is inserted into the slot and cuts the tape. This procedure is then repeated with another piece of tape. The two cut ends of the tapes are placed together and joined by a small piece of splicing tape. The splicing tape is pressure-sensitive and contains a special adhesive on one side that causes the two pieces of tape to be joined. Splices made by this procedure are effectively permanent, although it is possible to separate the two pieces of recording tape by carefully removing the splicing tape.

Tape cutting and splicing have a wide variety of uses. Tape loops are made by splicing together the two ends of a single piece of tape. Unwanted material can be edited out of a tape by cutting and splicing. Two different sounds can be connected, or sounds can be joined to silence by using blank recording tape or *leader tape* made of paper or plastic. In addition, cutting and splicing can be used to eliminate only part of a sound, thus changing the sound's *envelope*, or *amplitude characteristics*.

AMPLITUDE AND VOLUME

Sound travels through the air, or other mediums, in the form of waves. Figure 4-2 presents an *oscilloscopic*, or graphic, representation of a simple acoustic waveform.[1] In this graph, amplitude is the vertical measurement of the wave and can be measured in terms of atmospheric pressure.

Point a on the graph represents the *crest*, or *positive peak*, of the wave, the point of its greatest positive pressure. Point b represents the *trough*, or *negative peak*, of the wave, the point of its greatest negative pressure. The amplitude of an acoustic sound wave is measured by its vertical distance above or below the "zero" pressure point, which is actually normal atmospheric pressure.[2]

Sound waves within the range of human hearing have pressure changes at rates, or *frequencies*, too fast for the perception of the amplitude

[1] An oscilloscope is a laboratory instrument capable of presenting a graphic representation of sound waves on a cathode-ray tube.

[2] If an acoustic sound wave is picked up by a microphone, the wave is converted into electrical impulses. An alternating current electrical wave travels through the medium of electrons. The characteristics of AC electrical waves are the same as for acoustic sound waves except that their amplitudes are measured in terms of *volts*, which are units of electromotive force.

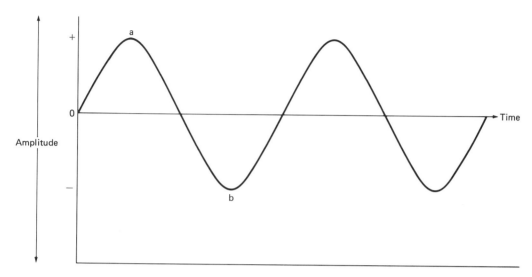

Figure 4-2   Amplitude of a Simple Waveform.

fluctuations of individual cycles. What is actually heard in terms of perceived amplitude, or volume, is the *root-mean-square (rms)* value of a wave.[3] This measurement provides a meaningful average of the changing intensity of a waveform.

The perceived amplitude of a sound is often referred to as its volume or loudness.[4] Dynamic markings, such as "p," "f," "mf," and so forth, are used to convey relative degrees of sound volume to performers. A more precise method of measuring the perceived amplitude of a sound is made possible through use of the unit of the intensity level of a sound. This unit is called a *decibel* and is abbreviated as *dB*. Decibel units are used to measure the relative amplitude characteristics of sounds.[5] The threshold of human hearing is measured as zero dB, while the threshold of pain is around 140 dB.

[3] Rms values are figured by taking the square root fo the square of the peak amplitude divided by two.

[4] In fact, amplitude is not the same as volume, nor, for that matter, is frequency really the same as pitch. A 20 dB increase in the intensity of a sound, for instance, will cause a perceivable change in pitch, even though the measurable frequency of the sound has remained constant. In their haste to quantify music information, some composers have equated amplitude with volume and frequeny with pitch, thereby causing some confusion. In this book, the terms *amplitude* and *frequency* have been modified by the term *perceived* when speaking of what the human ear hears.

[5] The decibel is a logarithmic unit of measurement. An increase of one dB is equal to a multiplication of the intensity level by a factor of about 1.258. For a more detailed discussion, see John Backus, *The Acoustical Foundation of Music* (New York: W.W. Norton & Co., Inc., 1969) pp. 79-93.

The range from "ppp" to "fff" could be approximately measured as from 40 to 100 db.[6]

THE ENVELOPE OF A SOUND

The *envelope* of a sound is a description of its amplitude characteristics with respect to time. A *simple envelope* consists of three stages: *attack time*, *sustain time*, and *decay time*. The attack time is the amount of time it takes a sound to go from zero dB to its greatest amplitude. The sustain time is the period of time a sound remains at its greatest intensity. The decay time is the amount of time a sound takes to fall back to zero dB. Figure 4-3 shows a simple envelope.

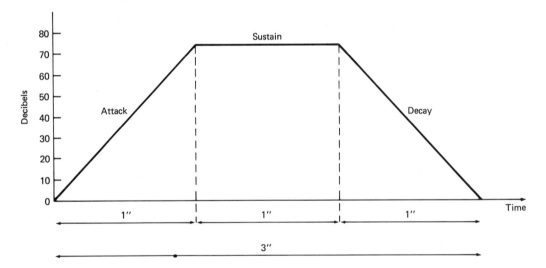

Figure 4-3   A Simple Envelope.

Here the attack, sustain, and decay times are all one second (1″) in duration. The duration of the entire envelope is three seconds. The amplitude is measured in a vertical scale of decibels. The attack, sustain, and decay times of an envelope are completely variable, and any combination is theoretically possible.

Acoustic sounds have characteristic envelopes that, in part, allow us to identify their sources. For instance, a piano sound has a very rapid

[6] This and other technical explanations in this book regarding the physics of sound, acoustics, or electricity, are, of necessity, somewhat simplified. It is beyond the scope of this book to deal thoroughly with these matters, and I have attempted only to give the nontechnical reader sufficient and comprehensive information for understanding important concepts. For an excellent introduction to the properties of sound, see Robert E. Runstein, *Modern Recording Techniques* (Indianapolis: Howard W. Sams & Co., Inc., 1974) pp. 20-40.

attack, a very short sustain time, and a variable but relatively long decay. Various pianistic effects produce different envelopes with regard to the decay time, but not to the attack and sustain times:

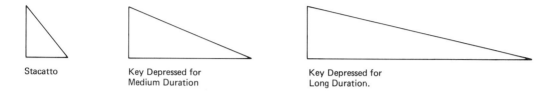

Stacatto   Key Depressed for   Key Depressed for
                        Medium Duration   Long Duration.

The characteristic envelopes, as well as their possible variations, of other instrumental and acoustic sounds are easily perceived and diagramed when thought of in this manner.

COMPOSING WITH CUTTING
AND SPLICING TECHNIQUES

Williams Mix *by John Cage*

Cutting and splicing techniques can alter the envelope characteristics of a sound because it is possible to cut the tape at any point, thereby eliminating part or all of the attack, sustain, or decay of the sound. It is also possible to modify the attack or decay characteristics, or to splice parts of different sounds together. The wide range of possible modifications make cutting and splicing some of the most used of all the tape manipulation techniques.

One of the most extensive uses of tape cutting and splicing within a single work is to be found in *Williams Mix*, by John Cage (b. 1912, Los Angeles). In 1951, Paul Williams, an unlicensed New York architect, gave Cage a grant of $5,000 for the purpose of producing a composition. As a result, Cage established the *Project of Music for Magnetic Tape*, of which *Williams Mix* was one of the completed projects, some others being Earle Brown's *Octet* and a piece by Morton Feldman. Cage involved several other composers in his project, including Louis and Bebe Barron (b. 1923 and 1928, New York City), Earle Brown (b. 1926, Lunenberg, Mass.) and David Tudor (b. 1926, Philadelphia).

As is the case for many other Cage works, the score for *Williams Mix* was composed by chance operations derived from the *I-Ching*, the Chinese *Book of Changes*. Coins were tossed to determine various aspects of composition, and sixteen charts were made from the results. These charts determined the rhythmic structure, envelopes of sounds, durations of silences, and general density of activity, as well as what category of sound would be used at any particular point.

Six categories of sound were created:

A. city sounds;

B. country sounds;

C. electronic sounds;

D. manually produced sounds, including music;

E. wind produced sounds, including songs;

F. small sounds requiring amplification in order to be heard.

Most of the original sound material was recorded by Louis and Bebe Barron. Almost six hundred separate recordings were made before the work of assembling the piece could begin.

The fifth page of the score for *Williams Mix* is shown in Figure 4-4 This is a full size drawing of eight tracks of ¼" tape running at 15 inches-per-second. It is literally a templet, or pattern, for the cutting and splicing of the tapes. The contents of each piece of tape is noted first by an uppercase letter, designating one of the previously mentioned six categories of sound. Following the category designation are three lowercase letters that refer, respectively, to the pitch, timbre, and volume of a sound. These three-letter groupings use only two letters: a "c" or a "v." A "c" indicates that an aspect of the sound has been controlled; a "v" refers to an absence of control. Thus the first sound on track 1 of system 1 on page 5 of the score is noted as "Dvvv," which means that it is a manually produced sound in which the pitch, timbre, and volume have not been controlled. Several categories overlap, and electronically mixed sounds, as on the second track of the first system, have double designations. Underlined capital letters indicate rhythmic characteristics produced by tape loops. Arrows indicate the use of repetitions. The vertical bar in the first system indicates a new structural part, and the numbers and letters above this line indicate information on timings and the use of charts. Blank spaces on the various tracks represent silences, created by using leader tape or blank recording tape.

Since the tape recorders used for *Williams Mix* were full-track monaural (only one track the width of the tape), Cage decided to control the envelope of the sound by cutting and splicing. In this case, the shape of the tape often literally represents the envelope of the sound. Some shapes are very involved (track 3, system 1). They require very careful and difficult cutting of the tape. Each piece of tape must be spliced onto another piece of recording or leader tape and both must be shaped to join smoothly. Several hundred pieces of tape had to be cut and spliced according to the 192 pages of the score, each of which lasts only 1 1/3 seconds. The amount of time involved in producing such a work is considerable; it took Cage and his associates nine months to assemble the original eight tapes.

After the splicing of the eight tapes was completed, they were mixed into a final stereo version, each track containing four of the original tracks. The result is kaleidoscopic. *Williams Mix* is a constantly changing cacophony

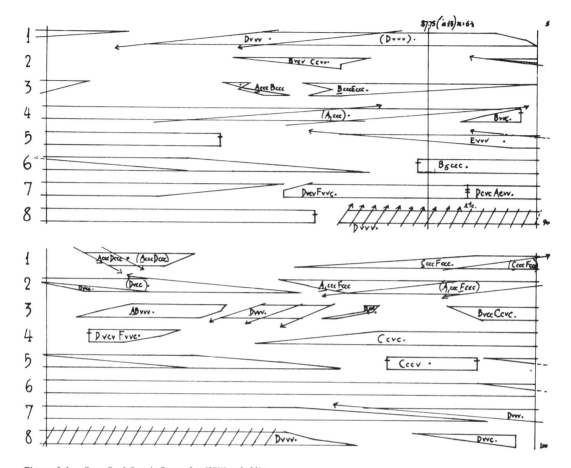

Figure 4-4   Page 5 of Cage's Score for *William's Mix.*

of sounds, a barrage of aural information.[7] Although *Williams Mix* is carefully constructed, the principle of construction is change. Therefore, there is no perceivable structure inherent in the music. Most of the sounds last for so short a time that they can hardly be identified, let alone connected to other events.

How, then, does one approach this and other similar works of Cage? What should one listen for and how should one listen to it? Cage himself offers an explanation from his own point of view:

[7]The only available recording of *Willimas Mix* is on Avakian JC-1. Since this recording was made during a concert in Town Hall in New York City on May 15, 1958, audience sounds are clearly audible. This recording was made by recording from the speakers, not by direct line. The audience reactions after the conclusion of the piece are the actual reactions of that audience, not part of the composition.

I wished, when I first used chance operations, to make a music in which I would not express my feelings, or my ideas, but in which the sounds themselves would change me. I would discover, through the use of chance operations, done faithfully and conscientiously, that the things that I thought I didn't like, I actually liked. So that rather than becoming a more refined musician, I would become more and more open to the various possibilities of sound. This has actually happened, so that my preference, as an individual, in terms of musical aesthetic experience, is not any of my music, and not any of the music of any other composer, but rather the sounds and noises of everyday life.[8]

Cage does not present a perceivably structured musical work in *Williams Mix*. Instead, he creates a sound world in which listeners may explore, pick, and choose what they like or dislike, make their own connections and structures, and, if they wish, ignore any or all of the possibilities. The score for *Williams Mix* and the realization of it that Cage made are not the same thing. Any number of other realizations could be made that would be different in their particulars but the same in their effect. *Williams Mix* is a 4¼ minute excursion into the world of sound that becomes music through perception.

DISCOGRAPHY

Cage, John.   "Williams Mix," in *The 25-Year Retrospective Concert of the Music of John Cage*, Avakian JC-1.

FOR FURTHER LISTENING

Cage, John. *Fontana Mix*.   Turnabout TV-34046 S.   This work from 1958 is similar, in this realization, to *William Mix* in both its concept and result.

Xenakis, Iannis.   *Concrete P-H II*.   Nonesuch H-71246.   Composed in 1958 for the Philips Pavillion of the 1958 Brussels World's Fair, *Concrete P-H II* consists of hundreds of small pieces of tape spliced together. The only source material is the sound of burning charcoal. The material is so arranged that a constant increase in the density of the sound is heard.

[8]John Cage in "Conversations with John Cage," in *Music before Revolution*, EMI (Electrola/Odeon) 16528954C, side 7.

5
SPEED CHANGE

SPEED CHANGE TECHNIQUES

Most tape recorders have a selection of speeds. Home units commonly offer speeds of 3 3/4 and 7 1/2 ips. Most people have experienced the effect of playing back a recording at a speed slower or faster than the original speed of the recording. With the availability of 3 3/4 and 7 1/2 ips, for instance, material can be reproduced an octave lower or higher and at a rate of one-half the original or twice as fast.

Studio tape recorders usually have higher speeds than those of home units. The reason for this is that higher speeds allow for better quality of sound recording. 15 and 30 ips are common speeds on professional machines. In addition, studio tape recorders are sometimes fitted with *variable speed units* that allow the speed to change continuously over a wide range. Some newer units can change speeds continuously over a range from 1 7/8 ips to 60 ips, allowing a five-octave spread. When the playback speed of a record tape is changed, both the *frequency* of the original material and its *rate* of presentation are affected.

The perceived frequency of a sound is usually referred to as its *pitch*. Pitches are traditionally named in terms of *pitch-class*. There are twelve pitch-classes in the Western tempered scale: A, A#, B, C, C#, D, D#, E, F, F#, G, G#. Enharmonic spellings of these pitch-classes are also possible.[1] The particular octave placement, or transposition, of these pitch-classes is called *register*. When we refer to "middle C" or C4, we denote both a pitch-class and a register.[2]

The frequency of a wave is the number of times per second that it passes through all of its values between its positive and negative peaks and returns to its starting value. Each traverse of the wave is called a *cycle*. The measurement of cycles per second (cps) is a *Hertz* (Hz). Figure 5-1 illustrates the frequency of a simple waveform. In this oscilloscopic representation, frequency is seen to be the horizontal measurement of the wave, while amplitude is again the vertical measurement. Starting at the "zero" line at point "a," the wave moves through the crest to the trough and back again to the "zero" line at point "b." Thus the wave has completed one cycle. The amount of time taken to complete this cycle is one second, thus the frequency of this wave is 1 Hz.

In electro-acoustic music, the composer is not limited to the use of the twelve pitch-classes previously discussed. The entire frequency spectrum of human hearing, approximately 20 Hz to 20,000 Hz, is open for consideration and use. The technique of speed change, also called *tape transposition*, allows composers of tape music to variously alter the perceived frequency of any sound event. Speed change can also be used to alter the timbre of a sound, by altering the nature of its *overtone structure*.

The simple waveforms illustrated in Figures 4-2 and 5-1 are *sinusoidal* waveforms, usually referred to as *sine waves*. These waveforms to not exist in nature as isolated waveforms, but they can be produced by oscillators, and, as will be seen in Part II, are very useful in electronic music. Sine waves consist of only one frequency. Acoustic sounds are much more complex because they consist of several frequencies or *harmonics* sounding simultaneously.

OVERTONE STRUCTURES

When we say that the frequency of A4 on the piano is 440 Hz, we are referring to the *fundamental* frequency, or first *harmonic*, of that sound. Above this frequency are other frequencies, or overtones, that are multiples of the

---

[1] Enharmonic spellings refer to pitches that sound the same but are spelled differently. An example of this is A-flat and G-sharp.

[2] For a discussion of pitch register symbols, see Gardner Read, *Music Notation*, 2nd ed. (New York: Taplinger Press, 1969), pp. 43-44. Pitch register symbols used in this book are those recommended by the Acoustical Society of America.

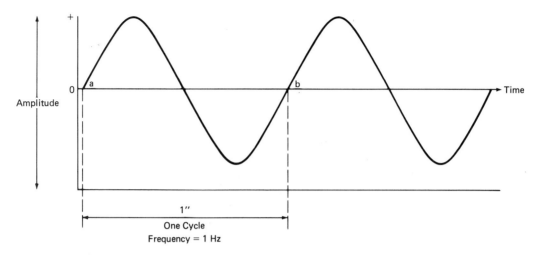

Figure 5-1   Frequency of a Simple Waveform.

fundamental. Thus an A4 on the piano with a fundamental, or first harmonic, of 440 Hz would have a first overtone, or a second harmonic, of 880 Hz, two times the fundamental. The third harmonic would be three times the fundamental, or 1,320 Hz, and so forth.

The possible first ten harmonics for a sound with a fundamental of 440 Hz are listed in Table 5-1.

Not all overtones are present in every sound. Each sound has its own individual overtone structure. In addition, each harmonic of each sound has its own amplitude and envelope. The amplitudes of overtones are generally less the farther they are from the fundamental.

It is this complex arrangement of harmonics at different amplitudes and with different envelopes that primarily constitutes the timbre of a sound. The sound of a flute, for instance, is strong in its first three harmonics. A clarinet sound is strong in its odd (1, 3, 5, 7, etc.) harmonics. A violin sound is more complicated than either of these, since it is strong in its first eighteen harmonics, although primarily in harmonics 1, 2, 5, 6, 7, 8, and

Table 5-1

HARMONIC	OVERTONE	FREQUENCY
1st	(Fundamental)	440 Hz
2nd	1st	880 Hz
3rd	2nd	1320 Hz
4th	3rd	1760 Hz
5th	4th	2200 Hz
6th	5th	2640 Hz
7th	6th	3080 Hz
8th	7th	3520 Hz
9th	8th	3960 Hz
10th	9th	4400 Hz

9. Timbre, then, may be said to depend on the overtone structure and general envelope of a sound. It is on this basis that we are able to characterize and distinguish sound events.

COMPOSING WITH SPEED CHANGE TECHNIQUES

If a recorded sound is played back at a different speed, the timbre of the sound will be affected, since all the harmonics of the sound will be heard at correspondingly different frequencies. If the speed of the recording is slowed considerably, the fundamental may be below the range of audibility. In addition, the envelope of the sound will be lengthened. If a recorded sound is played back at a much faster speed, several of the higher harmonics may disappear, and the envelope will be compressed. In either of these cases, the result of speed change could produce so drastic a timbral modification that the original sound source could be impossible to identify.

Sonic Contours *by Vladimir Ussachevsky*

This modifying effect can be heard in the beginning of *Sonic Contours* (1952), by Vladimir Ussachevsky (b. 1911, Hailor, Manchuria). During the first twenty-nine seconds of *Sonic Contours*, a recording of a chord played on a piano is heard at normal and slower-than-normal speeds. The initial sound is the chord played at a considerably slower speed so that the fundamentals of the lowest pitches all but disappear and the overtones are heard more strongly than usual. The envelope of the sound has been expanded, and the resulting sound has the booming effect of a distant explosion. It would be difficult to identify the original source of this sound if it were not followed by the same piano chord reproduced at the original speed.

Dripsody *by Hugh LeCaine*

Dripsody, by Hugh LeCaine (b. 1914, Fort Arthur, Ontario), is a good example of what can be achieved by using speed change as a primary technique in a tape composition. The sound source for this piece, composed in 1955 at the University of Toronto Electronic Music Studio, is the sound of the fall of a single drop of water. This sound was recorded on a short piece of tape, about ½ inch long. This source tape was then reproduced and copied at many different speeds in order to produce sounds with fundamentals ranging from 45 to 8,000 Hz. The final composition was assembled from these transpositions of the original water drop by splicing together the individual pieces of tape.

The first sound in *Dripsody* is the water drop at its original pitch. Then transpositions of the water drop above and below the original pitch are added and the range is gradually expanded. The glissandi that enter at 0'35" (zero minuts and thirty-five seconds) are especially effective. It will be noticed that the envelopes of the lower pitches heard in this work are fractionally longer than the envelopes of the higher pitches. This is due to the expansion of the original envelope that occurs when it is reproduced at a slower speed. Since the overtone structure of the water drop sound is not very complex, there is little noticeable timbral change except at the highest or lowest transpositions. The portamento effect heard at 1′38″ is created by using using continuous speed change over the duration of the sound.

Exit Music II *by Kenneth Gaburo*

Another example of the effects of speed change can be found in *Exit Music II: Fat Millie's Lament* (1965), by Kenneth Gaburo (b. 1926, Raritan NJ). The structure of this work is ternary, and the outer sections consist of tape loops played at various speeds. The sound material for these loops consists of percussion and voice sounds. As the music fades in at the beginning of the piece, these loops are reproduced at speeds faster than the original recordings. The increase in tempo and the loss of higher overtones create a tinny, squeaky sound quality that is humorous in its effect. Gaburo evidently views Fat Millie's problems, which are compounded when she tries to sit down, as a source of amusement.

> Fat Millie (must)
> Squash her tuh (what?)
> Every time she sits.
> ----------I think.
> oo,ee,oo,ee,ooo,eeeeeeeeeesquack!
> tuh tuhtuhtuh   tuh   tuhwhack![3]

As the piece continues, loops of the same material at the original speed are slowly faded in and eventually become dominant. This creates the effect of slowing down the tempo of the music, and prepares the way for the middle section of the work that begins to fade in at 2′09″. This section is an excerpt from Morgan Powell's jazz composition *Odomtn* and is reproduced at its original pitch level. This quote, which, according to Gaburo, coincides with Millie's most painful moment, is at an even slower tempo than anything yet heard. It seems at once to be a comment on the raucousness and the seriousness of the situation.[4] At 3′22″, the music of the first section returns, although in an abbreviated form. The tape loops are presented at both the original and faster than original speeds. In *Exit Music II*, Gaburo has used speed change to produce humorous effects. The drastic speeding-up of

---

[3] Kenneth Gaburo, *Music for Voices, Instruments & Electronic Sounds*, Nonesuch H-71199. Poem used by permission of the composer.

[4] The echo-like, repetitive nature of the jazz material is created by tape delay, a technique discussed in Chapter 7.

sound material used here is analogous to "fast motion" effects created on film, and generally produces the same audience reaction.

DISCOGRAPHY

Gaburo, Kenneth.   *Exit Music II: Fat Millie's Lament*. Nonesuch H-71199.
LeCaine, Hugh.   *Dripsody*. Folkways FM 3436.
Ussachevsky, Vladimir.   *Sonic Contours*. Desto DC 6466.

FOR FURTHER LISTENING

Boucourechliev, André.   *Text II*. BAM LD-971   This work, composed in 1953, uses percussive material as its sound source. The original sounds receive extensive manipulation by cutting and splicing, and speed change. This produces the low-pitched material as well as the contrasting short-envelope high-pitched sounds. This recording is the combination of two tapes played simultaneously. Since the tapes are not synchronized, the combined result is variable with respect to temporal correspondence. This recording is only one of countless possible combinations.

Reibel, Guy.   *2 Variations en Étoile*. Philips 6740-001.   These two variations are from a set of six composed by Reibel. The first of the variations recorded here, *Metamorphose*, uses a continuously varying speed change to create portamenti and glissandi from the original percussive sounds.

6
DIRECTION CHANGE

DIRECTION CHANGE TECHNIQUES

Direction change is the simplest of the tape manipulation techniques: It involves merely the playing of a tape backward. As a result of this reversal, a literal retrograde of the material on the tape will be heard. Events will take place in reverse order. Moreover, it is important to realize that the aspects of individual sound events will also be reversed. For instance, an envelope having the shape ⟋‾‾‾‾‾‾‾⟍ when played forward, will have the shape ⟋‾‾‾‾‾‾‾⟍ when played backward. As another example, reverberation originally recorded at the end of a sound event will appear before the main body of the sound when played backward.

Direction change can produce interesting timbral modifications because it allows the listener to hear the configuration of a sound or a series of sounds in a manner that is impossible to achieve acoustically. However, the effects of direction change, or *tape reversal* as it is sometimes called, are rather obvious, and, therefore, somewhat limited. For this reason, direction change is seldom used as a primary technique in tape compositions. Direction change is usually used in conjunction with other tape manipulation techniques, especially speed change.

COMPOSING WITH DIRECTION CHANGE

A Piece for Tape Recorder
by Vladimir Ussachevsky

The effects of direction change can be heard in the beginning of Vladimir Ussachevsky's *A Piece for Tape Recorder* (1956), one of the early compositions of American tape music. The acoustic sound sources for this work are a gong, a piano, a single stroke on a cymbal, a single note on a kettledrum, the noise of a jet plane, and some nonelectronic organ chords. In addition, Ussachevsky used some electronic sound sources: four sine tones, produced by an oscillator; a short passage played on an electronic organ; and a click of a switch on a tape recorder.

The first minute-and-a-half of *A Piece for Tape Recorder* uses a great deal of direction change in conjunction with other tape manipulation techniques. The initial sound of the piece is that of a piano recorded on a tape loop that is played backward. Because the envelopes of the piano have been reversed by direction change, the sound is uncharacteristic of the piano.

At 0'06", a gong sound fades in. The source of this sound is almost unrecognizable, since the attack of the gong sound has been cut off and the remaining decay has been reproduced backward. At 0'14", the backward piano loop is heard again. This time, however, it is mixed with gong material played backward at slower speeds. These piano sounds fade out at 0'29", and the reversed gong decay is heard alone.

More backward electronic organ sounds enter at 0'38", but they are not looped. Pitch change is accomplished in this instance by a radical speed change.

At 0'47", a new gong sound is introduced. Here the attack and the end of the decay of the gong sound have been removed. What remains is the middle of the sound, which, in this case, is the beginning of the decay. This middle of the gong sound has been transposed by speed variation to seven pitches spanning a range of an octave-and-a-half.

At 0'58", a third gong sound is heard, this time using only the attack of the sound. The portamento effect is created by continuous speed change.

The rest of *A Piece for Tape Recorder* contains similar uses of direction change and other tape manipulation techniques.[1] The very title of this work reflects Ussachevsky's compositional perspective in 1956. He considered the tape recorder to be his instrument and composed with it by experimenting with the various changes that tape manipulations could create. Whatever his source material, Ussachevsky rigorously manipulated it to find the full range of possibilities. From these possibilities, Ussachevsky selected those elements that fulfilled his requirements:

---

[1] The use of combined tape manipulation techniques is more thoroughly discussed in Chapter 8.

Otto Luening (seated) and Vladimir Ussachevsky in The Columbia-Princeton Electronic Music Center, circa 1958. (Photo courtesy of Columbia-Princeton Electronic Music Center)

. . . the interrelation between the development of the material and the final form of the work certainly played a part in the composition of *A Piece for Tape Recorder*. The abstract aim was two-fold. First of all, I wanted to achieve a kind of large, asymmetrical arch on both a dynamic and a pitch scale. The ascent was to be accomplished through a series of little arches, while the descent would consist of a long, gently undulating line of a predominantly gray timbre, punctuated by fragments of the thematic material used in the first part. The second aim was to start the composition with a sound pattern possessing in large measure those qualities which would permit the listener to make associations with definite pitches and, at times, conventional rhythmic patterns. Gradually the timbres with a greater noise content would be introduced, but the motivic unity would persist. The composition was to end quietly with an impression that the last few notes were largely noise descending by discernible intervals of thirds, fourths, and sixths.[2]

[2] Vladimir Ussachevsky, "Notes on *A Piece for Tape Recorder*," *The Musical Quarterly*, 46, no. 2 (April 1960), 209.

DISCOGRAPHY

Ussachevsky, Vladimir. *A Piece for Tape Recorder*, Finnadar QD 9010 0798. Also available on CRI-112.

FOR FURTHER LISTENING

Ferrari, Luc.   *Visage V*. Philips 6740-001.   The third section of *Visage V* (1959) contains a variety of concrète material cut and spliced and played backward.

Luening, Otto and Vladimir Ussachevsky. *Incantation*. Desto 6466.   Composed in 1952, *Incantation* was the first collaboration between Luening and Ussachevsky. Extensive use of tape direction change is heard in this piece, particularly with material from vocal, flute, and piano sounds. The tape reversal is usually used in conjunction with speed change techniques.

7
TAPE DELAY

ACOUSTIC REVERBERATION

When a sound is generated, it radiates from the sound source in a arc.[1] As the sound waves move outward, some of them will reach the listener's ear directly. This is referred to as *direct sound*. Direct sound will not have encountered any obstacles between the source and the listener, and will have arrived at the listener's ear in a straight line.

Some of the other waves will travel to surrounding surfaces before they reach the listener's ear. If these surfaces are sufficiently hard, the waves will be reflected. Some of the reflected waves will also reach the listener's ear, but, since they must travel farther, they will arrive at the ear later than the direct sound. Sound waves perceived in this manner are called *reflected sound*.

Since reflected sound takes longer to reach the listener than does direct sound, the ear perceives the sound even after the sound source ceases

---

[1] Sound travels at a constant speed of 1130 feet per second in the medium of air at 70 degrees Farenheit.

to produce the sound. This continuation of the sound after it has stopped being produced is called *reverberation*.

The reverberation phenomenon is the combination of many reflections of a sound arriving at the listener's ear at different times and from different directions. The intervals of time between the reflections are so short, being less than from 20 to 25 milliseconds, that the ear cannot perceive them as individual events.[2] If the time intervals between reflected sounds are greater than 50 milliseconds, the ear is able to perceive the individual reflections. In this case, the phenomenon would be called *echo*. The difference between reverberation and echo is a perceptual difference, depending on the time between sound reflections.[3]

In acoustic sound, the amount and quality of reverberation or echo depends on the physical environment. Hard surfaces reflect sound waves, while soft surfaces absorb them. Large spaces generally allow for longer reflection times than do small spaces. The classic echo effect experienced in mountainous terrain is the result of great distances and hard rock.

In tape music, reverberation and echo, if desired, must usually be added to the sound material. If the source material for a tape composition is acoustic, some natural reverberation exists in the recording. However, some of this reverberation may be lost in performing various tape manipulation techniques. Even if this is not the case, the composer may wish to add additional reverberation or echo to the recorded material. There are three methods of adding reverberation or echo to taped sounds: acoustic reverberation, artificial reverberation, and tape delay techniques.

Acoustic reverberation is achieved by playing the recorded material back through loudspeakers into the desired acoustic environment and recording the reverberated sound. While this procedure will ensure a natural reverberation quality, other aspects of the sound may suffer as a result. The frequency range of the original material may be compressed, and the general quality of the sound is difficult to control.[4] Acoustic reverberation was used in many early tape compositions, but it is now a rarity.

ARTIFICIAL REVERBERATION

There are two types of artificial reverberation: mechanical and electronic. Mechanical artificial reverberation is achieved by using either a *spring reverberation unit* or a *reverberation plate.* In both of these devices, the sound

---

[2] A millisecond is equal to one one-thousandth of a second.

[3] Various experts disagree on the exact amount of time between sound reflections that is necessary to create the perception of echo. The range of from 20 to 50 milliseconds reflects these various opinions. It also allows for individual differences in aural perception.

[4] To overcome these problems, some studios built special reverberation chambers, but, in general, they were only partially successful.

travels through physically vibrating mediums, which are either a coiled spring or a large steel plate. The mechanical vibrations produce repetitions of the sound that are separated by short intervals of time. In this way, the effects of natural reverberation are simulated. Because of its lower cost, the spring reverberator is more common than the reverberation plate, although the quality of plate reverberation is superior.

Electronic artificial reverberation is achieved by using solid-state analog or digital technology to create a *delay line*, a series of delayed repetitions. These methods are, at present, rather expensive, and therefore are not in common use in tape studios. Electronic artificial reverberation and delay devices offer greater control over delay than mechanical units and will undoubtedly become more common in the future. However, they lack the random complex factors present in natural reverberation, and they cannot produce as natural-sounding a reverberation as plate reverberation.

TAPE DELAY TECHNIQUES

Tape delay techniques offer a variety of delay effects that are primarily heard as types of echo. These effects are dependent on the physical arrangement of the components of the tape transport. Figure 7-1 shows a typical tape transport found on professional machines.

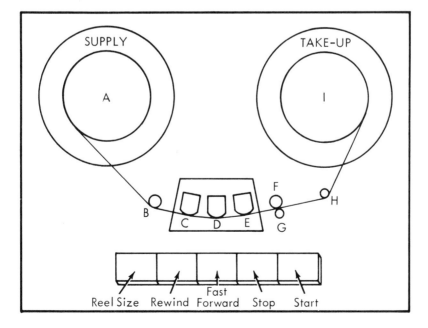

Figure 7-1   Components of a Tape Transport.

The letters in Figure 7-1 designate the following components:

A   Supply reel
B   Tape guide
C   Erase head
D   Record head
E   Playback head
F   Pinch roller
G   Capstan
H   Tape guide
I   Take-up reel

The transport has three motors. The capstan motor pulls the tape at a constant speed when the tape is forced between the capstan and the pinch roller. The supply and take-up motors supply proper tension and wind the tape.

Professional tape recorders have three heads for the functions of erasing, recording, and playing back the tape. Since these three heads are separated from each other, a small amount of time elapses as a particular point on the tape passes from one head to another. This causes a delay from the time a sound is recorded to the time it is reproduced. This is the basis for all single-recorder tape delay effects.

The nature of single-recorder tape delay effects depends on the configurations of the various tape heads. These configurations determine how many tracks can be recorded on the tape as well as the format of their recording and playback. The following are common head configurations and formats for ¼″ tape.

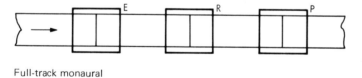

Full-track monaural

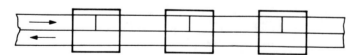

Half-track monaural

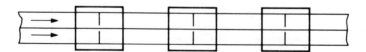

Half-track stereophonic

Quarter-track stereophonic

Quarter-track quadraphonic

If a full-track or a half-track monaural tape recorder is used, the only possible tape delay technique is *feedback delay*, also called *tape feedback*. In this situation, a signal is recorded onto the tape by the record head, played back from the playback head, and then fed back into the record head. This signal path can be illustrated by using the following shorthand where "R" stands for the record head and "P" designates the playback head: Signal → R → P → R. This creates a *feedback loop*, resulting in an unspecified number of repetitions of the signal. The amount of time between separations depends on the distance between the record and playback heads and the speed at which the tape travels.

With stereophonic or quadraphonic machines, it is possible to produce a limited number of delayed repetitions. This technique is known as *straight-line delay*. Using a half-track stereo machine, the signal can be routed as follows: Signal → R1 → P1 → R2 → P2. The outputs of both channels are mixed together, and the result is a single repetition of the recorded signal.

TAPE DELAY TECHNIQUES VS TAPE DELAY EFFECTS

When discussing tape delay, it is necessary to distinguish between techniques and effects. There are only two tape delay techniques: straight-line delay and feedback delay. Straight-line delay involves transferring a signal from the playback head of one channel to the record head of another channel. Straight-line delay always results in a limited number of repetitions. The number of repetitions depends on the number of channels used. Feedback delay is created by feeding the signal back into the record head of the channel that it was originally recorded on. This creates a feedback loop, which may involve one or more channels. Feedback delay will create an unspecified number of repetitions, since the signal path is a loop.

Single-recorder tape delay uses only one tape recorder. The possible signal paths for single-recorder tape delay are laid out in Table 7-1.

Table 7-1

HEAD CONFIGURATION	STRAIGHT-LINE DELAY	FEEDBACK DELAY
full-track monaural	(not possible)	R → P → R
half-track monaural	(not possible)	R → P → R
half-track stereo	R1 → P1 → R2 → P2	R1 → P1 → R2 → P2 → R1
quarter-track stereo	R1 → P1 → R2 → P2	R1 → P1 → R2 → P2 → R1
quarter-track quad	R1 → P1 → R2 → P2 → R3 → P3 → R4 → P4	R1 → P1 → R2 → P2 → R3 → P3 → R4 → P4 → R1

In straight-line delay, the outputs of all of the playback heads are mixed together in a *mixer,* a device that combines two or more signals and allows the volume of each input to be controlled.

Tape delay may also be performed by using two tape recorders simultaneously. Figure 7-2 illustrates a possible two-recorder delay.

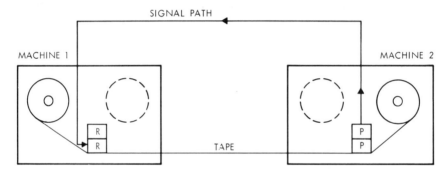

Figure 7-2   A Two-Recorder Tape Delay.

In this illustration, two half-track stereo machines are used. The signal is initially recorded and played back on one channel of machine 2. The signal is then routed from the playback head of machine 2 to the record head of machine 1. This rerecording of the signal is then played back on the other channel of machine 2. The outputs of both channels of machine 2 are mixed together. Since this is a type of straight-line delay, the effect will be a single echo. There will also be an extended delay time, due to the distance between the two recorders.

The most commonly used *tape delay effects* are *echo* and *extended echo.*[5] The difference between these two effects is rather subjective. Ex-

[5] The term *tape reverberation* is often used to describe tape echo effects, but this is technically and perceptually incorrect. Reverberation effects (repetition delay times shorter than 50 milliseconds) are technically possible using tape delay techniques at speeds of 30 ips or greater. However, this is seldom done. Reverberation in tape music is usually created by artificial means.

Signal phasing and *flanging* are two other possible tape delay effects, but they are almost always done electronically instead of by tape delay. A discussion of signal phasing and flanging effects is beyond the technical scope of this book. For information on these effects, especially as applied to the world of commercial recording, see Richard Factor, *Phasing and Flanging* (New York: Eventide Clockworks, Inc.).

tended echo has longer delay times between repetitions but there is no set measurement. Usually, extended echo effects are thought of as being achieved by a two-recorder delay system, as shown in Figure 7-2. Both echo and extended-echo effects can be created by either the straight-line or the feedback delay technique.

COMPOSING WITH TAPE DELAY TECHNIQUES

In Kenneth Gaburo's *Exit Music II*, a composition previously discussed, the effect of extended echo delay can be easily heard. The middle section of *Exit Music II* uses a single extended echo to create a repetition of the jazz material. The original material is stated on one channel and then, after about a one second delay, is repeated on the other channel. This creates a stereophonic effect, since the original statement and its repetition are separated by space as well as time.

Low Speed *by Otto Luening*

Otto Luening (b. 1900, Milwaukee, Wisconsin) has used tape echo in several of his early tape compositions. Together with Ussachevsky, Luening was one of the pioneers of tape music in the United States. Luening and Ussachevsky composed several works jointly and were co-directors of the Columbia-Princeton Electronic Music Center, which opened in 1959.

Low Speed (1952) is one of several of Luening's tape pieces that uses the flute as source material. The sounds of the flute in this work are reproduced at speeds slower than that of the original recording. This allowed the pitches of the flute to be extended below the normal range. In addition, this speed change caused the overtones of the flute sound to be heard more clearly than usual.

Luening uses feedback delay in *Low Speed*. Each statement of the flute is followed by several softer echoes of the original sound. Thus, by using only one melodic line with feedback echo, the composer is able to achieve repetitious combinations of melodic fragments.

Luna Park *by Tod Dockstader*

Another example of tape echo can be heard in *Luna Park* (1961), by Tod Dockstader (b. 1932, St. Paul, Minnesota). The main sound source in the first section of *Luna Park* is the sound of laughter. This material is reproduced at speeds faster than that of the original recording and treated by feedback delay. This produces a series of rapid echoes of the laughter, imparting a surreal quality to the sound.

Dockstader refers to his work as "organized sound," a term first used by Edgard Varèse. Dockstader's methods of organization are derived from the various tape manipulation techniques and different kinds of electronic sound processing. Beginning with a specific idea for a composition, Dockstader collects appropriate materials, experiments with their possibilities, and finally organizes the sound material in such a way as to convey the idea of the work.

Dockstader is a recording engineer and does not consider himself to be a musician in the traditional sense. Like most of his works, *Luna Park* is an instinctive organization of materials designed to convey subjective and somewhat programmatic ideas that are extramusical. The various techniques that Dockstader employs in his works are not intended to be ends in themselves but rather means to create specific moods and effects.

DISCOGRAPHY

Dockstader, Tod.   *Luna Park*. Owl ORLP-6.
Luening, Otto.   *Low Speed*. Desto DC 6466.

FOR FURTHER LISTENING

Kotonski, Wlodzimiez.   *Microstructures*. Philips 6740-001.   *Microstructures* (1963) uses percussive sounds derived from wood and glass. While a variety of tape manipulation techniques can be heard, the effects of tape delay are audible throughout most of the piece.

Luening, Otto.   *Fantasy in Space; Invention in Twelve Notes; Moonflight*. Desto DC-6466.   All of these early works by Luening were composed in 1952. They use tape delay techniques with flute sounds.

8
COMBINED TAPE MANIPULATION TECHNIQUES

As has already been noted in discussing the works mentioned in previous chapters, most musique concrète works use more than just one tape manipulation technique. The possibilities with combined techniques are greater than when just one technique is used. Greater variation of the sound material helps to create a more interesting work and allows the composer to explore a larger world of sound.

One of Pierre Schaeffer's original concerns with musique concrète was the exploration of a single sound or class of sounds. Schaeffer's first work, *Étude aux chemins de fer*, deals only with train sounds. This approach to the composition of musique concrète has intrigued many composers. Using only one type of sound creates limitations for the composer and forces him to explore the possibilities of his material. Such restriction also gives the composition a sense of unity, since all of the sound material is related.

Water Music *by Toru Takemitsu*

Water Music (1960), by Toru Takemitsu (b. 1930, Tokyo), exhibits extreme limitations on source material. The only sounds in *Water Music* are those of water drops. Unlike Hugh LeCaine's *Dripsody*, *Water Music* uses a variety of water-drop timbres, largely created by dropping water from different heights and into variously sized containers. Takemitsu also uses a wide variety of tape manipulation techniques.

The first event in *Water Music* is the sound of a single drop of water. This material has been amplified and reverberated, giving it an outsized quality. The second sound in the piece is the same as the first, transposed an octave higher by speed change. This is followed by other single-drop sounds presented at various pitches. Each event requires the individual recording, cutting, and splicing of a piece of tape.

At 0'13", a new form of the water-drop sonority appears. This event consists of two pitches, the first being, as it were, a grace note to the second. This effect is created by splicing two water-drop sounds together, shortening the first by cutting off the decay of its envelope.

At 0'16", an elongated form of the water-drop sound is introduced. The sustain portion of this sound's envelope has been lengthened, possibly by the splicing of additional material into the middle of the sound.

After a variety of single and double water-drop sounds have been presented, we hear many drop sounds spliced closely together and transposed to a high register by speed change. This occurs at 0'47". After a repetition of this statement, the same material is heard as a downward glissando at 1'02". This effect is created by continuous speed change.

At 1'04", the glissando is halted by two statements of the water-drop sound played backwards at a speed much slower than that of the original recording.

Tape loops are used for the first time in *Water Music* at 1'08". At first, the short loop of drop sounds is reproduced at such a fast speed that little pitch information can be heard. Soon the loop is heard at a slower speed, although still faster than normal. At this slower speed it is possible to hear the repetitious pitch pattern as well as the echo effect created by tape delay.

In the first minute-and-a-half of *Water Music*, Takemitsu uses all of the tape manipulation techniques to change various aspects of the water-drop sound. The rest of the piece contains similar manipulations of the material.

Water Music provides a curious listening experience, for it is at once related to the old and the new. Takemitsu's uses of silences and dramatic gestures are strikingly reminiscent of traditional Japanese theater music. Events are often surrounded by long silences, and climaxes are short and abrupt. At the same time, the sound material in *Water Music* is created in ways that are uniquely contemporary.

Water Music does not exist as a continuous linear structure. It is, rather, a series of events that belong together because of their common source. At the same time, these events are differentiated from each other by their placement in time and the various manipulations performed on them.

It is more important to listen to the specific qualities of each sound than the relationships between events.

Thema (Omaggio a Joyce)
by Luciano Berio

Another musique concrète work that uses only one class of sounds is *Thema (Omaggio a Joyce)*, by Luciano Berio (b. 1925, Oneglia, Italy). *Thema* was composed in 1958 at the Studio de Fonologia of the Radio Audizioni Italiane in Milan. The only sound source for *Thema* is the voice of Cathy Berberian reading from the beginning of the eleventh chapter of James Joyce's *Ulysses*. In the original version of *Thema*, and in some of the commercial recordings of the piece, the actual composition is prefaced by the reading of the text that Berio used in composing.

In composing *Thema*, Berio was concerned with developing transitions between words and music.[1] To achieve this, Berio experimented with the transformational possibilities of tape manipulation techniques. As a result, *Thema* is, in a way, a catalog of the possibilities of tape manipulation techniques used on vocal sounds. It is, therefore, important to consider some of the highlights of the piece.

Thema begins with the superimposition of several words from the beginning of the text. This is a technique that Berio makes great use of throughout the place. In creating these superimpositions of material, several tracks of the voice have to be mixed together into the final format, which, in this case, is stereophonic. The result of this superimposition of tracks is to create a chorus of voices from only one original voice.

At 0'42", Berio uses cutting and splicing techniques to create a unique sound picture of the word *blooming*.[2] First he cuts out all but the beginning "bl" sound of the word. Then many rerecordings of the "bl" sound are spliced together. This is the first heard in a high register, transposed by speed change. The material is then presented at a lower register, still higher than normal, and is finally heard at the original pitch. In this last presentation, Berio gradually adds portions of the word so that repetitions grow from "bl" to "bloo" to "bloom" to "blooming." This addition of parts of the word also has the effect of slowing the rhythm of the repetitions, since the length of each iteration increases as the word becomes complete. The effect of this passage is quite marvelous, since the word and its meaning are literally formed as we listen.

At 1'13", Berio creates extreme transformation of the vocal timbres. These few sounds are not recognizable as having come from a vocal source.

---

[1] *Thema* is discussed at length in the interview with Luciano Berio contained in Part III.

[2] The timings for *Thema* are given from the beginning of the actual piece and do not include the introductory reading of the text.

This effect, used at several points in *Thema*, is the result of multiple manipulations of the same material. In this instance, cutting and splicing, speed change, and direction change have all been used to transform the original material. In addition, the sound is also *filtered*, so that portions of the original frequency spectrum are removed. These extreme transformations are closely followed by an example of continuous descending speed change.

Berio uses a combination of cutting and splicing, speed change, and tape delay to create the timbres beginning at 1'23". These high-pitched events continue for several seconds and serve as background for the more intelligible vocal sounds.

Throughout *Thema*, Berio creates a constant motion between three general categories of sound: discontinuous (separated), periodic (repetitious), and continuous (as in the prolongation of the "s" sonority). There is also movement between relative degrees of recognizability and unintelligibility of the spoken material. In this way, Berio creates a continuous metamorphosis between speech and music. The result is a composition as interesting and fresh today as it was when first heard.

At certain points in *Thema*, the sound of the voice has been transformed to such a degree that its origin is no longer recognizable. This is the result of performing several tape manipulation techniques on the same material. Multiple manipulations of acoustic material can drastically alter its characteristics, as is evident in Vladimir Ussachevsky's *Of Wood and Brass* (1965).

Of Wood and Brass
by Vladimir Ussachevsky

Of Wood and Brass was composed in four sections, each of which uses different source materials. The first section (0'00"-0'56") uses primarily the sounds of a trombone and an electronic oscillator. The trombone sounds have been changed by multiple tape manipulations, including cutting and splicing, speed change, and direction change. The resulting sonorities are far removed from typical trombone timbres.

The second part of *Of Wood and Brass* (0'57"-1'53") is made from trumpet sounds. Primarily because of extreme speed change, the trumpet sounds are greatly changed from the quality of the original material.

Section three (1'54"-3'12") uses the sound of a xylophone. In addition to tape manipulation, the timbre of the xylophone has been further changed by the process of *ring modulation*. This is accomplished by using a *ring modulator*, an electronic device that is in most electro-acoustic music studios. The ring modulator has two inputs, and either acoustic or electronic material can be fed into the device. The output of the ring modulator is the sum and the difference of all of the frequencies fed into the ring modulator. For example, if two sine waves of 300 Hz and 700 Hz were fed into the inputs of a ring modulator, the output would be the sum of the two frequencies, which is 1000 Hz, and the difference, which is 400 Hz. In the third section of *Of Wood and Brass*, Ussachevsky has fed the xylophone material into one input of the ring modulator, and a sine wave into the other input. The metallic-sounding quality of the xylophone material is the result of the ring modulation process. The timbre has been changed because the frequency information is different.

The fourth section of *Of Wood and Brass* is made from trombone and Korean gong sounds. The portamento effect created on the trombone is recognizable, even though it is reproduced at a lower speed. The use of tape manipulation techniques and ring modulation, accounts for the transformation of the trombone and gong material.

In composing *Of Wood and Brass*, Ussachevsky wanted to "remove the final sound materials as far as possible from the quality of the original instrumental sounds."[3] As a result, new timbres are created that often bear little resemblance to the original sonorities.

In the previous discussions of musique concrète compositions, care has been taken to deal with the works in some detail, especially in the consideration of technical procedures. This has been done to provide the reader with specific examples of the tape manipulation techniques and how they can be used. By this point, it is hoped that the reader will have gained some facility in hearing and discerning the technical processes involved in musique concrète. For this reason, and because of the practical limitations of this book, the remainder of this chapter will be devoted to brief discussions of selected examples from the literature. Works using vocal, instrumental, and traditionally extramusical sounds will be explored, as well as compositions that use a minimum of tape manipulation techniques.

Psalmus *by Krzysztof Penderecki*

The human voice has been a favorite source of material for many composers of musique concrète. Vocal sounds lend themselves to a wide variety of possible transformations and can be used with or without words. In *Thema*, Berio bases his composition on Joyce's text, sometimes concentrating on the sound of the words rather than on the words themselves. In *Psalmus* (1961), by Krzysztof Penderecki (b. 1933, Debica, Poland), wordless voice sounds are used. In this, his only tape composition, Penderecki uses the sonorities of soprano and baritone voices to explore the inflection possibilities of the Polish language. Speed change is used for transposing the sustained sounds, while cutting and splicing techniques provide many of the shorter envelopes and repetitions. Cluster chords, groups of closely spaced pitches sounding simultaneously, are created by the superimposition of several recordings. Many of the vocal effects heard in *Psalmus*, such as the rapid articulation of consonants and the use of clusters, are found in Penderecki's more recent vocal music.

---

[3] Vladimir Ussachevsky, from notes on *Of Wood and Brass*, CRI 227 USD.

Berio's *Thema* and Penderecki's *Psalmus* are representative of many musique concrète works that use vocal sounds. The continuing interest in the use of vocal material for tape composition, especially when combined with spoken poetry, has resulted in a new class of compositions called *text-sound*. Text-sound works are sometimes associated with concrète poetry and are often referred to as *sound poetry*. Text-sound compositions are characterized by the primary use of the spoken word as opposed to sung words or wordless vocal sounds. Although the term *text-sound* originated in Holland around 1967, it is primarily thought of as a Swedish movement, since most text-sound compositions are by Swedish composers. In recent years, the movement has also gained popularity in Europe and the United States.

Text-sound works are often concerned with expressing specific ideas and thoughts. These works contain little manipulation of the spoken words, since, as in most poetry, the meanings of the words are important and must be understood. *Vietnam* (ca. 1970) by Lars-Gunnar Bodin (b. 1935, Stockholm) and Bengt Emil Johnson (b. 1936, Stockholm) is an example of this type of text-sound work. The piece consists almost entirely of spoken phrases dealing with the war in Vietnam. Since the work is frankly political and seeks to relate a particular point of view, there is almost no tape manipulation except between certain spoken phrases.

English Phonemes (1970), by Arigo Lora-Totino (b. 1928, Turin, Italy) represents a different kind of text-sound composition. This work is more concerned with the sounds of speech than with the meaning of words. In the first part of *English Phonemes*, three lists of related words, called themes, are spoken by male and female voices. After an initial statement of the themes, the order of the words and their phonemes are rearranged to create what Lora-Totino refers to as "a progressive semantic reduction."[4] In the second part of *English Phonemes*, the material of the first part is subjected to tape manipulation and electronic processing, such as filtering. As a result, the meanings of the words are destroyed. What is left are the phonemes of the words, and noises created from the phonemes.

MUSIQUE CONCRÈTE COMPOSED FROM INSTRUMENTAL SOURCES

Traditional musical instruments offer composers a wide variety of sound sources for musique concrète compositions. The transformation of instrumental timbres by tape manipulation techniques has already been discussed with reference to Ussachevsky's *Of Wood and Brass*. François Bayle (b. 1932, Tamatave, Madagascar) takes a different approach to the use of instru-

---

[4] A phoneme is the smallest part of speech.

mental sounds in *L'Oiseau-chanteur (The Songbird)*. *L'Oiseau-chanteur* (second version, 1963) is the third part of *Portraits de L'Oiseau-qui-n' existe-pas (Portraits of the Bird-that-does-not-exist)*, music composed for images by Robert Lapoujade. In *L'Oiseau-chanteur*, Bayle uses French horn, oboe, and harpsichord to produce short phrases. These instrumental sounds are extended by the use of electronic and other concrète material. While the instrumental sounds receive almost no direct modification, they are prolonged by the electronic and concrete material through cutting and splicing techniques. The result is an extension of the characteristic instrumental timbres.

Iannis Xenakis (b. 1922, Braila, Rumania) uses new, as well as traditional, instrumental techniques in generating the sound material for *Orient-Occident III* (1959-1960). Orient-Occident III is a second revision of a work originally composed for a UNESCO film by Enrico Fulchignioni that deals with comparisons of European, Asian, and African art. At the beginning of *Orient-Occident III*, Xenakis uses a cello bow drawn over various objects, such as cardboard boxes, metal rods, and gongs. At one point, Xenakis uses an excerpt from his orchestral work *Pithoprakta* transposed to a low register by speed change. In addition to the instrumental material, Xenakis incorporates traditionally extramusical sounds, such as signals from the ionosphere converted into sound. Xenakis uses a wide variety of sources in *Orient-Occident III* to deal with making transitions. Overlapping, superimposing, and cross-fading (sometimes called dovetailing) sections are used several times in the piece. Often there is no transition but a direct splicing of one section to another.

Francois Bayle in studio 116C of the Groupe de Recherches Musicales, Institut National de L'Audiovisuel. (Photo by Guy Vivien, courtesy of Groupe de Recherches Musicales)

Most of Xenakis's musique concrète uses sound material that is not tradi-tionally considered musical. This area of sound offers the composer the largest range of possibilities. Several compositions previously discussed, such as Schaeffer's *Études of 1948*, Cage's *Williams Mix*, LeCaine's *Dripsody*, and Takemitsu's *Water Music*, use traditionally extramusical sounds. Xenakis has composed with a wide variety of such material. In *Diamorphoses II* (1957), Xenakis uses what he refers to as "ugly sounds," such as jet plane sounds, crashing railroad cars, and sounds of earthquakes. These sounds are sub-jected to various transformations by cutting and splicing, speed change, and direction change of the tape. At several points in *Diamorphoses II*, a high-pitched portamento is heard. This material is produced by using a Greek sheep bell transposed by continuous speed change.

In *Concrete P-H II* (1958), Xenakis uses the sounds of burning char-coal. Hundreds of short pieces of tape were spliced together to produce the final composition.

Bohor I (1962) by Xenakis uses the sound of a Laotian mouth organ and the sounds of jewelry being dropped and scraped. By means of super-imposing many tracks or layers of material, Xenakis creates a large sound mass that slowly increases in intensity. Speed change accounts for the wide frequency range and the various timbres of the piece. *Bohor I* is essentially a long (21'56") crescendo of a sound mass whose internal structure is in con-stant flux.

Pierre Henry (b. 1927, Paris) chose an unusual combination of sounds for his *Variations on a Door and a Sigh* (1963). The sources used in this piece are those of a door (creaking, shutting, and so on), a sigh (various breath sounds), and a type of musical saw. From this material, Henry creates twenty-five short variations reflecting on various musical and environmental situations. Henry uses all of the tape manipulation techniques to produce a tour de force of imagination with very limited means.

Another musique concrète work that uses an unusual sound source is *Bowery Bum* (1964), by Ilhan Mimaroglu (b. 1926, Istanbul, Turkey). Mimaroglu uses only the sound of a rubber band in *Bowery Bum*. Cutting and splicing techniques are used to form the melodic fragment heard at the beginning of the work. Additional splicing, along with speed and direction change, creates the variations of the original material.

MUSIQUE CONCRÈTE
WITH MINIMAL TAPE MANIPULATION

All of the works discussed so far have used varying degrees and kinds of tape manipulations. Many compositions involve the use of multiple manipulations to create specific effects. In contrast to this approach , some composers have used a minimum of tape manipulation to achieve their goals.

I Am Sitting In A Room (1970), by Alvin Lucier (b. 1931, Nashua, New Hampshire) is unique in the literature of musique concrète. *I Am Sitting In A Room* consists of a brief statement spoken by the composer and recorded on tape. The original recording is then played through a loudspeaker into a room, and rerecorded, by means of a microphone, on a second tape recorder. This results in a *second generation* tape, a second recording of the original tape. This process is repeated until a fifteenth generation tape is recorded. As a result, the natural resonant frequencies of the room become increasingly reinforced with each successive generation of the tape.

I Am Sitting In A Room uses a kind of acoustic feedback. The tape is played and rerecorded over and over into the same acoustic environment. Eventually, due to this feedback process, only the resonant frequencies of the room are reinforced, and the original speech is obliterated. This process could be used with any sound, and the results will differ according to the characteristics of the source material, the acoustic environment, and the microphone and loudspeakers that are employed. Except for the splicing together of the fifteen generations of recordings, Lucier uses no tape manipulation techniques in this work.

Another musique concrète composition that uses minimal tape manipulation is *Presque Rien No. 1* (1970), by Luc Ferrari (b. 1929, Paris). *Presque Rien No. 1* is an example of a genre of musique concrète that deals with a sort of diary in sound. *Presque Rien No. 1* presents the sounds of daybreak on a beach. There are the sounds of cars, voices, animals, insects, and such, that naturally occurred when Ferrari made the recording. Ferrari has exercised little control over the results except for two manipulations. He has cut out some portions of the original recording and spliced the remaining sections together. This creates a slightly contracted perspective of the original material. Secondly, he has made the insect-like sounds that enter during the middle of the piece slowly increase in volume until they alone are heard at the end of the work. Except for these changes, *Presque Rien No. 1* presents the chance sounds of a particular day at a particular beach.

This brief survey of the musique concrète literature has only begun to demonstrate the possibilities of the medium. Through the wide variety of source material, the use of tape manipulation techniques, and the application of electronic processing, more fully discussed in Part II, the composer of musique concrète has an almost unlimited range of sound possibilities.

DISCOGRAPHY

Bayle, François.   *L'Oiseau-chanteur*. Candide 31025.

Berio, Luciano.   *Thema (Omaggio à Joyce)*. Turnabout 34177; Philips 836-897.

Bodin, Lars-Gunnar and Bengt Emil Johnson.   *Vietnam*. Sverige Radio.

Ferrari, Luc.   *Presque Rien No. 1*. DGG 2543004.

Henry, Pierre.   *Variations on a Door and a Sigh.* Philips DSY 836-898.

Lora-Totino, Arrago.   *English Phonemes 1970.* Source Record No. 5 in *Source: Music of the Avant Garde*, 5, no. 1 (1971).

Lucier, Alvin.   *I Am Sitting In A Room.* Source Record No. 3 in *Source: Music of the Avant Garde*, 4, no. 1 (1970).

Mimaroglu, Ilhan.   *Bowery Bum.* Turnabout TV-34004S.

Penderecki, Krzysztof.   *Psalmus.* Philips 6740-001.

Takemitsu, Toru.   *Water Music.* RCA VICS-1334.

Ussachevsky, Vladimir.   *Of Wood and Brass.* CRI 227.

Xenakis, Iannis.   *Bohor I; Concret P-H II; Diamorphosis II; Orient-Occident III.* Nonesuch 71246.

FOR FURTHER LISTENING

Bayle, François.   *Solitude.* Philips 6740-001.   This is a loosely programmatic work composed in 1969. It deals with aural aspects and impressions of a popular music concert of the period. There are the sounds of crowds, street traffic, sirens, electric guitars, and excerpts from performances by Duke Ellington, The Soft Machine, and Boris Vian. The tape manipulations are easily heard and create a pleasant collage.
    Vapeur. BCM LD-072.   *Vapeur* (1962) uses the sounds of harp, bass clarinet, string bass, and cymbals. The initial sounds are unaltered, but the instrumental timbres are slowly extended by tape manipulation techniques.

Carson, Philippe.   *Turmac.* BAM LD-072.   *Turmac* (1962) was created from machine sounds. There is little sound transformation in this work. Tape loops, splicing, and speed change are used to some degree, but most of the piece is the result of mixing together various tracks.

Dockstader, Tod.   *Quartermass.* Owl ORLP-6.   *Quartermass* (1964) is an extensive exposition of Dockstader's ideas. Although the sound of an oscillator is used in the work, most of *Quartermass*'s sources are acoustic. Among other sounds, there are those of ballons, cymbals, radio static, and adhesive tape.

El-Dabh, Halim.   *Leiyla and the Poet.* Columbia MS 6566.   *Leiyla and the Poet* (1961) is based on the ancient Arabic ode *Majnum Leiyla.* The work follows the program of the poem in which a madman and a poet try to convince Leiyla to go different ways. Voices, excerpts of music of the Middle East, and an electronic oscillator are used as sources. Tape manipulation is used sparingly.

Henry, Pierre.   *Voile d'Orphée.* Philips 836-887.   Composed in 1953, *The Veil of Orpheus* is one of the earliest extended musique concrète compositions. The use of tape recorders provides much greater technical flexibility than is heard in *Symphonie pour un homme seul*. *Voile d'Orphée* uses a large variety of sounds treated by tape manipulation techniques. Many of the work's ideas, such as the use of harpsichord sounds, and the particular use of voice material, have become characteristic of several more recent French works. *Voile d'Orphée* also foreshadows similar dramatic works by Henry and other French composers.

Kayn, Roland. *Cybernetics III*. DGG 2543-006.   Vocal and animal sounds are the basic material of *Cybernetics III* (1969). Kayn creates interesting analogies between human and animal sounds by tape manipulation, especially speed and direction change. He also uses electronic processing techniques, such as filtering and ring modulation.

Mache, François-Bernard. *Terre de feu*. BAM LD-072; Candide 31025. *Terre de feu* (1963) is primarily a study in the effects of speed change. The original material is percussive and metallic and is changed into sounds reminiscent of the sounds of fire and water.

Malec, Ivo. *Luminétudes*. Philips 6521 017.   This 1968 work by the Yugoslavian composer demonstrates further possibilities of cutting and splicing as primary techniques. Although a wide variety of sounds are used, the listener is struck less with their natures or manipulations than with their juxtapositions with each other and with silences.

Mimaroglu, Ilhan. *Le Tombeau d'Edgar Poe*.   Turnabout TV 34004. This piece, composed in 1964, uses a recording of a reading of Mallarmé's poem *Le Tombeau d'Edgar Poe* as its only sound source. The vocal material undergoes extensive transformation by tape manipulation. Mimaroglu has produced what he considers to be a melodrama with musical-literary associations not unlike those found in some later text-sound works.

Parmegiani, Bernard. *Danse*. Candide CE 31025.   The main sound source in *Danse* (1962) is a collection of wordless vocal sounds. This material is accompanied by various instrumental timbres. A wide variety of tape manipulations and electronic processings creates an interesting array of transformations, with a continuum between the vocal and instrumental timbres.

Schaeffer, Pierre. *Étude aux objets*. Philips 6521 021.   This group of five works was originally composed in 1959 and revised in 1966-67. More sophisticated than the *Études of 1948*, these works use instrumental sounds treated in ways that are logical extensions of Schaeffer's ideas. The titles of the five sections describe their natures: *Expanded Objects; Related Objects; Multiplied Objects: Extended Objects; Reassembled Objects or Stretto*.

Takemitsu, Toru. *Vocalism Ai*. RCA VICS 1334.   *Ai* is the Japanese word for love. In *Vocalism Ai* (1960) the word *ai* is pronounced by a male and a female voice in many different ways and further varied by tape manipulations. The result is a wide variety of sounds made from a single source and an exploration of the variety of meanings of love.

10 + 2: 12 American Text Sound Pieces. 1750 Arch Street. (Available from 1750 Arch Records, Box 9444 Berkeley, CA 94700)   For English speaking listeners, this is one of the best introductions to the world of text-sound. There are a dozen varied works by eleven different composers including John Case, Charles Dodge, and Robert Ashley. Techniques employed in the various pieces range from garden variety tape recording (*crickets* by Aram Saroyan) to computer-synthesized speech (*Speech Songs* by Charles Dodge).

Vandelle, Romuald.   *Crucifixion* (excerpts). BAM LD-070.   *Crucifixion* was composed in 1960. It is typical of a genre of French works that are tape music presentations of dramatic, often religious, themes. These works are sometimes composed for radio broadcast, such as Pierre Henry's settings of the Gospels, or for theatrical presentation, such as Henry's *Voile d'Orphée*. *Crucifixion* depicts various stages of the crucifixion of Christ. A narrator introduces each section of the work. The piece is based on instrumental and vocal sounds.

PART

II

Electronic Music

9

ELECTRO-ACOUSTIC
MUSICAL INSTRUMENTS

PRECURSORS

The earliest electronic music was made by electro-acoustic musical instruments.[1] The origins of these instruments can be found in the long history of mechanical musical instruments.[2] While there are many considerations contributing to people's interest in designing, building, and listening to mechani-

[1] An interesting question arises when considering the definition of musical instrument. The dictionary definition is, roughly, anything that produces sound and is used musically. This definition has only been acceptable because of an unvoiced historical assumption that a musical instrument can be played in real-time. Until recently, this qualification remained unstated because the concept of not-real-time did not exist. Now, however, this qualification has become a necessary part of the definition of a musical instrument. An electronic music synthesizer, for example, may or may not be an "instrument," depending upon how it is designated and used. This has resulted not only in different design philosophies but also in divergent compositional aesthetics and theories. This matter is discussed further in Chapter 13.

[2] For an excellent discussion of mechanical musical instruments, see Alexander Buchner, *Mechanical Musical Instruments* (London: Batchworth Press, 1959).

cal musical instruments, three reasons stand out as being the most important. First, mechanical instruments are capable of autonomously imitating human musical activity. The imitation of human actions continues to be a fascination of composers using all manner of automata. Second, mechanical instruments can produce music that is impossible to perform with human means. A player piano, for instance, can play at faster tempos than any pianist. Third, mechanical musical instruments can preserve a given performance and reproduce it. For example, performances by pianists and composers have been preserved on player piano rolls. In varying degrees, these qualities are also typical of electro-acoustic musical instruments.

The first application of electricity to musical instrument design was made by J.B. Delabord, who invented the *Electric Harpsichord* in 1761. In this instrument, electricity was used to assist the *action*, or mechanism between the keyboard and the strings. Later similar instruments, such as Hipp's *Electromechanical Piano* (1867) and Gray's *Electroharmonic Piano* (1876), are motordriven acoustical instruments, not electro-acoustic musical instruments.

CLASSIFICATION OF ELECTRO-ACOUSTIC MUSICAL INSTRUMENTS

Electro-acoustic musical instruments are those in which the sound is in some way transmitted through electrical circuits. There are two general types of electro-acoustic instruments: *electrical* and *electronic*. *Electrical musical instruments* are those in which the initial sound is produced in a mechanical way. This category includes such instruments as the original Hammond Organ and electric guitars. *Electronic musical instruments* are those in which the sound is electronically generated. The Yamaha organ is an example of an electronic instrument. Both electrical and electronic musical instruments require amplification in order to be heard at normal listening volumes.[3]

---

[3] The classification of electro-acoustic instruments is not standardized. The present categories of *electrical* and *electronic* are used to simplify a confusing situation. Previous attempts at classification include those by Curt Sachs in *The History of Musical Instruments* (New York: W. W. Norton & Co., Inc., 1940) and Sibyl Marcuse in *Musical Instruments, A Comprehensive Dictionary*, (New York: Doubleday & Co., Inc., 1964). Sachs refers to the general class of electro-acoustic instruments as *electrophones*, while Marcuse uses the term *electrophonic instruments*. The term *electrical instrument* as used in this book refers to the same instruments as Sachs's term *electromechanical* and Marcuse's category of *electromechanical* (including *electrostatic*, *electromagnetic*, and *photoelectric*). The use of *electronic instrument* in this book is the same as Marcuse's us of the term. Sachs uses the outdated name *radioelectric instruments* to refer to electronic instruments.

The earliest discoveries in the relationship between electricity and the production of sound were accidental. One such case is the discovery of *galvanic music* by Dr. C.G. Page of Salem, Massachusetts. In 1837, Page was experimenting with a primitive battery, a coil, and some horseshoe magnets. He knew that the wet-cell battery, invented by Volta in 1800, stored an *electrical charge* and was capable of furnishing an *electric current*, or flow of electrons. Page also understood that electric currents are caused to flow by *voltage*, which is an electrical pressure, through an *electric circuit*, the path along which the current moves. However, Page was not aware of the properties of coils or of the concept of *induction*, the process by which a body with electrical or magnetic properties creates similar properties in a neighboring body without direct contact. Page was surprised to discover that when the coil was attached to the battery and one or both poles of the magnet were placed by the coil, a ringing sound was heard in the magnet when connections to the battery were either made or broken. He suspected that the sound was caused by the reverberation of the snapping sound made when connections to the battery were made or broken. Actually the coil became magnetized by the flow of current from the battery, and, through *electromagnetic induction*, the magnets were caused to vibrate whenever the circuit was made or broken.

In the years following Page's discovery, there were several experiments with the electrical production of sound, but no actual attempts to produce electrical instruments. One of the earliest electrical instruments was patented in 1885 by Ernst Lorenz. Lorenz called his invention *Elektrisches Musikinstrument*. This instrument used electrical vibrations to drive an electromagnet that was connected to resonating boards, thus translating electrical vibrations into sound. Lorenz's instrument looked not unlike a set of telegraph keys.

In 1899, William Duddell, an English physicist, invented the *Singing Arc*. This instrument used carbon arc lamps, whose discharge paths were interrupted by controlled electrical vibrations, to create sound.[4] The rate of the initial electrical vibrations, or oscillations, was controlled from a specially designed keyboard. When Duddell played his Singing Arc for the London Institution of Electrical Engineers, the music was simultaneously heard in two nearby laboratories, the arc lamps of these laboratories being on the same circuit as Duddell's Singing Arc. The Singing Arc, when played, created oscillations in the main line and caused other arc lamps on the same circuit to produce the music. Duddell speculated on the possibility that concerts

---

[4] Carbon arc lamps were commonly used for public lighting in the late nineteenth century. In the arc lamp, an intensely hot light was created by having an electrical current flow between two carbon *electrodes* or poles.

could be given in conjunction with lighting service but did not pursue the idea.

The work of Lorenz and Duddell was largely experimental, and did not result in any kind of musical activity other than isolated experimental presentations. By comparison, the achievement of Thaddeus Cahill is monumental.

THADDEUS CAHILL
AND THE TELHARMONIUM

Thaddeus Cahill was born in Iowa in 1867. At an early age, he became interested in the physics of musical sounds. When he was fourteen, he constructed his own telephone receiver, because the Bell company had refused to sell him one for his experiments. At the age of eighteen, Cahill dropped out of Oberlin College to devote more time to inventing. In 1890 he moved to Washington, D.C, where he worked as a clerk in the House of Representatives, took law courses at night at Columbia University, and invented the electric typewriter. In 1894, Cahill was admitted to the bar and began the practice of law, which he continued for several years.

In 1902 Cahill moved his laboratory from Washington to Holyoke, Massachusetts. By this time, he had already patented, and begun to build, the first *Telharmonium*, or *Dynamophone*. In 1906 Cahill built a larger and improved version of the Telharmonium and moved it from Holyoke to New York City. The machine filled thirty boxcars and weighed over two hundred tons; it had cost Cahill over $200,000. This was one of the largest and most expensive musical devices ever constructed.

The concept of the Telharmonium was based on known principles. Cahill was familiar with electric generators, or *alternators*. He knew that alternators produced a current that changed its direction between positive and negative values. This pattern of direction change could be graphically represented by a sine wave pattern. Cahill also knew that the recently invented telephone operated on the principle that acoustic vibrations could be converted into similar flucuations in electrical current by a microphone and reconverted into sound by a telephone receiver. Cahill figured that the output of an alternator could be fed directly into a telephone line without use of a microphone. As a result, an audible sine tone would be produced. The rate at which the alternator turned would determine the pitch of the sine tone, and several synchronized alternators could produce overtones of the harmonic series. Thus, complex timbres would be possible.

In 1906 Cahill installed the improved Telharmonium in Telharmonic Hall at 39th and Broadway. The basement of Telharmonic Hall contained the 145 alternators and other machinery necessary for the production of sound.[5] Upstairs, separated from the noise of the machines, was the console from which the Telharmonium was played. The console contained two organ keyboards that controlled pitch over a range of 40 to 4,000 Hz (B0 to E7). The relative amplitudes of various harmonics were determined by draw-stops above the keyboards, and the overall volume was controlled by a foot pedal.

Cahill intended to distribute the music of the Telharmonium by means of special telephone wires. For a monthly fee, subscribers would have their choice of operatic, classical, sacred, or popular music. The music would be heard through cone speakers, similar to, but larger than, those used on early phonographs.

The initial response to the Telharmonium was very positive:

> . . . the player, by using the proper keys and stops can construct the tones of any instrument he wishes. He can have the clear note of the flute, the heavy burr of the cello or the squeal of the fife. The qualities of all instruments—the vivacity of the piano, the emotion of the violin, the purity of the clarinet—are thus within instant reach of the player upon a machine of this type. The present instrument with 145 alternators, while producing the most extraordinary results, will not reach all of the combinations necessary, let us say, to produce the marvelously complex music of an orchestra, but the inventor is already planning a much larger machine, with hundreds of alternators, upon which eight or ten musicians may perform together, making possible heights of musical harmony never before imagined.
>
> Will the new instrument tend to affect the present musical art?
>
> If it reaches in practice anything like the perfection of its experimental performances, it will undoubtedly become a most valuable addition to the range of musical possibilities. As a pure economic proposition, it will furnish really good music much cheaper than the ordinary small orchestras; and there will be little danger of strikes of musicians. After a machine is installed in a city, a dozen or twenty highly skilled performers may easily supply thousands of restaurants, churches, schools, and homes with music.[6]

But the Telharmonium was not a success. There were a number of technical problems that were too difficult or too expensive to solve. Not enough subscribers could be found, and those who did subscribe complained of poor

---

[5] Cahill felt that at least three hundred alternators were necessary for a truly complete instrument. The expense, however, was too great.

[6] Ray Stannard Baker, "New Music for an Old World," *McClures Magazine* (July 1906), pp. 300-301.

service. Eventually, the public wearied of the novelty of the Telharmonium, and by 1909, the company had failed.

Although the technology of his time could not support his ideas, Cahill was responsible for several remarkable innovations, such as envelope and timbre control.[7]

The inventions of Lorenz, Duddell, and Cahill are electrical instruments, since they involve some mechanical production of sound. In order that electronic musical instruments might exist, it was necessary for *electronic audio oscillators* to be invented. These oscillators are electronic circuits that oscillate, producing frequencies in the audible range. Experimentation with electronic oscillations began shortly after Lee DeForest's invention of the *Audion* in 1906. The Audion, now known as the *triode*, is a type of vacuum tube that made amplification possible, and opened the way for experiments with electronic oscillators by DeForest and other scientists.

EARLY ELECTRONIC MUSICAL INSTRUMENTS

The *Theremin*, introduced in 1919 by Leon Termen in Moscow and Leningrad, is one of the earliest electronic instruments.[8] Unlike previous electro-acoustic instruments, it did not imitate any previous acoustic instrument. It is also the oldest electro-acoustic musical instrument still in use. The sound of the Theremin is made by two *ultrasonic* sine oscillators that produce frequencies higher than the audible range. One of these oscillators has a fixed frequency, the other oscillator is variable. To change the frequency of this oscillator the Theremin player moves one hand toward, or away from, a vertical metal rod. As the player's hand changes distance with regard to the rod, the interaction of the difference in *capacitance*, or electron storage potential, between the performer and the instrument causes the variable oscillator to change frequency. This creates a *difference tone* between the two oscillators. The difference tone lies in the audible range. It is these amplified difference tones that produce the sound of the Theremin. The volume of the instrument is similarly controlled by moving the other hand near a metal loop. The Theremin is a *monophonic* instrument, capable of producing only one pitch at a time. The theremin is probably best known for making the vibrato-portamento sounds heard in old horror and suspense films, such as Alfred Hitchcock's *Spellbound*.

Two monophonic electronic keyboard instruments were invented in 1928: Friedrich Trautwein's *Trautonium* and Maurice Martenot's *Ondes*

[7] In 1929, Laurens Hammond proved the commercial feasibility of Cahill's basic invention by constructing the Hammond Organ. This instrument is, in fact, a small, inexpensive, and practical version of the Telharmonium. For more detailed information on the Telharmonium, see "History of Electronic Music, Part One," *Synthesis*, vol. 1, no. 1, (1971).

[8] The word *Theremin* is a French corruption of the inventor's name.

Martenot. These instruments differ primarily in their method of timbre control. The Ondes Martenot produces a sinusoidal waveform that contains no overtones. If a more complex timbre is desired, overtones can be added by pressing one or more buttons located to the left of, and below, the keyboard. This creation of timbre through addition of harmonic content is known as *additive synthesis.* The Trautonium produces an initially complex waveform, making a complex timbre. If a simpler timbre is desired, it is necessary to filter out some of the overtones. Creating specific timbres by eliminating harmonics is known as *subtractive synthesis.*

The Trautonium was originally developed by Trautwein for experimental purposes. It never developed into a popular concert instrument, but it was used in schools throughout Germany since it had an untempered frequency range, making it useful for ear training. In 1948, the composer and inventor Oskar Sala (b. 1910) developed the *Mixturtrautonium.* Although it uses and elaborates Trautwein's original concept of subtractive synthesis, the Mixturtrautonium is not an electronic instrument, since the sound is generated from spun gut strings and then amplified. There are two keyboards, allowing *polyphonic* performance, where two or more notes may be produced simultaneously. Only one Mixturtrautonium was built, and it has been primarily used by Sala. The Mixturtrautonium can be heard in *Five Improvisations on Magnetic Tape* (1961) by Oscar Sala. Unfortunately, the unadulterated sound of the instrument is seldom heard in these improvisations. The great use of tape manipulation techniques and electronic processing create sounds that are reminiscent of a reverberated electronic organ.

The sound quality of the Ondes Martenot is distinct, since it never becomes very complex. Unlike the original Trautonium, the Ondes Martenot combines a tempered scale from the keyboard with the possibilities of portamento from a flexible metal strip, or *ribbon control.* Timbre and envelope are variable to a degree, and volume is controlled by a special key or by a knee-lever, similar to that of a harpsichord. The Ondes Martenot is one of the few early electronic instruments to have been successful. Hundreds of compositions incorporating the instrument have been written, mostly by French composers. Oliver Messiaen (b. 1908, Avignon, France) has composed several works for the Ondes Martenot. Perhaps the most famous is his ten movement *Turanglia-Symphony* (1948), a work that uses Ondes as a solo instrument. More unusual is Messiaen's *Fête des Belles Eaux*, composed in 1937 for a sextet of Ondes Martenot. The work was composed for a water show on the Seine that took place during the 1937 Paris Exposition. Since Messiaen wanted only the sounds of the monophonic Ondes, six instruments were necessary to allow a sufficient availability of pitches and textures. *Fête des Belles Eaux* demonstrates all of the various possibilities and characteristics of the Ondes, without overusing specific capabilities such as portamento.

In 1929, Laurens Hammond began producing the Hammond Organ. Strictly speaking, this very successful instrument is not an electronic organ.

Since the signal is produced electromagnetically, the Hammond Organ is really an electrical instrument. In the original Hammond Organ, there are a series of alternators. In each of these, a tone wheel, a rotating iron disc, produces a flux in the current provided by an electromagnet. This creates an alternating voltage, making a sinusoidal pattern that is then amplified. This scheme is actually a miniaturized version of Cahill's Telharmonium, and, like that instrument, produces sine waves. Since there are twelve alternators, each containing several tone wheels, sine waves in the normal harmonic series can be added together to make a variety of timbres. While the harmonics 2, 3, 4, 6, 8, 10, 12, and 16 are available and can be added in varying proportions, the original Hammond organ tends to sound like itself more than like a pipe organ. This, however, never seemed a drawback, and the instrument has been one of the most commercially successful electro-acoustic instruments. Although it has been widely used in popular music, the Hammond Organ has been all but ignored by composers of art music. Karlheinz Stockhausen's *Momente* (1962-1964) is a notable exception.

THE DEVELOPMENT OF ELECTRO-ACOUSTIC MUSICAL INSTRUMENTS

Between 1930 and 1950 over a hundred electro-acoustic instruments were invented. Here, in chronological order, are just a few: Emicon (1930); Hellertion (1931); Piano-harp (1932); Vivatone (1932); Electronde (1933); Croix sonore (1934); Partiturophon (1935); Electrochord (1936); Pianotron (1938); Melodium (1938); Novachord (1938); Ondioline (1941); Electronic Sackbut (1945); Clavioline (1947); Solovox (1947); Melochord (1949); Elektronium 91950). None of these instruments has survived in contemporary use. Some of them were too limited or unconventional to justify their acceptance. Others were basically experimental and provided stepping stones to more contemporary instruments.

Historically, the most successful electro-acoustic instruments are those that most closely resemble conventional acoustic instruments in both performance design and sound production. As a result, there are two general classes of contemporary electro-acoustic instruments: electronic organs and amplified conventional instruments.

Electrical organs have been generally phased out in favor of the electronic type. The reasons for this are simple: electronic organs can offer greater flexibility and variety. Indeed, some of the newer electronic organs incorporate features formerly found only on so-called synthesizers, and in general are so sophisticated in their designs and abilities that it can be difficult to distinguish between electronic organs and synthesizers.[9] Electronic

[9] This problem is further compounded by designs of some recent synthesizers; they look like electronic organs. This topic is further discussed in future chapters.

organs, as a group, have been successful because they are keyboard instruments and do not require major reorientation for the average keyboard performer.

Amplified conventional instruments have become quite common. While the electric guitar is the most notable, literally all conventional acoustic instruments have been amplified and electronically modified. The names of instruments designed for electro-acoustic production are usually modified by the term "electric," such as electric guitar, electric violin, electric piano, and so forth. In these instruments, the sound-producing mechanism is similar to, or the same as, the acoustical version except that it is amplified. In addition, these electrical instruments may also incorporate timbre-modifying devices. Any acoustical instrument can be easily amplified by means of a *contact microphone* attached to any resonating part of the body of the instrument.

DISCOGRAPHY

Messiaen, Oliver.   *Fêtes des Belles Eaux*. Erato LDE 3202; Musical Heritage Society 821.

Sala, Oskar.   *Five Improvisations on Magnetic Tape*. Westminister 8110.

Stockhausen, Karlheinz.   *Momente*. Nonesuch H-71157; Wergo 60024.

10
ELECTRONIC MUSIC AND OPTICAL SOUND TRACKS

OPTICAL SOUND TRACKS

During the first half of the twentieth century, almost all electronic music was produced by electro-acoustic musical instruments. The technical resources for studio composition did not yet exist. But by 1925 Lee DeForest had perfected a new way of recording and reproducing sound by optical means: *optical sound tracks*. This led to a type of electronic music produced by photoelectric devices.

Optical tracks are made by converting electrical impulses taken from a microphone into photographic images on film. This conversion is accomplished by having the electrical impulses open and close a light valve that exposes the film stock. This optically recorded sound information is put on the sound track of a film, the thin strip on one side of the width of the film. As the film is projected, the sound track passes an *optical reader*. This consists of a light source and a *photoelectric cell*, or *photocell*, which is usually a small glass bulb that contains special electrodes. As the optical track moves past the photocell, the changing pattern of lightness and darkness varies the amount of light reaching the photocell. This causes the electrical output of the photocell to vary. This output is amplified and the images are thus converted back into sound.

While optical tracks were originally invented for the purpose of recording and reproducing acoustical sounds, it was soon realized that optical tracks could also be used to create sound by drawing or photographing directly on the optical track. Because of the graphic nature of this medium (most of the work was done by animators rather than composers) electronic sound produced by optical tracks is often called *drawn sound* or *animated sound*.

Oskar Fischinger and *Ornamente Sound*

One of the earliest experiments in animated sound was conducted by the noted engineer and animator Oskar Fischinger (b. 1900, Gelnhausen, Germany; d. 1967, Los Angeles). On Easter of 1932, Fischinger was resting in the heat of a Berlin spring afternoon. As his wife, Elfriede, walked past the bedroom, she inadvertently dropped a key. Hearing the sound of the key falling on the wood floor, Fischinger left the bedroom and went into his film animation studio. Hours later, he emerged with a series of unusual drawings he called *ornamente sound*.

Having recognized the key falling to the wood floor solely from the resulting sound, Fischinger surmised that sounds must have distinct characteristics, or *shapes*, that could be graphically represented. Could it not be possible, Fischinger wondered, to produce sound directly by photographing drawings onto the optical track, thereby visually illustrating the qualities of sound?

Some of Fischinger's ornamente sound drawings are shown in Figure 10-1. When run through the optical reader of a sound projector, these drawings produce distinctive sounds that do not exist in nature. Fischinger soon learned that changes in the area and density of the images would control the pitch and volume of the sound, and the general shape of the drawing

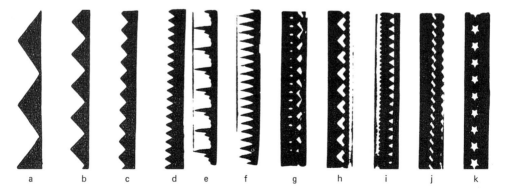

a   b   c   d   e   f   g   h   i   j   k

Figure 10-1   Examples of Ornamente Sound Drawings.

would create the timbre. In Figure 10-1, for instance, examples a, b, c, and d would produce the same kind of timbre at the same volume, but at increasingly higher pitches. All of the other examples would produce different timbres.[1]

In the early 1930s, several animators investigated methods of creating sound through the use of optical tracks.[2] Most of this work was experimental, and little of its survives. Of the more recent efforts in composing electronic music with optical tracks, undoubtedly the most important are those of John and James Whitney and Norman McLaren.

The Work of John and James Whitney

During 1943 and 1944, John Whitney and his brother James Whitney produced *Five Film Exercises.* The music for these films was created by photographing the movements of pendulums and printing the results on the sound track. The motions of pendulums produce sinusoidal waveforms when reproduced on optical tracks. By using several pendulums simultaneously, and by reexposing the same film stock over and over, additive synthesis could be achieved, and complex timbres created. In addition to these techniques, the original film could be exposed at very slow rates and later on reproduced at rates as much as sixty times that of the original. This allowed the Whitneys the capabilities of variable speed effects and a large frequency range. All of these techniques were facilitated by a special machine that the Whitneys designed. After the film was exposed, it could be easily edited for desired juxtapositions.

As John Whitney notes, "Our art was, by comparison, without historical precedent and our apparatus was equally new and requiring invention."[3] The music for *Five Film Exercises* is one of the earliest extant works of electronic music. Even more interesting, it is far more sophisticated and complex than much of the music produced in the electronic music studios

[1] For more detailed information on optical sound recording, see Howard M. Tremaine, *Audio Cyclopedia*, 2nd ed. (New York: Howard W. Sams & Co., Inc., 1969).

[2] For a discussion of early experiments with *animated sound*, see Roy M. Prendergast, *A Neglected Art* (New York: W. W. Norton & Co., Inc., 1972), pp. 186-197. Some of the information presented here is questionable, especially with regard to early experiments. This is due to the lack of primary source material on the subject and the mistakes that exist in most secondary references. It is probably impossible to write a correct, documented, and thorough history of *animated sound.* For this reason, I have omitted questionable events from the text of this book and have dealt only with what can be documented by reliable primary sources.

[3] John Whitney, "Moving Pictures and Electronic Music," in *DIE REIHE*, v. 7 (1960), p. 61. Copyright © 1960 by Universal Edition, Vienna, Copyright © 1965, English edition. Copyright assigned to Universal Edition Publishing, Inc. Used by permission of European American Music Distributors Corp., sole U.S. Agent for Universal Edition.

of the early 1950s. The music works particularly well as an accompaniment to the abstract, but technically unrelated, animated images of the film.

The Whitneys did not continue their work in composing with sound tracks. There were certain problems with the pendulum system that seemed insurmountable. However, the Whitneys' concerns were primarily visual rather than musical.

The Work of Norman McLaren

Norman McLaren (b. 1914, Stirling, Scotland) was one of the first animators to work with animated sound. He has also created many films with optically produced electronic music: *Book Bargain* (1936); *Allegro* (1939); *Rumba* (1939); *Dots* (1948); *Loops* (1948); *Pen Point Percussion* (1950); *Now is the Time* (1951); *Two Bagatelles* (1952); *Neighbors* (1952); *Blinkity Blank* (1954); *Rhythmetic* (1956); *Korean Alphabet* (1967) (visuals by Kim in Tae); *Synchromy* (1971).[4] McLaren has used both hand-drawn and photographed sound tracks with fascinating results. The music for *Neighbors*, for examples, so well suits the images that it is difficult to imagine one without the other. Perhaps the most interesting of these films is *Synchromy*, a film in which one sees and hears the same thing simultaneously.

In *Synchromy*, McLaren has used the optimal track for the visuals. McLaren first composed the music for *Synchromy*, creating a light and humorous background. He then "recorded" the music on the optical track by photographing it, frame by frame. For this he used a method first developed by Rudolph Phenninger in the early 1930s for his film *Tonal Handwriting*. McLaren constructed sixty cards, each measuring 1 by 12 inches. On these cards are drawings of alternating black and white spaces. Each card represents one pitch of the chromatic scale, thus giving a five-octave range. The appropriate card is photographed as called for by the musical score, and thus the soundtrack is created. The visual part of *Synchromy* graphically displays the same soundtrack, although the image is often shown in multiples and color has been added to make the film more interesting.

OPTICAL TRACK MUSICAL INSTRUMENTS

Optical tracks have also been used to make photoelectric musical instruments. In 1935, Yeugeny Sholpo, who worked at the Leningrad Conservatory and the Moscow experimental studio, built *Variophones*, instruments

---

[4] The film *Pen Point Percussion* is a documentary on the animated sound process as practiced by McLaren. Similar information is also contained in a documentary on McLaren, *The Eye Hears and the Ear Sees*. These and most of McLaren's films are available from The Canadian Film Institute, 75 Albert Street, Suite 1105, Ottawa, Ontario K1P5E7.

using preprinted optical tracks to make sound. More recent instruments include the commercial *Welte Organ* and the *Optigon*. The Welte Organ was built in Germany in the 1950s. The optical tracks of this instrument were printed on twelve large identical glass discs that turned at different speeds conforming to the tempered scale. Each disc produced several timbres with octave transpositions. The discs were removable and could be changed to provide different timbres. A complicated system of lamps, prisms, photocells, and keying devices made the instrument operable. Theoretically, this system would allow one to play any desired sound from an organ keyboard.[5]

The Optigon used a system similar to, but much simpler than, that of the Welte Organ. The optical tracks were printed on thin plastic discs, and only one disc was used at a time. The instrument resembled a small cord organ and was marketed, rather unsuccessfully by Mattel, Inc., as a toy during the early 1970s.

Electronic music created by optical tracks occupies a curious niche in electro-acoustic music. As a medium of composition, it interested almost no composers and very few film-makers; McLaren's work is unique. As a type of instrumental design, photoelectric sound production has been commercially unsuccessful. In fact, outside of the United States optical sound recording is almost an anachronism; most films now use magnetic sound tracks. Compared to magnetic sound recording, optical tracks offer poor quality sound, clumsy manipulation, and rapid deterioration.

[5] For more detailed information on the Welte Organ, as well as photoelectric sound generation in instruments, see Alan Douglas, *The Electronic Musical Instrument Manual*, 5th ed. (London: Sir Isaac Pitman & Sons, Ltd., 1968), pp. 108-114 and pp. 290-293.

11
CLASSICAL STUDIO ELECTRONIC MUSIC
The Cologne Studio and its Precursors

Classical studio electronic music is predicated on the use of the tape recorder and tape manipulation techniques. The basic difference between musique concrète and classical studio electronic music is the type of material used as sound sources. While musique concrète uses acoustic source material, the sound sources for classical studio electronic music are electronically generated sounds.

SIMPLE ELECTRONIC WAVEFORMS

There are four simple *waveforms* or *waveshapes* that are commonly used in the production of electronic music: *sinusoidal* or *sine, sawtooth, square,* and *triangle*. The names of these waveforms are derived from the shapes they produce when visually represented on an oscilloscope. Each particular shape represents a graph of the voltage change, the change of electrical pressure, in time. These four waveforms are illustrated in Figure 11-1.

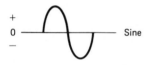
Sine

Sawtooth

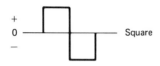
Square

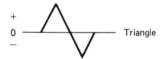
Triangle

Figure 11-1 Simple Waveforms.

Each of these waveforms has a characteristic timber that is a result of the particular structure of each waveform's harmonics and their relative amplitudes. A description of these characteristics is known as *Fourier analysis*, named after Jean Baptiste Joseph Baron Fourier (1768-1830), a French mathematician and physicist. Fourier analysis tells us that any *periodic* waveform, one that repeats exactly, can be analyzed or described as a series of sinusoidal waveforms, or *components*, that exist in integral multiples of the fundamental frequency. This, of course, is the harmonic series.[1] Fourier analysis also describes the relative amplitude and phase characteristics of each harmonic. These characteristics of frequency, amplitude, and phase are known as the *frequency spectrum*, or simply *spectrum*, of a waveform.[2]

[1] This has already been discussed in Chapter 5.

[2] The reverse procedure of Fourier analysis is *Fourier synthesis;* it is the building up, or synthesizing, of a waveform from sinusoidal components. Fourier synthesis can be similar to, or identical to, additive synthesis in electronic music, depending on the particular situation. For more information on Fourier analysis and synthesis, see Wayne A. Slawson, "Sound, Electronics, and Hearing," in *The Development and Practice of Electronic Music,* ed. Jon H. Appleton and Ronald C. Perera (Englewood Cliffs, NJ: Prentice-Hall, Inc., 1975), pp. 35-40.

Since the basic waveforms used in electronic music are periodic, their spectra are easily analyzed. Sine waves have already been discussed; they are the simplest of all possible waveforms and, therefore, cannot be further analyzed.

Sawtooth waves contain all harmonics in the harmonic series, and the amplitude of each harmonic is the inverse of its position in the series.

Square waves are types of *rectangular*, or *pulse*, *waves*. Square waves contain only the odd numbered harmonics. This is because the square wave is fifty percent positive, which means that fifty percent of its cycle has a positive voltage. Another way of saying this is that a square wave has a 1:2 *duty cycle*. As a result, every other harmonic (2,4,6,8,etc.) is missing. Thus, a square wave contains only odd (1,3,5,7,etc.) harmonics, and the relative amplitude of the harmonics are the same as for sawtooth waves: The amplitude of each harmonic is the inverse of its position in the series.

Many different types of *pulse waves* are possible. The harmonic content of a pulse wave is determined by its duty cycle. For example, a pulse wave with a duty cycle of 1:4 will be 25 percent positive, and every fourth harmonic will be missing. Square wave oscillators are fixed and can only produce square waveforms. Variable pulse wave oscillators have controllable duty cycles and can produce a variety of pulse, or rectangular, waveforms.

Triangle waves contain only odd harmonics, and the relative amplitude of each harmonic is the square of the inverse of that harmonic's position $\frac{1}{n^2}$. It is this difference in the relative amplitude of the triangle wave's harmonics that causes it to sound different from the square wave.

In addition to these periodic waveforms, another commonly used sound source in electronic music is *white noise*, or *white sound*. White noise is the result of all frequencies within the audible spectrum sounding simultaneously at randomly varying amplitudes. The result is a hissing, wind-like sound.[3]

Electronically generated sound waves are the basic material of all electronic music. Electronic oscillators have been used in electronic musical instruments since 1920, but the classical electronic music studio dates only from the early 1950s. What differentiates classical studio from other types of electronic music is that it is a studio approach to composition and is primarily dependent on the tape manipulation techniques for the processing of sound.[4]

---

[3] White noise is sometimes referred to as *coloured noise* in British sources. *Pink noise* has been used to refer to the lower spectrum of white noise (under 1,000 Hz), and *blue* noise has been used to refer to the higher frequencies.

[4] The studio approach to the composition of electro-acoustic music was roughly formulated by Pierre Schaeffer. There are obviously close relationships to practices in the visual arts. See the interview with Morton Subotnick in Chapter 18 for an elaboration of this point.

Louis and Bebe Barron in their studio in 1965. (Photo by Walter Daran.)

It will probably never be known who was responsible for the first studio-composed work of electronic music. This is not because of a lack of claims; it is due to a lack of historical clarity. Electronic music was not born as a studio art, as was musique concrète, but rather as instrumental performance music. The studio approach to electronic music developed gradually, and it was probably not until 1951 that anything resembling the classical electronic music studio existed.[5]

LOUIS AND BEBE BARRON

In 1951, at least two classical electronic music studios were established: the studio of Louis and Bebe Barron in New York City, and the NWDR studio in Cologne, Germany. Louis and Bebe Barron began experimenting with the manipulation of taped sounds in 1948. Working independently, and unaware of Schaeffer's work until 1950, the Barrons developed their own techniques and attitudes. In 1951, the Barrons began building electronic oscillators and composed their first electronic music composition, *Heavenly Menagerie*.

The Barrons developed an aesthetic of composition based on the characteristics of their equipment. "We began to explore the possibilities of simple circuits [that] had characteristic behavior patterns. The desiderata was that the behavior should not be regulated, but rather nonlogical. The most interesting sounds often came from circuits that were not stable."[6]

[5] Lowell Cross lists several "electronic music" compositional events in his article "Electronic Music 1948-1953," in *Perspectives of New Music*, 7 (Fall-Winter, 1968), 59-61. What many of these actually were remains nebulous.

[6] Louis Barron, in conversation with the author.

The result of this approach was that the Barrons' music tended to consist of short sections, spliced together. Each section is presented in its characteristic form and there is usually no further development. This style of composing lends itself well to dramatic application, and it is no wonder that Louis and Bebe Barron are best known for their electronic music film scores, which include *Bells of Atlantis* (1953), *Miramagic* (1954), *Forbidden Planet* (1956), *Jazz of Lights* (1956), and *Bridges* (1969).

THE COLOGNE STUDIO

The NWDR (Nordwestdeutscher Rundfunk: the Northwest German Radio) studio in Cologne represents an entirely different, and historically more usual approach to the classical electronic music studio. The Cologne studio was founded in 1951 by three men: Herbert Eimert (b. 1897, Bad Kreuznach, Germany; d. 1972), Robert Beyer (b. 1901, Germany); and Werner Meyer-Eppler (b. 1913, Antwerp; d. 1960, Bonn). Of these three, only Eimert was a composer. He was a graduate of the Kölner Konservatorium and a devotée of Schoenberg's twelve-tone theories. Eimert's own work *Antonale Musiklehre* (1924) was one of the earliest dissertations on Schoenberg's method.

Werner Meyer-Eppler was a physicist and mathematician and one of the pioneers in information theory. He also had a continuing interest in electro-acoustic music, and in 1949 he wrote *Elektrische Klangerzeugung*, one of the first surveys of the field.

Robert Beyer was, among other things, an inventor and author whose work occasionally dealt with electro-acoustic music.

On October 18, 1951, Eimert, Meyer-Eppler, and Beyer established the Cologne studio. The location was chosen because of the new NWDR facilities. The guiding light and first director of the Cologne studio was Eimert. He saw serial composition as the only truly intelligent way of approaching contemporary composition. Inevitably, he saw electronic music as the next logical development of serial technique: "Only in electronic music has the real sense of these developments (in serial technique) been realized."[7] The key for Eimert was in the ability to control: ". . . only

---

[7] Herbert Eimert, "What is electronic music?," *DIE REIHE* (The Row), 1 (1958), 8. Copyright © 1955 by Universal Edition, Vienna, Copyright © 1958 English Edition. Copyright assigned to Universal Edition Publishing, Inc. Used by permission of European American Music Distributors Corp. sole U.S. agent for Universal Edition. Eimert's article is one of the most fascinating of the early writings on electronic music. It is at once a proclamation and a defense of the medium. Eimert is steadfast in his beliefs, and he attempts to delineate not only the proper aesthetic but also the definitive materials of electronic music. Eimert had little time for Schaeffer and other composers who pursued far less "rational" paths. Although Eimert's ideas and terminology may seem somewhat anachronistic today, an understanding of his ideas is necessary for a true comprehension of the European music of the 1950s and 1960s.

in coming to electronic music can we talk of a real musical control of nature."[8] Eimert believed that more control over the elements of music allowed for greater specificity in the compositional process; this resulted in the ultimate goal of achieving a greater, and therefore better, musical order.

THE WORK OF HERBERT EIMERT

Eimert was very influential in the early development of electronic music in Germany. As director of the Cologne studio he was responsible not only for its physical but also for its psychological makeup. He selected both the equipment for the studio and the composers who would work there. Since Eimert was very careful about the funding of his project and the documentation of its production, the Cologne studio soon became the best known of the early classical electronic music studios.[9]

Eimert's ideas are perhaps best reflected in his own compositions. Eimert's *Struktur 8* (1953) is based on serial techniques but uses only eight pitches instead of twelve. The source material is electronically generated and systematically varied by means of filtering, ring modulation, and reverberation.[10] The style of *Struktur 8* is *pointillistic*, a common characteristic of much classical studio electronic music, especially that from the early days of the Cologne studio.[11]

Eimert was also interested in the possibilities of using speech sounds in tape composition. Although he was familiar with Schaeffer's work, Eimert

[8] Ibid., p. 10.

[9] One of Eimert's most important contributions was the establishment of the periodical *DIE REIHE*, which was devoted to contemporary music as viewed by Eimert and his associates. Published between 1955 and 1962, *DIE REIHE* was the main forum for European serial and post-serial composers. The eight volumes of *DIE REIHE* are available in the original German edition from Universal Edition, and in English translation from European-American Music Corporation.

[10] Only an excerpt of Eimert's *Struktur 8* is available on disc. It exists on a curious recording issued by Wergo: WER60006. The record is largely a lecture by Eimert, assisted at one point by Meyer-Eppler, and illustrated by short musical excerpts and examples. Since the information is largely verbal and in German, it is of little value to those who do not understand the language. The result is a record with more dogmatic than documentary intent. The information on side one of this disc is available to readers of English in Eimert's article "What is electronic music?," *DIE REIHE*, 1 (1958), 8. Side two of the record does present excerpts of some of Eimert's early works. The first four excerpts are the most interesting, the fourth of these being from *Struktur 8*, and the first three *probably* being, in order, from *Klangstudie I* (1952), *Klangstudie II* (1952-53), and *Ostinate Figuren und Rhythmen* (1953).

[11] *Pointillism* is a term used to describe a style of twentieth century music where the musical events appear isolated and separated from each other, especially with regard to pitch, duration, and register. The result is a music of short and disjointed sound events. The term was first used in music to describe the later works of Anton Webern. Pointillistic originally described a style of French impressionist painting in which the artist used separate dots of basic colors instead of brush strokes of mixed colors to define an image.

had little regard for such an intuitive approach to composition. Eimert's interest in, and use of, speech sounds probably dates from 1949, when Meyer-Eppler first became aware of the *Vocoder*, a device for analyzing and synthesizing voice sounds first developed by Bell Telephone Laboratories. Meyer-Eppler developed his interest in electronic music and speech synthesis simultaneously as is evidenced by the title of his book *Electronic Tone Generation, Electronic Music, and Synthetic Speech* (Bonn, 1949). His interests were shared by Eimert, and together they conducted several investigations of speech sounds, utilizing Meyer-Eppler's knowledge of information theory and phonetics. They rigorously and systematically explored the effects of tape manipulation techniques and electronic processing techniques, such as filtering and ring modulation, on speech sounds. The result of most of these experiments was the transformation of speech into abstract sounds.

Eimert's *Selektion I* (1959) displays the outgrowth of his experiments with Meyer-Eppler, as well as Eimert's own compositional philosphy. The basic material for *Selektion I* is both concrète and electronic. The concrète material is derived from a spoken text that delineates the technical and compositional processes of the work. After this material has been manipulated and processed, it is no longer recognizable as speech but resembles the electronic material of the piece with which it is mixed to form the completed work. The construction of both the concrète and electronic materials of *Selektion I* was accomplished by following strict procedures derived from concepts of serial composition. Both the process and the result are very different from Schaeffer's music. In Eimert's music there is no exploration of an intuitive or improvisational nature. The final versions of the speech material are used in the same manner as the electronic material; indeed, the difference in the perceivable qualities of the sounds are slight.

The Cologne studio was fully operational by 1953. Its makeup was typical of a well-equipped classical electronic music studio: There were several electronic oscillators that produced primarily sine and sawtooth waveforms, white noise generators, ring modulators, various types of filters, *gates* (devices for controlling the amplitude, or envelope characteristics, of a sound), reverberators, a Monochord and a Melochord (both electronic music keyboard instruments, later removed from the studio on philosophical grounds), several tape recorders (both one and four channel machines) including some with variable speed capability, tape-loop players, and the usual tape editing equipment.

KARLHEINZ STOCKHAUSEN

One of the best known composers associated with the Cologne studio is Karlheinz Stockhausen (b. 1928, Madrath, Cologne). Stockhausen's formal education in composition began in 1950 when he studied with Frank Martin at the Cologne Academy. Under Martin's tutelage, Stockhausen became familiar with the works of Bartók, Stravinsky, and, especially, Schoenberg. In 1951, Stockhausen met Herbert Eimert. Eimert introduced him to the later works and ideas of Anton von Webern (1883-1945), a Viennese composer who greatly expanded Schoenberg's twelve-tone method and who was responsible for the initial developments of serial techniques. Eimert also involved Stockhausen in the contemporary music world of Cologne and Germany, particularly in programming for the West German Radio. Although Eimert appears to be the largest single influence on Stockhausen, there were several others. Stockhausen was impressed with the music of Pierre Boulez (b. 1925, Montbrison, France) and Messiaen, particularly Boulez's *Second Piano Sonata* and *Le Soleil des eaux*, and Messiaen's *Four Studies* for piano. Stockhausen was also impressed with the ideas of Meyer-Eppler, especially his work in information theory and its applications to music.[12]

In 1952, Stockhausen went to Paris to work at the ORTF studio and study at the Conservatoire with Messiaen. During this time, Stockhausen kept in close contact with Eimert, who was putting the finishing touches on the Cologne studio. In 1953, Stockhausen was invited by Eimert to be co-director of the Cologne studio. Later, Stockhausen became the sole director, a position he held until 1978.

So much contradictory material has been written by and about Karlheinz Stockhausen and his work that it is almost impossible to unravel. Stockhausen is one of the most important figures in mid-twentieth-century music, but the basic reasons for his eminence are often overlooked. Stockhausen and his music emerged from a background firmly rooted in history and tradition. Unlike some other composers of his generation, Stockhausen embraced his musical heritage, particularly as he saw it revealed in Webern, and built upon it. His developments of serial and post-serial thought were, in his mind, the logical extensions of the past. His work was the promise of fulfillment.

Stockhausen developed many of the techniques and philosophies of mid-twentieth-century music. His ideas about musical form, compositional process, musical notation, extension of musical resources, and classical electronic music studio techniques were often pioneering. In addition, Stockhausen has documented his work perhaps more carefully than any other twentieth-century composer. He has left a trail of scores, recordings, and writings that are testaments to his accomplishments.

One of the most important aspects of Stockhausen's career is the parallel it has made to much of the development of contemporary music from 1952 to about 1974. He helped rescue rationality from the chaos of

---

[12] These were the major influences on Stockhausen's intellectual and musical life. However, Jonathan Harvey believes that the complex personality that is Karlheinz Stockhausen can only be explained as the result of an equally complex background. Harvey deals with this subject in his book *The Music of Stockhausen* (Los Angeles: University of California Press, 1975).

World War II by promoting Webern and serialism. Working within the twentieth-century concept (perhaps mythological) of a progressive evolution, Stockhausen developed and expanded his ideas into ever increasing complexity, sophistication, and, above all, rationality. The development of systematic complexities eventually led to a reduction of their essences and, finally, to their abandonment. Stockhausen's later works are largely intuitive and improvisational, and sometimes rather conceptual.[13]

Stockhausen's Study II

Study II (1954) was Stockhausen's first important work of electronic music. This work was preceded by two other tape pieces: *Étude* (1952), composed at the Paris studio, and *Study I* (1953), composed at Cologne. *Study II* typifies the techniques and procedures of classical studio electronic music, as well as Stockhausen's compositional thinking at the time. The source material for *Study II* consists entirely of sine waves. This was considered to be the purest sound source for electronic music composition, since it is the most elemental and allows, almost demands, that the composer construct his own timbres. "Such sinus tones were the first elements with which we com-posed (literally put together) various spectra according to the structural demands of a particular composition. *Each single sound is therefore the result of a compositional act.* The composer determines the various characteristics, also called *parameters*."[14]

In composing *Study II*, Stockhausen chose to base the piece on the number 5.[15] In dealing with pitch, he decided to create an available scale of frequencies separated by the constant interval of $25\sqrt{5}$, or 1.066494942, or 1.07. This interval is slightly larger than a half-tone or minor second. Starting at 100 Hz, Stockhausen multiplied each successive frequency by $25\sqrt{5}$:

$$100 \times 25\sqrt{5} = 106.6494942 = 107 \text{ Hz};$$
$$107 \times 25\sqrt{5} = 114.1149588 = 114 \text{ Hz};$$
$$114 \times 25\sqrt{5} = 121.5804234 = 121 \text{ Hz; etc.}$$

[13] See Jonathan Harvey's discussion of *Aus den seiben Tagen,* one of Stockhausen's early "intuitive" works.

[14] Karlheinz Stockhausen, "Electronic and Instrumental Music," *DIE REIHE,* 5 (1959), 61. It should be noted that Stockhausen's use of the word *parameter* is technically incorrect. *Parameter* is a mathematical term that primarily refers to any quantity whose value changes with the circumstances of its application. This makes little sense when applied to concepts such as pitch, rhythm, or dynamics. Milton Babbitt has suggested an alternative terminology for use when dealing with music in terms of specifically measurable quantities. Babbitt suggests the use of the term *dimension* for a general area and the term *element* for a specific identity within that area. Thus, the element of A4 would exist within the dimension of pitch. This approach makes sense in dealing with quantification and is probably what most composers want to relate when they use the term *parameter.* However, it is questionable whether all qualifiable aspects of sound are quantifiable. In normal parlance, it seems reasonable to speak of such properties as pitch and dynamics as aspects of sound, or even as elements of sound.

[15] Perhaps this was related to the fact that he was simultaneously composing *Piano Piece V.*

This intervallic ratio does not produce whole numbers, so Stockhausen had to round off his frequency calculations.[16] This procedure yielded a scale of eighty-one frequencies between 100 Hz and 17,200 Hz. It is interesting to note that no octaves can be produced in this tuning of approximately ten divisions to the octave.

Having produced his usable pitch material, Stockhausen proceeded to create his *note mixtures*, which are chord-like combinations of five frequencies each.[17] Predictably, there are five different tupes of "note mixtures," or chords, that are determined by having the constant intervallic ratios between pitches be 1, 2, 3, 4, or 5 times $25\sqrt{5}$. Each frequency in each chord type can serve as the base (lowest) frequency, therefore allowing for five chords in each type. Table 2 shows the frequency components for the first twenty-five chords in this scheme.

Table 2

CHORD TYPE	CHORD NUMBER	FREQUENCIES
I	1	100, 107, 114, 121, 129
I	2	107, 114, 121, 129, 138
I	3	114, 121, 129, 138, 147
I	4	121, 129, 138, 147, 157
I	5	129, 138, 147, 157, 167
II	6	100, 114, 129, 147, 167
II	7	114, 129, 147, 167, 190
II	8	129, 147, 167, 190, 217
II	9	147, 167, 190, 217, 246
II	10	167, 190, 217, 246, 280
III	11	100, 121, 147, 178, 217
III	12	121, 147, 178, 217, 246
III	13	147, 178, 217, 263, 319
III	14	178, 217, 263, 319, 386
III	15	217, 263, 319, 386, 469
IV	16	100, 129, 167, 217, 280
IV	17	129, 167, 217, 280, 362
IV	18	167, 217, 280, 362, 469
IV	19	217, 280, 362, 469, 607
IV	20	280, 362, 469, 607, 785
V	21	100, 138, 190, 263, 362
V	22	138, 190, 263, 362, 500
V	23	190, 263, 362, 500, 690
V	24	263, 362, 500, 690, 952
V	25	362, 500, 690, 952, 1310

[16] Curiously, Stockhausen seems to have done this with some inconsistency, even though he says that the rounding off was directed by the possible frequencies obtainable on the oscillator he used.

[17] Even though Stockhausen refers to these individual frequencies as *partials*, these *note mixtures* are not truly like harmonic series, since all of the frequencies are at equal amplitudes, and these frequencies are not integral multiples of a fundamental. See Karlheinz Stockhausen *Studie II* (London: Universal Edition, 1956), p. vi.

These chords are graphically displayed in Figure 11-2. As in the previous list, chord numbers are designated at the lowest frequency of each chord.

This entire procedure for the formation of chords, or *note mixtures*, is repeated nine times. This results in a total of 193 chords or mixtures: $9 \times 25 = 225 - 32$ duplicate chords = 193.

The chords may be present one at a time or in combinations of 2, 3, 4, or 5. Chord types may be mixed with each other. It is this construction and mixture of sine tone chords that gives *Study II* its particular timbral flavor.

To complete the scheme of fives, Stockhausen divides the piece into five sections. Each section can be characterized by specific qualities: I (0'00"-0'52"; pp. 1-8) deals with sounds of light density, usually only 1 five-note chord at a time and of generally medium duration; II (0'53"-1'20"; pp. 8-13) uses much denser combinations of sine waves, often of 5 five-note chords; III (1'21"-1'40"; pp. 13-15) is characterized by very short envelopes of primarily single chord sounds; IV (1'41"-2'13"; pp. 16-20) has widely spaced chord combinations that cover a large frequency spectrum and are presented with long envelopes; V (2'14"-2'54"; pp. 21-26) is a combination of all of the four previous types of material.

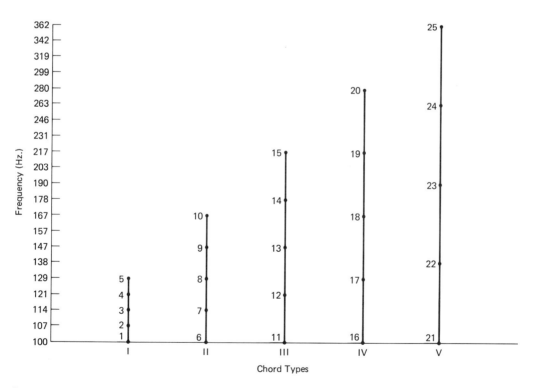

Figure 11-2   Chord Types (note mixtures) used in Study II.

Stockhausen also creates a decibel scale for dealing with amplitudes ranging from 0 dB (which he describes as at least equal to 80 phons) down to −30 dB. This is a volume scale with relative values for the amplitudes of the sounds. The scale is divided into thirty equal divisions of 1 dB increments. This decibel scale does not seem to be governed by the number 5.

Stockhausen does not explain how he made his final compositional decisions for *Study II*.[18] It may be safely assumed, however, that serial techniques played some part. Also evident is the development of the idea of *Klangfarbenmelodie* (tone color melody). This idea was first used by Schoenberg in his *Five Orchestra Pieces* (1909) where he assigned the notes of a melody to be played successively be different instruments. This elevated the importance of timbre to a more predominant role; the change of timbres can be followed by the ear, as can the change of pitches. Webern elaborated the idea of Klangfarbenmelodie so that the timbral changes became the melody in the sense that they are more apparent than pitch structures. In *Study II*, as well as other early works of Eimert and Stockhausen, Klangfarbenmelodie has been developed to the point where the pitches, or frequencies, are important, in part because they determine the timbres, timbres that never before existed.

After Stockhausen's materials had been created and ordered, he prepared a score of *Study II*, the first page of which is shown in Figure 11-3. Each page of this score has only one system, divided into three parts. The top portion indicates the chords, or note mixtures, being used. The chords are represented by shaded rectangles placed on a frequency grid. The shading of the chord boxes ranges from transparent (one chord) to black (five chords) depending on how many chords are sounding simultaneously. The bottom portion of the system indicates the shape and relative amplitude of the envelope of the vertically corresponding chord box(es) by placing shapes representing the envelopes on a decibel grid. The middle portion of the system is a sort of splicing chart representing, in centimeters at 30 ips, the length of the individual pieces of tape.

Having formulated the materials, their ordering, and the score for *Study II*, Stockhausen was ready to begin the realization of the work. Each of the five frequencies of each of the 193 chords was recorded at a uniform amplitude (this is the first, or original, generation of the recorded sound). A 4cm piece of tape of each frequency was cut out of the original tape. The five 4cm pieces of tape for each chord were then spliced together end to end, beginning with the lowest frequency. Next, each of these pitch sequences

---

[18] The epitome of Stockhausen's formalized thinking is to be found in *Plus Minus* (1963); the ultimate reduction of his principles of construction is in *Kurzwellen* (1968). The fully developed *Plus Minus* system is not evidenced in *Study II*, but those elements of the system drawn from Webern and Eimert are obviously present. To what degree the ordering of elements of the piece were serially structured is not clear. The use of information theory, so central in *Plus Minus*, is only slightly relevant to *Study II*, since Stockhausen did not take classes from Meyer-Eppler until 1954.

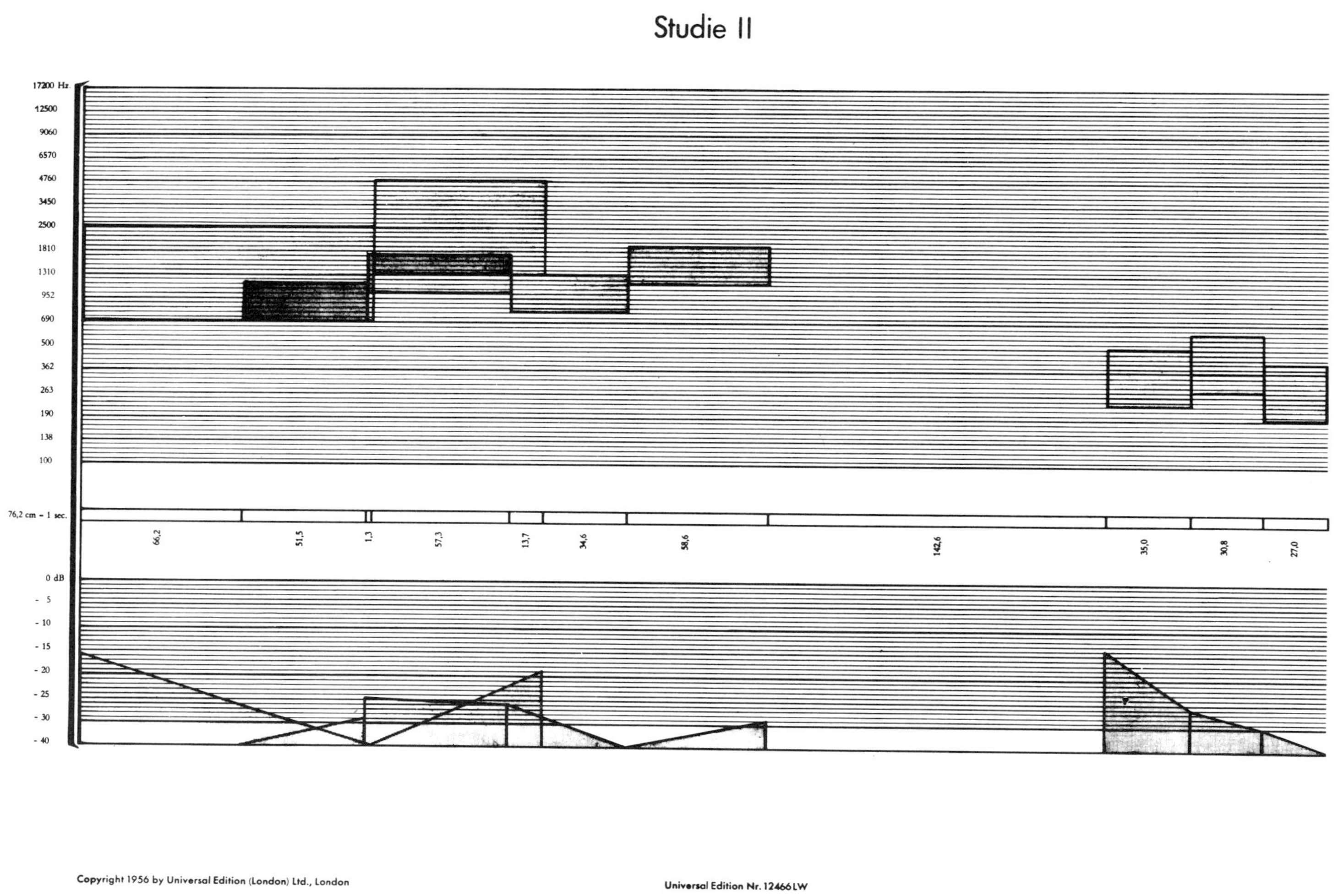

Studie II

Figure 11-3 Page 1 of *Study II*.

was played back in an echo chamber that had about a ten second reverbera-tion time. This had the effect of blurring the five frequencies together into one sound aggregate, or chord, although the various frequencies would still "enter" in order, creating a stepped attack. The reverberated chord was recorded on another piece of tape (second generation). This tape was cut and formed into a tape loop. The loop was played back while its volume was manually regulated according to the desired envelope. This result was recorded (third generation) and used in the final master of *Study II*.[19]

After each chord has been thus recorded, according to the required timing lengths in the score, it was necessary to mix the various chords together where called for. Thus, as illustrated in Figure 11-3, the second, third, fifth, and sixth chords could be recorded and spliced together to form one piece of tape, and the first and fourth chords could be recorded and spliced together to form a second piece of tape. These two pieces would then be played back simultaneously and recorded on another tape (fourth generation). This would produce the first succession of chords heard in *Study II*. This is followed by a period of silence for which a piece of blank or leader tape would have been spliced on.

The method of construction that Stockhausen used for *Study II* is typical of classical studio technique. Most classical studio electronic music works were put together by such laborious, time-consuming methods. It is easy to understand how even a short work of classical studio electronic music could take many months to complete.

Study II is a classic example of classical studio electronic music. It is rationally planned, ordered, executed, and documented.[20] It was produced with painstaking effort by using tape manipulation techniques and additive synthesis. While the use of tape manipulation techniques remained a standard feature of the classical electronic music studio, other ways of creat-ing timbral variation, besides additive synthesis, were developed: *amplitude modulation*, *frequency modulation*, and *subtractive synthesis* performed by a variety of *filters*.

TIMBRAL DEVELOPMENT THROUGH AMPLITUDE MODULATION

Amplitude modulation (AM) is a process by which the amplitude of a signal is changed.[21] In music, the effect of this process is referred to as *tremelo*, a slight, usually periodic, variation in the volume of a sound. Suppose a singer

---

[19] Stockhausen uses only attack ◿, sustain ▭, or decay ◺ shapes in creating the envelopes for *Study II*. They are never combined for one chord. When an attack shape is required, the second genera-tion tape loop was played forward; when a decay shape was needed, the tape loop was played backward.

[20] However, as is true of much serial music, the audible results, while being explainable, are not fully predictable.

[21] Modulation can occur in either AC or DC signals. In speaking of audio signals, reference is, of course, to AC waves.

wished to produce a tremelo. They would initially produce a sound at a particular volume, then, while still producing the same sound, they would sing slightly louder and then slightly softer than the original volume. By doing this in a periodic, repetitious fashion, a tremelo would be produced. In creating a tremelo effect, the singer must take three things into account: the *rate* or speed of change (how fast or slow), the *range* or degree of change (how loud or soft), and the *pattern* or configuration of the change (how the volume changes in time).

When amplitude modulation is produced electronically, it is necessary to have two different signals: the *carrier signal* and the *modulating signal*. The carrier signal is the original signal whose amplitude will be changed. In amplitude modulation, the amplitude of the carrier signal is analogous to the original volume of the sound produced by the singer. The modulating signal modulates, or changes, the amplitude of the carrier just as the singer affected the rate and the range of tremolo in a specific pattern.

When a singer produces a tremolo, the various aspects that produce the effect are considered in approximate terms. However, in amplitude modulation produced with electronic signals, these aspects can be exactly measured by considering the *amplitude of the carrier* and the *amplitude, frequency, and waveshape of the modulating signal*. The amplitude of the carrier signal determines the original, or *median, amplitude*. The amplitude of the modulating signal determines the range of modulation. The frequency of the modulating signal determines the rate of modulation. The waveshape of the modulating signal determines the pattern of modulation.

Let us suppose we are to amplitude modulate a 700 Hz sine tone by a 5 Hz sine tone. Since the operative word is "by," the 700 Hz signal is the carrier signal, and the 5 Hz signal is the modulating signal. The amplitude of the carrier is, let us suppose, x, and the amplitude of the modulating signal is y. The original, or median, amplitude therefore is x. The positive range of modulation will be between $x+y$ and $x-y$. The rate of modulation between these two values will be 5 times per second. The pattern of modulation will be sinusoidal. Figure 11-4 illustrates this modulation. Note that in amplitude modulation only the amplitude of the carrier is changed; the frequency of the carrier is not affected.

In the previous example, the rate of change was 5 Hz. This is slow enough to allow the human ear to perceive the change in amplitude, and therefore it would produce a tremelo effect. However, if the rate of change goes above about 20 Hz, it is no longer possible to perceive the amplitude changes of the carrier as amplitude changes. Rather, the fluctuations of amplitude at fast rates are perceived as new frequencies called *sidebands*. In amplitude modulation, two sidebands are produced: the sum of the frequencies of the carrier and the modulator, and the difference of these two frequencies. In addition, the original frequency of the carrier is also audible. Therefore, if the carrier were a 700 Hz sine wave, and the modulator were a 200 Hz sine wave, the result of amplitude modulation would be 900 Hz (sum) and 500 Hz (difference) and 700 Hz (original frequency of the carrier).

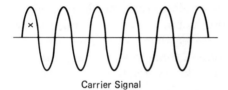

Carrier Signal

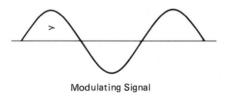

Modulating Signal

Resultant Amplitude Modulated Signal

FIGURE 11-4 Amplitude Modulation.

As can be easily seen, the only distinction between the results of amplitude modulation and the previously discussed ring modulation is the presence of the carrier frequency. Ring modulation is a type of amplitude modulation in which, ideally, only the summation tone and the difference tone of the input frequencies are present.[22]

TIMBRAL DEVELOPMENT
THROUGH FREQUENCY MODULATION

In *frequency modulation* (FM), the frequency of the carrier is changed or modulated. Musically, this effect is referred to as *vibrato*. A singer can easily produce a vibrato by slightly wavering above and below the original pitch. In frequency modulation, the frequency of the carrier signal determines the original, or median, frequency. The amplitude of the modulating signal determines the range of modulation. The frequency of the modulating signal determines the rate of modulation. The waveshape of the modulating signal determines the pattern of modulation. As can now be seen, the

[22] In practical use, a certain amount of the original frequencies usually leak through, and are present in, the ring modulated signal.

functions of the modulating signal are identical in both amplitude and frequency modulation; the only difference is in the aspect, amplitude or frequency, that is changed.

Let us suppose we are to frequency modulate a 700 Hz sine tone by a 5 Hz sine tone. The amplitude of the carrier is x and the amplitude of the modulator is y. The original, or median, frequency, is 700 Hz. The range of modulation is a function (F) of y and varies with it; the frequency of the carrier will modulate equidistantly above and below 700 Hz. Therefore, if $Fy=z$, the range of modulation will be $700 \pm z$.[23] The rate of modulation is 5 Hz. The pattern of modulation is sinusoidal. The result of this particular example would be heard as a vibrato. This is illustrated in Figure 11-5. Note that the amplitude of the carrier remains constant in frequency modulation.

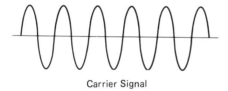

Carrier Signal

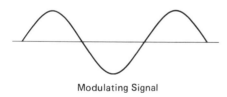

Modulating Signal

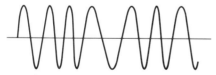

Resultant Frequency Modulated Signal

Figure 11-5 Frequency Modulation.

[23] The maximum variance of the carrier above or below the frequency of the unmodulated signal is called the *peak frequency deviation*. It is measured in Hertz, and is a function of the amplitude of the modulating signal. In the present example, if the carrier of 700 Hz is modulated to a high of 900 Hz and a low of 500 Hz, the peak frequency deviation would be 200 Hz ($900 - 700 = 200$; $700 - 500 = 200$).

When the frequency of the modulating wave goes above about 20 Hz in frequency modulation, sidebands are produced. However, these sidebands are far more numerous than those produced by amplitude modulation or ring modulation. As a result, the timbres produced by frequency modulation can be complex.[24]

In the previous examples of amplitude modulation, ring modulation, and frequency modulation, only sine waves have been used. Of course, any waveform can be used to perform these processes. The more complex the waveforms, the more complex the results. This is because sidebands will be produced for each harmonic of the waveform.

Amplitude modulation, ring modulation, and frequency modulation provide the composer of electronic music with a vast number of possible timbres. They are easier to produce than timbres arrived at by pure additive synthesis. They also allow for further modification by various types of *filtering*.

TIMBRAL DEVELOPMENT THROUGH FILTERING
AND SUBRACTIVE SYNTHESIS

A *filter* is a device that removes part of the audible spectrum of a sound. There are two general types of filters: *fixed* and *variable*. In a fixed filter, the *passband* is not adjustable. The passband of a filter is the part of the fre-

---

[24] The sidebands in frequency modulation are figured by the *frequency modulation index*. This is calculated by the following formula:

$$\text{modulation index} = \frac{\text{peak frequency deviation}}{\text{modulator frequency}}.$$

Let us suppose the 700 Hz carrier is modulated by a 50 Hz modulator. Using the same peak frequency deviation as in footnote 23, the formula would be $MI = \frac{200}{50} = 4$.

This means that there would be four significant sidebands on either side of the carrier frequency; this would be a total of eight sidebands.

The intervallic distance of neighboring sidebands is equal to the frequency of the modulating wave (50 Hz). Therefore, the following significant sidebands would result:

> 900
> 850
> 800
> 750
> 700 Hz Carrier
> 650
> 600
> 550
> 500.

Further detail on the process and results of frequency modulation is outside the scope of this book. For additional information, see Allen Strange, *Electronic Music* (Dubuque: William C. Brown Co., Publishers, 1972), pp. 12-20, and Hubert S. Howe, *Electronic Music Synthesis* (New York: W. W. Norton & Co., Inc., 1975), pp. 13-16.

quency spectrum that is allowed to pass through the filter. The passband is described with reference to its *bandwidth* and its *center frequency*. The bandwidth is the difference between the *cutoff frequencies* of the passband, the highest and lowest frequencies allowed to pass through the filter at full amplitude. Those frequencies not passed, that is, those that are attenuated 3 dB or more from maximum amplitude, are called the *stopband.* The center frequency is simply the center of the passband. As an example, suppose the high cutoff frequency of a filter is 700 Hz and the low cutoff frequency is 500 Hz. The band is then from 500 Hz to 700 Hz; the bandwidth is 200 Hz; the center frequency is around 600 Hz.[25]

A collection of fixed filters is called a *filter bank*. The filters are usually arranged in a contiguously ascending format and, taken together, extend over the audible range. Often, filter banks are arranged so that each filter covers the same relative frequency range, such as one octave or one-third of an octave. In addition, each filter sometimes has its own independent *attenuator,* or volume control. The output of a filter bank is often a *combined output* in which all of the filter outputs have been mixed together.

Variable filters are adjustable with regards to their attenuation, center frequency, and, sometimes, bandwidth. *High-pass filters* are variable filters with adjustable low cutoff points. These filters attenuate, or decrease, the amplitude of frequencies below this point. The high cutoff point is fixed, usually above the range of hearing. If the low cutoff point is raised, the filter is said to "close," because the bandwidth is contracting. As the low cutoff point is lowered, the filter is said to "open," because the band and the bandwidth are expanding.

Low-pass filters are variable filters that work in an opposite fashion. Here the low cutoff point is fixed, and the filter attenuates frequencies above the variable high cutoff point.

The other common type of variable filter is the *band-pass filter.* In a band-pass filter, the bandwidth and the center frequency may be regulated independently. Thus, a band with a center frequency of 1,000 Hz could have a narrow or a wide bandwidth. A bandwidth of 500 Hz could be moved to a high or low band placement, thus changing the center frequency. Table 11-1 illustrates types of filtering changes on a band-pass filter.

Filters, used singly or in combination, allow for further signal processing and timbral modification. Subtractive synthesis, used in electroacoustic musical instruments as well as tape music, is accomplished by using filters to remove selected portions of the spectrum of a sound, thus creating a simpler, less complex timbre. Any acoustic or electronic sound except, of course, sine waves, can be filtered.

---

[25] The center frequency is actually the *geometric mean* rather than the *arithmetic* mean. The geometric mean is the square root of the product of the high and low frequencies. For example, $\sqrt{500 + 700} = 592$. Since we perceive logarithmically, however, the arithmetic mean of 600 Hz is close enough for most purposes.

Table 11-1

CHANGE OF BANDWIDTH:

Bandwidth	Center Frequency	Band
2,000 Hz	1,000 Hz	0 -2,000 Hz
1,000 Hz	1,000 Hz	500-1,500 Hz
100 Hz	1,000 Hz	950-1,050 Hz

CHANGE OF CENTER FREQUENCY:

Bandwidth	Center Frequency	Band
500 Hz	1,000 Hz	750-1,250 Hz
500 Hz	500 Hz	250-750 Hz
500 Hz	1,500 Hz	1,250-1,700 Hz

The process of *equalization* is similar to filtering. An *equalizer* is a device that allows portions of the frequency spectrum to be amplified or attenuated. Equalizers have two or more bands, usually calibrated in decibels. They are used, not to eliminate portions of the frequency spectrum, but rather to adjust the volume relationships among the available bands.[26] Treble and bass controls on amplifiers allow for garden variety equalization, or *EQ*. *Graphic equalizers* often look like fixed filter banks since they both have several bands.

Amplitude modulation, ring modulation, frequency modulation, and filtering greatly expanded the timbral vocabulary of electronic music. By the middle 1950s, these techniques were standard procedures in most electronic music studios. The technique of additive synthesis, as seen in *Study II*, continued to be used in composing electronic music. More often, however, the composer would develop a complex timbre by using amplitude modulation, ring modulation, or frequency modulation, and then filter it to achieve the desired result. This kind of subtractive synthesis was not only easier and less time consuming than additive synthesis, it also provided more possibilities: a single complex sound could be filtered in a great many ways. All of these various techniques were explored by Stockhausen in his work *Gesang der Jünglinge* (*Song of the Youths*—1955-56).

Stockhausen's Gesang der Jünglinge

Gesang der Jünglinge was Stockhausen's first work of tape music after *Study II*. The similarities between these two works are primarily structural, since Stockhausen continued to develop his serial thinking. In other, perhaps more aurally apparent areas, the works seem rather dissimilar. *Gesang der Jünglinge* is not a purely electronic work; of equal importance to the electronically generated material are the sounds of a boy's voice. An-

[26] Plus or minus 10 to 12 dB is the usual range of equalizers.

other difference between *Study II* and *Gesang der Jünglinge* is the formation of timbres and their resulting qualities. In *Study II*, additive synthesis was the only technique used for constructing timbres; in *Gesang der Jünglinge*, Stockhausen used both additive and subtractive techniques as well as various kinds of modulation.

In constructing the timbres for *Gesang der Jünglinge*, Stockhausen formulated two timbral scales: one electronic, the other concrète and made from sounds of a boy's voice. In doing this, Stockhausen sought not only to relate the electronic and voice materials, but also to extend the concept of Klangfarbenmelodie. Each of the two timbral scales has eleven elements, or categories, of timbre. The materials for the scale of electronic timbres are

1. Sine tones,
2. Frequency modulated sine tones, periodically modulated,[27]
3. Frequency modulated sine tones, statistically modulated,
4. Amplitude modulated sine tones, periodically modulated,
5. Amplitude modulated sine tones, statistically modulated,
6. Periodic combinations of the first five categories,
7. Statistic combinations of the first five categories,
8. White noise with constant density,
9. White noise with statistically varied density,
10. Periodic sequences of filtered beats,[28]
11. Statistic sequences of filtered beats.

This scale of electronic timbres is arranged in an order of increasing complexity, beginning with sine tones and going to white noise.[29] A second scale of timbres, made from the sounds of a boy's voice, is similarly arranged. Stockhausen constructed analogies between elements of the two timbral scales. For instance, simple vowel sounds are analogous to sine waves; harsh consonants, such as "ch," are similar to white noise.

Stockhausen also created scales, or rows, for ordering the aspects of pitch (six scales), duration, and dynamics. He was thus able to serially compose *Gesang der Jünglinge* by referring numerically to a specific pitch, duration, dynamic, and timbre for each electronic or vocal event.

[27] The terms *periodic* and *statistic* characterize the modulating signal. A periodic modulation is a repetitive one in which the characteristics of the modulating signal do not change. A statistic modulation is one whose characteristics of change are calculable but not repetitious.

[28] These *beats* are clicks produced by oscillators between 1 and 20 Hz. These frequencies are below the range of human hearing, but they do produce audible clicks when amplified and played through loudspeakers. The clicking sound is the result of the physical movement of the speaker cone.

[29] It seems that amplitude modulated sounds should have preceded frequency modulated sounds, since the latter are more complex.

The title of *Gesang der Jünglinge* refers to the third chapter of the book of *Daniel* where the three youths, Shadrack, Meshack, and Abednego are thrown into the fiery furnace by King Nebuchadnezzar. The text is drawn from the *Benedicite* canticle of the Apocryphal version of the same book, and is spoken and sung in German by one boy. Stockhausen had dissected the text into syllables, phonemes, and phones, and, as closely as possible, tried to record the desired resultant voice sounds directly on tape. Where the boy was not able to provide Stockhausen with the desired quality of sound, the vocal sound was electronically modified or processed to accommodate Stockhausen's scheme.[30] Stockhausen also rearranged and combined words and parts of words in order to approximate various levels of comprehensibility as well as create new juxtapositions of meaning. In the final version of *Gesang der Jünglinge*, these effects may be used singly or in combination to produce everything from a comprehensible solo to a cacophonous choir of voices.

Stockhausen's *Gesang der Jünglinge* is one of the compositions generally regarded as a classic of early electro-acoustic tape music. Technically, it represents state-of-the-art technology in 1956 for both electronic and concrete processing and manipulation. This work shows an extensive development of Stockhausen's compositional thinking, especially in regard to those serial concepts drawn from Webern and Eimert. In composing *Gesang der Jünglinge*, Stockhausen enlarged Eimert's techniques of the transformation of voice sounds and vocal-electronic sound analogies. Stockhausen also utilized Meyer-Eppler's ideas of information theory in ordering syntax and timbre.[31]

DISCOGRAPHY

Barron, Louis and Bebe. *Forbidden Planet* (soundtrack). Planet Records PR 001 (P.O. Box 3977, Beverly Hills, CA 90212).

Eimert, Herbert. *Selektion I*. Philips 835 485/86AY; Mercury SR-2-9123.

———. *Struktur 8*. Excerpt found in *Einführung in die Elektronische Musik (Introduction to Electronic Music)*. Wergo WER 60006.

Stockhausen, Karlheinz. *Gesang der Jünglinge*. DGG 138811.

———. *Study II*. DGG LPEM 19322; DGG 16133.

[30] In extending the range of the boy's voice, Stockhausen used a *Springer machine*, also known as an *information rate changer*. This curious, amazing, and often infuriating device is capable, on a good day, of changing either the pitch or duration of a sound without affecting the other aspect. For further information, see Gustav Ciamaga, "The Tape Studio," in *The Development and Practice of Electronic Music*, ed. Jon H. Appleton and Ronald C. Perera (Englewood Cliffs, NJ: Prentice-Hall, Inc. 1975), pp. 108-110.

[31] For a more thorough discussion of *Gesang der Jünglinge*, see Karlheinz Stockhausen, "Actualia," *DIE REIHE*, 1 (1958), 45-51. This article not only discusses *Gesang* but also explains Stockhausen's thinking at the time. The article is variously informative, confusing, sophisticated, naive, argumentative, and hostile; but it is always interesting.

Eimert Herbert. *Epitah für Aikichi Kuboyama.* Wergo WER 60014. Much of Eimert's later work followed in the path of *Selektion I. Epitaph für Aikichi Kuboyama* (1960-62) deals with the processing and manipulation of speech, especially processing by ring modulation. Aikichi Kuboyama was a Japanese fisherman and a long-suffering victim of the fallout of the bombing of Hiroshima. He died in 1966.

Ligeti, György. *Artikulation.* Philips 835 485/86 AY; Wergo 60059; Mercury SR-2-9123′ Limelight LS-86048. *Artikulation* was realized by Ligeti (b. 1923, Diciosanmartin, Transylvania) and Gottfried Michael Koening in 1958 at the Cologne studio. The piece deals with the expression of speech patterns and inflections by means of electronic sounds. The resulting "conversation" of electronic sounds displays all of the manipulations and processings of the classical electronic music studio. In theory and concept, *Artikulation* owes much to the ideas and work of Eimert and Stockhausen. It is also a precursor to two acoustic works by Ligeti: *Aventures* (1962) and *Nouvelles Aventures* (1962-65), both referred to as "mimodramas."

Stockhausen, Karlheinz. *Hymnen.* DGG 2707 039. *Hymnen* (1966-67) is one of the monumental works of the classical studio. The recorded version consists of a small universe of electronic and concrete sounds, composed around the national anthems of several countries. Stockhausen extensively used what he calls *intermodulation* in *Hymnen.* By this term he refers to one event, such as an anthem, being modulated (ring, amplitude, or frequency) by another event. For instance, if the frequency changes of one anthem are used to amplitude modulate another anthem, Stockhausen would say that the *harmony* of the first has modulated the *rhythm* of the second, thus *intermodulation.* *Hymnen* involves every technique of tape manipulation and signal processing known at the time. Structurally, *Hymnen* is much more intuive and subjective than any of Stockhausen's previous works. Stockhausen insists that *Hymnen* is not a collage.

Stockhausen, Karlheinz. *Telemusik.* DGG 137012. *Telemusik* was composed in 1966 at the NHK studio in Tokyo. This was the first piece in which Stockhausen used his procedures of intermodulation (see above remarks on *Hymnen*), combining elements of folk music from Africa, the Amazon, Bali, Brazil, China, Japan, Hungary, Spain, Russia, and Vietnam with electronic sounds. The folk music elements are almost always processed beyond recognition. *Telemusik* is clearly divided into thirty-two sections, each of which is percussively articulated by a Japanese temple instrument, such as a wood block or chime.

12

CLASSICAL STUDIO ELECTRONIC MUSIC
The Development of the Classical Studio

In the 1950s and early 1960s, the Paris and Cologne studios were the leading centers of electro-acoustic music in Europe. Although an increasing number of studios came into being, Paris and Cologne dominated the world of electro-acoustic music. They represented two very different schools of thought and came to typify the styles, approaches, psychologies, and interests of musique concrète and electronic music. Only toward the middle of the 1950s did crossover between the two camps become likely. At that point some concrète material might be found included in Cologne works such as *Selektion I* and *Gesang der Jünglinge*. But this concrète material was usually speech sounds, often treated in a manner identical to that of the electronic material. In addition, electronic signals did find their way into compositions of the Paris schools, but these sounds were usually little more than adjuncts to the concrète material. Seldom, during the 1950s, was an all-concrète work produced in Cologne, or an all-electronic work produced in Paris.

Between 1953 and 1960, most of the major electro-acoustic music studios of Europe were established. These studios followed the combined approaches of the Paris and Cologne studios, although the primary concern tended to be with electronic, rather than acoustic, sound material. While there were some private studios established during the 1950s, most of the installations were funded by public sources. In Europe, the sponsoring institutions were often government-operated radio broadcasting services. This followed the pattern of the Paris and Cologne studios and seemed logical, since the type of equipment and personnel required was already a part of the radio studio. In the United States and Canada, most electronic music studios were founded at universities and were considered part of their educational and research facilities.

Each of the classical electronic music studios was unique. Much of the equipment was specially designed or modified for each studio. Since there was no standarization, each studio tended to have its own technical personality. In conjunction with this, the aesthetics of the studios' founders often dictated, by the selection of personnel and equipment, the nature of the compositions produced. It is thus possible to speak of various schools of classical studio electronic music. These schools are represented by the aesthetic and technical similarities of works composed in certain studios. Sometimes these qualities are quite audible to the experienced listener; at other times the similarities are primarily theoretical or conceptual. For these reasons, it is usually best to consider the classical studio electronic music of the 1950s along with the studios where it was created.

THE NHK STUDIO

Works by Toshiro Mayazumi and Minao Shibata

One of the earlier electronic music studios was established in Tokyo. The Radio Nippon Horo Kyokai (NHK) studio was founded in 1954 by a group of technicians and program producers interested in electronic music. They were strongly influenced by ideas of the Cologne studio, whose technical reports they used as the basis for their experiments. Toshiro Mayazumi (b. 1929, Yokohama) was the first Japanese composer to become interested in tape music. His *Musique Concrete x, y, z* (1953) and his trilogy *Music for Sine Waves by Proportion of Prime Numbers, Music for Modulated Waves by Proportion of Prime Numbers*, and *Invention for Square Waves and Sawtooth Waves* (circa 1954) were, respectively, the first Japanese works of musique concrète and electronic music. Mayazumi worked with the technicians of the NHK studio and with composers Makoto Maroi (b. 1930, Tokyo) to select the equipment for the studio. Since Mayazumi had visited the Paris studio in 1952 and Maroi had worked in Cologne in 1955, the influence of both studios was evident, although the Cologne approach prevailed. The original equipment of the NHK studio included a Melochord, a Monochord, several oscillators, thirty-two band-pass filters, and several tape recorders.

Mayazumi's *Mandara* (1969) deals, as do many of his works, with concepts drawn from Buddhist philosophy. The title, *Mandara*, refers to the uncertainty and confusion of earthly existence. *Mandara* has two main sections. The first, 0′00″-5′09″, consists entirely of electronic sounds. The initial material is predominantly sinusoidal, short-enveloped, with portamento pitch characteristics. These bird-like sounds are transposed to different registers by speed change. At 0′53″, long envelope sounds with slightly more harmonics enter and form a background to the higher pitched original material. The pitch character of the shorter sounds changes at 1′35″: The register is lowered, the portamento ceases, and some very slight frequency modulation is noticeable. At 2′18″, noise sounds enter. These are filtered into various limited ranges and enveloped and combined in ways that resemble human breathing. Thus in the first section of *Mandara*, Mayazumi moves from pitched, short sounds to nonpitched, longer enveloped sounds. The breathing quality of the noise material allows a transition to the second section of the piece, since this uses voice sounds. These voice sounds first appear to be coming out of very low-pitched noise because, like the noise, the voice material has had all but the very low frequencies filtered out. Gradually, the voice material assumes its normal frequency range and can be heard as a background of mumbling Japanese voices from which single voices frequently emerge for brief periods. Sometimes a koto can be heard accompanying the typical Japanese inflections of these voices. At 10′16″, the very end of the piece, a brief excerpt of one of Adolf Hitler's public addresses can be heard. Mayazumi's comment is obvious, although it would not be understood as positive by Western ears.

Mandara is not a real-time composition. There is a great deal of superimposition of sounds in order to create a dense layering effect of many events occurring simultaneously. In contrast to this is *Improvisation* (1968), a real-time composition realized at the NHK studio by Minao Shibata (b. 1916). Real-time compositions are rare in classical studio electronic music because of the difficulty in producing, processing, and controlling a lot of material at one time. Shibata's *Improvisation* therefore tends to concentrate on one or two events at a time. Most of the events are not enveloped but are continuous sounds. The short envelope sounds heard entering at 0′17″ could be the result of amplitude modulation, where one of the oscillators is a *sub-audio frequency* (below 20 Hz). Later in the piece, at 4′15″, other short envelope sounds occur that are the result of manual *gating*, control of the amplitude of the sound.

Shibata uses portamento a great deal in *Improvisation*. Sometimes this is the result of using speed change on tape recorders, recording the signal on a variable speed machine, and then recording the manipulated result immediately on a second machine. More often, however, the portamento is created by manually changing the frequency of the oscillators. Shibata uses a great many oscillators in *Improvisation* and this helps to give the texture a greater density. Often, many oscillators can be heard to portamento simultaneously, all moving in the same direction and maintaining the same fixed pitch interval. This consistent following of oscillators is sometimes referred to as *tracking.*

The waveforms used in *Improvisation* are primarily sawtooth. This is because Shibata wanted to make use of the filters in the NHK studio, and sawtooth waves offer the greatest possibilities for filtering, since they contain the most harmonics of all electronic waveforms.

THE RAI STUDIO

Works by Bruno Maderna
and Henri Pousseur

Like the NHK studio in Tokyo, the RAI studio in Milan was based on the concepts developed in Cologne. The Studio di Fonologia Musicale of the Radio Audizioni Italiane was established in Milan in 1955 by Luciano Berio and Bruno Maderna (b. 1920, Venice, Italy; d. 1972, Darmstadt, Germany). The RAI, or Milan, studio had equipment similar to that of the Cologne studio. This is not surprising, since Berio and Maderna had both spent time at the Cologne studio.

One of the first purely electronic works to be completed in the Milan studio was Maderna's *Continuo* (1958). *Continuo* uses very complex sound materials created by extreme amplitude and frequency modulation. These processes produce sounds with very rich spectra. The actual differentiation of the material is accomplished by tape manipulation techniques or electronic processing. The piece begins with the sound material in a very reverberated form. This has the effect of "smearing" the frequency information of the sound, creating an ethereal effect. This material is also presented with long envelopes. When several layers of these sounds are mixed together, an impression of continuous, but changing, sound fields is created. Gradually, Maderna changes the nature of the material without removing the initial layers of sound. The original material continues, but new layers, or voices, of sound are added. This new material has increasingly less reverberation and shorter envelopes. As the envelopes shorten, the timbre and pitch of the material changes more quickly. This is the continuum of the title: a process by which the sound material is differentiated and changed. Eventually, two distinct classes of sounds can be heard, beginning at 3′09″, but they are both derived from the same original source, treated in different ways.

Without specific information from the composer, and none seems to now exist, it is not possible to speak of exactly how Maderna constructed *Continuo.* Maderna's compositional thinking was a combination of German serialism and Italian lyricism. The exact proportions of these influences in *Continuo* are difficult to assess. This is not true of another work done in the Milan studio, *Scambi* by Henri Pousseur (b. 1929, Malmedy, Belgium).

Scambi (Exchanges) is not simply an electronic music composition, it is also a series of compositions, as well as a procedure for creating a certain kind of musical work. There were five versions of *Scambi* composed during 1957 and 1958; two of these were by Pousseur, two by Berio, and one by Marc Wilkinson.

The idea behind *Scambi* was to create sound structures that would allow the listener the freedom of making his or her own perceptions without having to be concerned about a preconceived form or notion. To accomplish this, Pousseur believed that it was necessary to avoid the periodic, or repetitious, nature of traditional music. Such avoidance would ensure the lack of any imposed hierarchy or teleology.

Pousseur used only one sound source in *Scambi*: white noise. The original material consists of eleven half-octave bands of noise between 140 Hz and 6400 Hz. Each band was first processed by being passed three times through a special *amplitude filter* that had been constructed for the Milan studio.[1] This amplitude filter cut off all signals under a certain specified amplitude and was adjustable to one of five settings. Pousseur combined the original eleven bands of noise into groups of three on the basis of their adjacency. This resulted in nine combinations, represented here by Roman numerals, while the original bands are represented by Arabic numerals:

1	2	3
2 = I	3 = II	4 = III
3	4	5
4	5	6
5 = IV	6 = V	7 = VI
6	7	8
7	8	9
8 = VII	9 = VIII	10 = IX
9	10	11

Each of these combinations was run through each of the five settings of the amplitude filter, resulting in forty-five basic sound units. These were recorded on thirty foot tape loops at 15 ips. Each of these forty-five original loops was rerecorded on a second machine using smaller loops of between three and thirty seconds duration. During this process, the speed of the first machine was randomly changed.

The small tape loops were then spliced together in such a way as to form one of four possible pitch-tempo transformations:

[1] The function of this amplitude filter could be duplicated by a combination of an *envelope detector*, also called an *envelope follower*, and a *gate*.

high — fast ⟷ high — slow
high — fast ⟷ low — slow
low — slow ⟷ low — fast
low — slow ⟷ high — slow.

Each of these pitch-tempo transformations lasted between twenty-one and forty-two seconds.

This material was then twice passed through reverberators to form a second class of material differentiated by timbre. Pousseur characterized the reverberated sounds as "homogeneous" and the unreverberated materials as "dry." This allowed for four additional types of sequences, two by transformation of a timbral nature,

dry   → homogenous
homogenous → dry,

and two being timbrally static,

dry   → dry
homogenous → homogenous.

With this sound material, which was now differentiated according to pitch, tempo, and timbre, Pousseur constructed thirty-two long sequences by splicing. Each of these sequences was again passed through the amplitude filter. During this final processing, certain portions of the elements of pitch, envelope, and general dynamics were allowed to be determined by chance operations of the amplitude filter as well as other devices. Silences were also determined at this point.

Any given realization, or version, of *Scambi* is the playing, in whatever order, of the final thirty-two sound sequences. The form is derived from the context of the procedure. The movement of the work is between opposing characteristics. The construction of the piece is its performance.

Any number of versions of *Scambi* are possible, since Pousseur has not provided a definitive score. He has left, rather, a series of procedures that intentionally include random elements. However, all of the possible versions of *Scambi* would be very similar in general terms, even if they would differ in their particulars. This is because the basic sound material, white noise, as well as the types of processings and manipulations, has been specified by the composer.

Like many twentieth-century composers, Pousseur has been more interested in controlling and predicting the general characteristics of music than the specific details. Thus, in listening to *Scambi*, one is aware of the overall nature of the music, rather than the precise character of the sounds. Pitch, for example, is not very important in its older sense as a series of perceivable pitch-classes; instead, pitch is relevant in terms of range and register, for it is in these qualities that change can be perceived.

ELECTRONIC MUSIC
IN THE NETHERLANDS

In contrast to the studios so far discussed, the Utrecht studio in the Netherlands has a rather complicated lineage. Initial interest in electronic music in the Netherlands was expressed by Walter Maas (b. 1909), a champion of new Dutch music and the founder of the Gaudeamus Foundation and the Gaudeamus awards for new music. In 1953 Maas invited Werner Meyer-Eppler to visit Holland and deliver a series of lectures on electronic music at the Netherlands Radio Union. As a result, attempts were made to establish an electronic music studio at the NRU in Hilverson under Meyer-Eppler's guidance. A full-fledged studio never developed, although a few isolated electro-acoustic works were realized at the NRU facilities between 1954 and 1957. The radio-associated electronic music studio that had proved successful elsewhere in Europe was not to be in Holland. Still, several Dutch composers continued to experiment with the media. Chief among these was Henk Badings (b. 1907, Indonesia). In 1956, with Maas's help, Badings convinced the electronics firm of Philips to open its laboratories to him. This was the beginning of the Philips studio in Eindhoven.

THE PHILIPS STUDIO

Works by Henk Badings, Edgard Varèse, and Dick V. Raaijmakers

Badings's first work composed at the Philips studio was *Cain and Abel*, a ballet score commissioned by the Nederlands Ballet for the 1956 Holland Festival. In composing *Cain and Abel*, Badings was expected to demonstrate the range of the available equipment. This included the usual array of oscillators, filters, modulation devices, and tape recorders found in most classical electronic music studios, as well as an electronic clavichord. It is this instrument that gives much of *Cain and Abel* its quality of being performed on an electronic keyboard instrument.

    Cain and Abel is typical of Badings's electronic music. It displays a concern for the development of complex timbres rather than relying on simple waveforms. The tonal quality is characteristic of Badings's music, and although he often extended traditional functional tonality by inventing new tunings, he never abandoned the familiar pitch structures of older music. The composition of *Cain and Abel* also gave demonstration of the speed at which Badings usually worked, for it was completed in only ten days.

    Perhaps the best known tape composition done at the Philips studio was *Poème Électronique* by Edgard Varèse (b. 1885, Paris; d. 1965, New

York), *Poème Électronique* was commissioned by Philips for its pavilion at the 1958 Brussels World Fair. The Philips pavilion of this exposition was designed by the noted architect Le Corbusier with assitance from Xenakis. The inside of the three-peaked circus tent structure was made up of hundreds of parabolic and hyperparabolic surfaces along which were arranged some four hundred loudspeakers. The final version of *Poème Électronique* was recorded on a three channel tape. Each channel of each of the many sections of the work was individually routed to a particular number and arrangement of speakers. This routing was accomplished by a fifteen channel *control tape*, a tape containing information not meant to be heard but used to control certain aspects of the actual composition. In the case of *Poème Électronique*, the control tracks determined the routing of the sound material as well as certain visual and lighting effects that were used to accompany the music. These visuals, selected by Le Corbusier and consisting of projections of photographs, paintings, collages, and various kinds of script, had no reference or correspondence to the music. Since no synchronization was attempted, the resulting correspondences, or lack there-of, were accidental. *Poème Électronique* made the Philips pavilion one of the highlights of the Brussels Exposition and drew over fifteen thousand visitors daily for six months.

Despite its name, *Poème Électronique* is not, strictly speaking, electronic music, although it does contain some sections composed of electronically generated sounds. Each of the work's sections is clearly differentiated from adjacent sections by the nature and treatment of the sound elements. In addition to electronic sounds, these elements include bells, percussion instruments, voices, sirens, jet planes, and other concrète sources. As is typical of Varese's concept of *organized sound*, these sections are themselves often constructed out of smaller sections of homogeneous material, and placed side by side without obvious relationships. Many of the sections of *Poème Électronique* are presented without any tape manipulation or electronic processing and therefore retain certain immediate associational values that do not relate to the adjacent sections.

Dick Raaijmakers (b. 1930, Maastricht) is another composer who worked at the Philips studio. Raaijmakers's composition *Contrasts* (1959) is a good example of how a small amount of source material can be extended by manipulation and processing. In the first section of *Contrasts*, two ideas are presented. The first idea is primarily rhythmic in nature and consists of percussive sounds created by very narrow filterings of sawtooth waves.[2] In the second idea, heard first at 0'03", pitch is obviously important as a con-

---

[2] The designation *rhythmic* when applied to a musical idea means that the most important information to be heard in this idea lies in the relationship of the temporal elements of the music. This is different from a musical situation in which pitch or timbre would be of primary importance. Obviously, all sound events, including musical ideas, are combinations of the elements of what is perceived as pitch, rhythm, and timbre, as well as secondary characteristics, such as dynamics or register. However, one or more of the primary elements of pitch, rhythm, or timbre usually tends to be most important in the musical idea.

tinuous melody in canon at the unison.[3] By using a constantly increasing tape-speed change, these two ideas are repeated several times with faster tempos and rising pitches. Several filterings can also be heard. In the second part of *Contrasts* (1'08"), the same technique is used with nine different filterings of white noise. The low-pitched background material heard in both sections is created by extreme speed change.

In 1960, as a result of a collaboration between Philips and the University of Utrecht, the first university studio was established in the Netherlands. The Utrecht studio took over the functions of the Philips studio in addition to serving as a center for research and teaching. Since 1964, the Utrecht studio has also been known as the Institute of Sonology.

THE UTRECHT STUDIO

Works by Frits Weiland
and Gottfried Michael Koenig

One of the earliest works completed in the Utrecht facilities was *Study in Layers and Pulses* (1961) by Frits Weiland (b. 1933, Bilthoven). This work is in three sections, the first of which consists of continuous low-pitched electronic sounds. At first, only one sound is heard; then, one by one, other similar sounds enter until a layered sound mass is created. The tremolo effect that is sometimes present is the result of *heterodyning*, a type of amplitude modulation caused by combining signals whose frequencies differ very slightly. The *beats*, or *beat frequencies*, produced by heterodyning are the difference between the frequencies of the two signals.[4]

The second part of Weiland's *Study* (2'15") consists of a continuation of the original material with the addition of short envelope "pulses." These pulses were not created by cutting and splicing techniques but by taking advantage of a feature of the type of oscillators usually found in classical electronic music studios. These oscillators did not have the capacity to continuously "sweep" over a larger frequency range. Rather, the one or two octave spread of the oscillator was transposed by adjusting a frequency range control knob. By manipulating this control, Weiland was able to create the short envelope sounds that are added in the second part of the piece. Like the continuous sounds of the first section of *Study*, the short sounds are added in every increasing numbers, creating a denser texture.

The third section of *Study in Layers and Pulses* (3'30") continues the layering process with the addition of various noise bands at increasingly higher registers. This continues until a loud noise band with a wide range eventually obliterates all of the other material; when this noise band suddenly disappears, only the initial low-pitched sound remains, and the work is concluded.

[3] A *canon* is a type of polyphonic work in which one part or voice is imitated by one or more of the other parts.

[4] Heterodyning is sometimes referred to as *nonlinear mixing*.

Studio No. 1 of the Institute of Sonology at the University of Utrecht in 1967. (Photo courtesy of Stichting Film en Wetenschap)

Studio No. 1 in 1974, with Goffried Michael Koening (seated) and Stan Tempelaars. (Photo courtesy of Stichting Film en Wetenschap)

Another composer who has worked in the Utrecht studio, and who was artistic director of the Institute of Sonology from 1964 to 1979, is Gottfried Michael Koenig (b. 1926, Magadeburg). Koenig has composed a series of works that all bear the title *Funktion (Function)* followed by the name of a color. *Funktion Blau* (1966), *Funktion Grun* (1967), and *Funktion Gelb* (1967-68) are some of the compositions in this series that have been commercially recorded. The *Funktion* part of the titles refers to a particular setting of a *variable function generator*, a device in the Utrecht studio for producing complex audio signals and *control signals*. Up to two hundred individually controllable amplitude steps can be set on the function generator. The result of any particular arrangement would be a complex waveform that could be used to control a sound-producing unit, such as an oscillator, or a sound-processing unit, such as a filter or a reverberator. Just as Varèse used control tracks prerecorded on tape to control the location of sound in *Poème Électronique*, so Koenig used the complex waveforms of the Utrecht studio function generator to control various aspects of his *Funktion* compositions. For instance, if Koenig uses the function generator to control the waveshape of an oscillator, a change in the function generator's particular sequence of amplitudes would result in a different control signal that would change the waveform of the oscillator.[5] After creating the desired control signals, Koenig recorded them on tape; these control tracks could later be used in assembling the final composition. The control signals or control tracks are, of course, not an audible part of the music; they control aspects of the music as determined by the composer.

The *Funktion* series of compositions are methodical experiments in the control of electronic sound material. The basic timbres, very rich in harmonics, are similar in all of the works. The changes that occur are similar in a general sense, although specific changes may be unique in their particulars. The final versions of the works are assembled by cutting and splicing according to a scheme calculated by a computer. The result is an aural landscape that constantly changes within narrowly specified limits. Particular changes have little significance, since no functional hierarchy is intended. It is like a series of variations in which the theme is only implied and the ordering is not important.

THE STUDIO OF THE POLISH RADIO

Symfonia *by Boguslaw Schäffer*

In 1957, the Studio of Experimental Music of the Polish Radio was founded in Warsaw by the composer and musicologist Josef Patkowsky. It quickly became an important training center for young composers, as well

---

[5] This, of course, is the principle of external voltage control that makes integrated electronic music systems or *synthesizers* possible. This is more fully discussed in Chapter 13.

as a research facility for the more established. One of the most dominant figures at the Warsaw studio has been Bogusław Schäffer (b. 1929, Cracow). Schäffer's work *Symfonia* (1966) deals with one of the basic problems of electronic music: the combining of artistic intention with technological facility.

By the late 1950s, the technology of the electro-acoustic music studio has developed far beyond the humble beginnings of Pierre Schaeffer's first experiments. Schaeffer's technological resources were easily dealt with by one person with only a modicum of experience. As the technology of the studio developed, greater demands were placed on the composer. Many established, older composers who wished to experiment in the electro-acoustic mediums were unwilling to acquire the necessary new skills to deal with all of the studio equipment. To make matters worse, the individuality of design in classical electronic music studios required a reorientation for each studio. To solve these problems, it became common for studios, especially those in Europe, to have engineers available to assist composers in the technical aspects of composition. This seemed only logical in these radio-centered studios, since the concept of artistic, as opposed to technological, talent already existed in terms of programming. Thus, although this was not always the case, the studio engineer had the responsibility for technically realizing the composers' ideas. This situation made the studio engineer, not only a collaborator, but also an interpreter of the composers' wishes.

In composing *Symfonia*, Bogusław Schäffer created a situation where the studio engineer, in this case Bohdan Mazurek, was necessary to the interpretation and realization of the work.

Symfonia, as initially produced by Schäffer, is a written score, consisting of abstract images. Page one of *Symfonia* can be seen in Figure 12-1. The images of the score are discussed at some length in the preface to the work. Each image represents a certain kind of sound event, and these events, in conjunction with their abstract representations, are partially defined in the preface. For instance, a certain shape may be said to represent a "short, full sound." What this means precisely, however, is never specified. Instead, anyone wishing to realize *Symfonia* must interpret the composer's incomplete specifications.

Symfonia consists of four movements done in this manner. Each movement uses different representational symbols (abstract visual shapes) that are defined by certain characteristics particular to that movement. Since the composer's ideas are intentionally vague, the score of *Symfonia* is only a point of departure for the realized work. Thus the Schäffer-Mazurek realization, the only recorded version, is one of countless possibilities. There can be no definitive version.

In the 1950s the development of electronic music in the United States lagged behind what was happening in Europe and Japan. This was due partially to lack of government patronage of the arts. In addition, there were no government-subsidized radio stations that could serve as centers for the establishment of studios.

BOGUSŁAW SCHÄFFER
1964—66

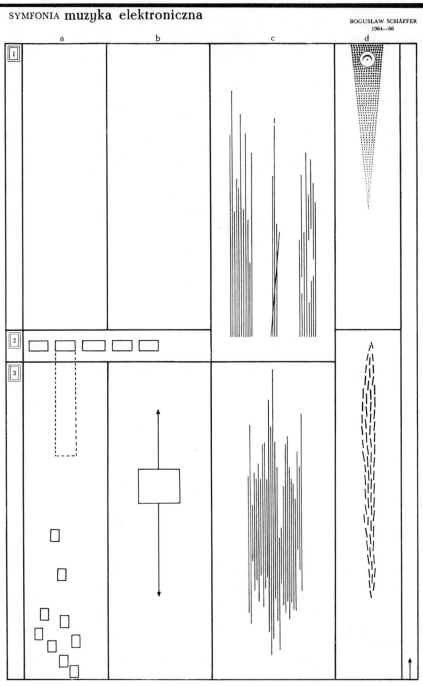

0"- 20"

Figure 12-1   Page 1 of *Symfonia.*

110

Although composers such as Louis and Bebe Barron, Vladimir Ussachevsky, Otto Luening, and Tod Dockstader did important pioneering work in electronic music, they did so on private and independent bases; during the 1950s there were no real centers of electro-acoustic music activity in the United States. For this reason, the early development of the electronic music studio was primarily a European phenomenon. As is true of most areas of the contemporary arts in America, the establishment and growth of electronic music centers in the United States was due largely to the interest of colleges and universities, with some assistance from private foundations.

THE UNIVERSITY OF ILLINOIS STUDIO

The first university electronic music studio in the United States was established at the University of Illinois in 1958 under the directorship of Lejaren Hiller (b. 1924, New York City). The original aims of the Experimental Music Studio were to encourage research, composition, and teaching in the areas of computer music, electronic tape music, acoustics, and instrumental design. While the University of Illinois has been an important center for the production of new music, early activity in the studio was more of a research nature and directed largely towards computer music and the computer generation of musical scores. There was little interest in classical studio electronic music.

There was, however, interest in invention during the early days of the Experimental Music Studio. James Beauchamp, who was on the faculty of Electrical Engineering, was interested in instrument design and contributed greatly to the studio. One of his inventions, a *Harmonic Tone Generator*, was used by Kenneth Gaburo to compose *Lemon Drops* (1965). *Lemon Drops* presents a basically keyboard performance situation with a sparse use of tape manipulation techniques, most noticeably speed variation. This jazz-like work appears largely improvisational in spirit and bears little resemblance to most electronic music of the period.

THE COLUMBIA-PRINCETON
ELECTRONIC MUSIC CENTER

Works by Mario Davidovsky
and Bulent Arel

The second institutionally sponsored electronic music studio in the United States was the Columbia-Princeton Electronic Music Center. It was officially established on February 20, 1959, with the help of a $175,000 grant from the Rockefeller Foundation to Columbia and Princeton Universities. The first directors of the Center were Vladimir Ussachevsky, Otto Luening, and Milton Babbitt.

University of Illinois Experimental Music Studio in 1958. (Photo courtesy of University of Illinois at Urbana-Champaign)

University of Illinois Studio D (digital studio) in 1979. (Photo courtesy of University of Illinois at Urbana-Champaign)

One of the studios of Columbia-Princeton Electronic Music Center in 1981. Left to right are Mario Davidovsky, Director; Pril Smiley, Associate Director; and Art Kreiger, Staff Member. (Photo courtesy of Columbia-Princeton Electronic Music Center)

The Columbia-Princeton Electronic Music Center holds a unique position in the history of electro-acoustic music in the United States. Being the first of its kind, the Center attracted many composers from outside of its parenting universities. "From 1960 to 1970 more than 225 compositions by more than 60 composers from 11 countries were produced at the Columbia-Princeton Electronic Music Center."[6] Since the Center contained several studios (eventually five), several composers could work at one time. Much of the Center's original equipment was specifically designed for its well-equipped studios. The size of the Columbia-Princeton Electronic Music Center and the number of composers who have worked there since its founding have made it one of the most influential studios in the field of electro-acoustic art music.

Two of the first composers to work at the Columbia-Princeton Electronic Music Center were Mario Davidovsky (b. 1934, Buenos Aires) and Bulent Arel (b. 1919, Istanbul). The electronic music of Davidovsky and Arel share certain stylistic characteristics that have often been associated with music composed at the Center. One of the most important stylistic elements is a general pointillism stemming from serial and post-serial thinking. Envelopes of individual events tend to be very short and are often

[6] Otto Luening, "Origins," in *The Development and Practice of Electronic Music*, ed. Jon H. Appleton and Ronald C. Perera (Englewood Cliffs, NJ: Prentice-Hall, Inc., 1975), p. 21.

grouped together into short, quick phrases. The timbres tend to be of basic electronic qualities, consisting of simple waveforms or elementary modulated sounds. There is an overall high density of information resulting from many sound events occurring in a short amount of time. Often, however, the events are not related in a perceptually functional way, so that what the listener comprehends is a series of gestures characterized by general, rather than specific, qualities. While these qualities are certainly not found in all music composed at the Center, they do exist in a sufficiently large number of compositions to allow them to be collectively identified as roughly constituting a style of classical studio electronic music.

All of these qualities are found in Mario Davidovsky's *Electronic Study No. 3* (1965) and create what Davidovsky refers to as a "filigree-like texture." As in most of Davidovsky's electronic music, cutting and splicing techniques are central to its construction. Individual electronic sounds are recorded and spliced together in the desired configuration. Several tracks of spliced material are superimposed and mixed together to form the final work.

Electronic Study No. 3 is dedicated to Edgard Varèse. Although Davidovsky is not specific about his dedication, it is perhaps revealing that many of Varèse's ideas are carried out in the work. Varèse wished to liberate pitch from the tempered scale, and Davidovsky has obviously done so here. *Electronic Study No. 3* contains many passages of *microtonal* pitch material, which uses intervals smaller than minor seconds (half-steps). In addition, no attempt is made to functionally relate simultaneous or successive pitches except by gestural qualities. For instance, the beginning of the piece presents a high-pitched sound of long duration initially articulated by a short percussive sound. Against this sustained tone, a series of low-pitched, short envelope sounds slowly descends. The specific pitches are less important than are the characteristics of their movement, one stationary, the other descending. Together they create an oblique polyphonic gesture. The rest of *Electronic Study No. 3* contains similar musical gestures, often presented in fast tempi. Thus one is generally aware of the direction of pitch movement (ascending, descending, stationary, irregular) and the polyphonic results of combinations of lines (parallel, oblique, contrary, similar) more than specific pitch content.

Varèse was also interested in composing with consecutive blocks of material rather than with continuous exposition. *Electronic Study No. 3* is composed of many short sections articulated sometimes by a silence and at other times by a sound of relatively long duration. This is not unlike the method that Varèse used in *Poème Électronique*. Although Davidovsky's material is more homogeneous than was Varèse's, contrasts are quite audible in *Electronic Study No. 3*.

Mention should be made of Varèse's ideas of spatial location and movement, also evident in *Poème Électronique*. Although *Electronic Study*

No. 3 does not use such an elaborate location system, the original version of the work is quadraphonic. Davidovsky uses location and movement to separate and define individual ideas.

Bulent Arel's *Stereo Electronic Music No. 2* (1970) is similar to Davidovsky's music with regard to the general stylistic qualities previously discussed. The music is often pointillistic, there are plenty of quick arabesque phrases, and the timbers are obviously electronic. There are, however, other stylistic features of Arel's music that are different from Davidovsky's and that constitute important elements of Arel's style.

Pitch is often perceptually important in Arel's music. This is evident in the beginning of *Stereo Electronic Music No. 2*. Here, long envelope sounds emphasize certain pitches by virtue of their duration; the shorter envelope material that interrupts does not have the same importance in pitch information. The pitches of the longer sounds become functionally relevant by relating to each other in ascending or curving patterns. Often, certain pitch ideas are transposed a half-step higher. While these qualities of pitch material are not always present in *Stereo Electronic Music No. 2*, they are frequent enough to constitute a stylistic feature of the work, a characteristic that is also evident in Arel's other works.

Arel's music often seems more continuous than Davidovsky's, or, at least, it seems to divide itself into larger, more comprehensible sections. This is due to Arel's use of repetition, and perhaps more important, extension of compositional ideas. *Stereo Electronic Music No. 2*, for example, can be heard as an investigation of contrasting long and short envelope sounds; this idea is established at the beginning of the work and reappears throughout.

THE UNIVERSITY OF TORONTO STUDIO

I of IV *by Pauline Oliveros*

The third institutionally sponsored electronic music studio in North America was founded at the University of Toronto. The Toronto studio was established in May 1959 under the direction of Arnold Walter (b. 1902, Hannsdorf, Moravia; d. 1973, Toronto) wth the technical assistance of Hugh Le Caine (b. 1914, Port Arthur, Ontario), then of the National Research Council of Ottowa. Like most classical studios, much of the electronic music equipment in the Toronto studio was especially designed and built for it. This included such items as the *Hamograph*, a device for controlling the rhythmic and dynamic aspects of sound, a large spiral-form steel mesh reverberator, and an organ-type keyboard for controlling the pitch of oscillators. Since the Toronto studio was well funded and cared for, it became one of the largest and most desirable studios of the early 1960s. Many composers came there to study and work.

University of Toronto Electronic Music Center. (Photo courtesy of UTEMS)

In 1966, Pauline Oliveros (b. 1932, Houston, Texas) visited the Toronto studio and composed a series of four works titled by their chronology: *I of IV, II of IV, III of IV, IV of IV*. *I of IV*, the only one of these works that was commercially recorded, is a real-time classical studio composition. The sound sources are twelve oscillators that can produce either sine or square waveforms. In order to achieve real-time control over the oscillators, thus eliminating the need for tape editing, Oliveros used the special keyboard designed for the Toronto studio. This allowed the oscillators to be "played" via the keyboard, as well as by direct manual control. The outputs of the oscillators were routed to two amplifiers, a mixer, a reverberator, and, finally, to two stereo tape recorders. Two recorders were used in order to achieve an extended tape delay system. The layout and tape path was similar to that outlined in Figure 7-2. The actual signal path was somewhat complicated, in order to achieve a complex system of delay effects. First the signal was routed to the record head of channel 1 of tape recorder I (IR1). It then followed the following path: IR1 → IP1 → IR2 → IP2 → IR1. This created a double feedback delay loop. Machine II was not used for recording, only playback. The signal paths between machines I and II were IIP1 → IR1, and IIP2 → IR1. Thus, an extended delay of eight seconds was achieved when material was played back on machine II. These extended delays have the effect of repetition, while the shorter feedback delays created on machine I actually contribute to the modification of the timbre and dynamics. The use of this tape delay system allowed Oliveros to repeat events and add them together, effects that would not otherwise be possible in a classical studio.

The extended delay can be heard at the very beginning of the piece where the initial attack of the sound is repeated at 0'08". This is the result of a sound being recorded on machine I and repeated, eight seconds later, by machine II. This initial attack can then be heard to repeat again and again at differing intervals caused by the combined effects of the feedback delay system of machine I and the extended delay provided by machine II. Even as these repetitions occur, new pitches are added through changes of the frequencies of the oscillators. These new additions can also be heard to repeat. Soon a rather dense texture is built up through changes of pitch and addition of repetitions.

The timbre of the sound in the opening of *I of IV* is created by a combination-tone technique developed by Oliveros. In this instance, she tuned eleven of the twelve oscillators to frequencies above 20,000 Hz; the remaining oscillator was tuned below 1 Hz. The result was the combination, or difference, tones that create the machine-like buzzing effect at the beginning of *I of IV*.

I of IV is also characterized by portamento melodies such as occur at 1'23" and wide-ranging pitch sweeps like those at 2'50". The latter are created by rapidly sweeping the internal frequency control of an oscillator.

While *I of IV* has an improvisational attitude about it, it also creates a somewhat surreal atmosphere. Although there are dynamic accents and articulations, there are no silences. There is always a sea of sound from which individual events spring, only to be slowly absorbed back into the swell. The rhythms created by the repetitions create an underlying continuity of motion, which may be temporarily superseded, but which always returns. Oliveros's concern with the sensual in music is evident in *I of IV*.[7]

THE YALE STUDIO

Second Electronic Setting
by Mel Powell

Unlike the classical electronic music studios discussed so far, the Yale Electronic Music Studio did not begin with large grants or specialized equipment. Founded in 1960 by Mel Powell (b. 1923, New York City), at Yale University, the Yale studio consisted primarily of whatever Powell and Bulent Arel were able to beg, borrow, or build. The original equipment complement consisted of several laboratory type oscillators, a ring modulator, a band-pass filter, a reverberator, and six monaural and stereophonic tape recorders, one of which had variable speed. Actually, this type of studio was more representative of the average classical electronic music studio than were the larger installations at Cologne or Columbia-Princeton.

[7] For further information on *I of IV*, see the interview with Pauline Oliveros in Part III.

The early output of the Yale studio was dominated by the work of Mel Powell. His *Second Electronic Setting* (1962) characterizes Powell's approach to the medium. The *Second Electronic Setting* is a concentrated, polyphonic work, consisting of up to thirty-six parts. In order to characterize the individual lines, Powell gave them differing timbral, rhythmic, and registral qualities.

The timbres in *Second Electronic Setting* are primarily created by the technique of additive synthesis, similar to that used by Stockhausen in *Study II*. However, unlike Stockhausen, Powell used the frequencies of the normal harmonic series to construct his timbres. The rhythmic qualities of the individual parts are largely a result of cutting and splicing techniques. Registral characteristics could be defined in the original recording or by a later speed change.

Just to accomplish the kind of precision and density of information that Powell achieved in the classical studio seems enough of a challenge. But, as is often the case in electro-acoustic music, the level of technical possibilities somewhat hampered, and even altered, Powell's efforts. In creating up to thirty-six simultaneous parts, it was necessary to produce so many generations of recordings that an unacceptable amount of hiss developed. Rather than abandon his goal, Powell modified it to fit the circumstances by always having one or more parts present in a high register, thereby masking the hiss. Another problem was the proper alignment of the various tracks. Often, many takes of certain combinations were necessary to achieve the correct result.

While timbre, rhythm, and register are important elements in *Second Electronic Setting*, the piece is primarily concerned with pitch material. All of the pitches are generated by a procedure of Powell's own invention. In this system, pitches are considered horizontally in groups of three. Beginning with any of the twelve pitch-classes, any other pitch-class could follow. The third pitch, however, must form the melodic interval of a minor second, unless this interval already existed between the first and second pitches; in that event, the third pitch could be any other pitch-class. Thus, the melodic interval of a minor second must appear once in every three pitches. The aural result of this procedure is to create a homogeneity in the pitch material of the *Second Electronic Setting* due to the statistical predominance of the interval of a minor second.

In listening to Powell's *Second Electronic Setting*, one is aware of the homogeneity of the music, even though one is drawn to its points of differentiation. The horizontal and vertical combinations of pitches occur too rapidly for the listener to register and connect each event, yet they are perceivable for the instant they exist. This, together with the differentiation of timbre and rhythm, creates a constantly changing matrix of sound, an interweaving and fluid complexity.

The decade from 1955 to 1965 was a sort of golden age for classical studio electronic music. During this period the major studios were established, schools were founded, styles developed, and techniques were explored. The electronic music composed during this time provided the foundation for the compositional and technological development of the future.

DISCOGRAPHY

Arel, Bulent. *Stereo Electronic Music No. 2.* CRI SD 268; Finnadar QD 9010 0798.

Badings, Henk. *Cain and Abel.* Composers' Voice CV 7803. (Donemus, Paulus Potterstraat 14, 1071 CZ Amsterdam, Holland).

Davidovsky, Mario. *Electronic Study No. 3.* Turnabout TV 34487; Finnadar QD 9010 0798.

Gaburo, Kenneth. *Lemon Drops.* Heliodor HS 25047.

Koenig, Michael Gottfried. *Funktion Blau.* Philips 6526 003.

———. *Funktion Gelb.* Wergo WER 324.

———. *Funktion Grun.* DGG 137 011.

Maderna, Bruno. *Continuo.* Philips 835 485/86AY; Limelight LS-86047; Mercury SR-2-9123.

Mayazumi, Toshiro. *Mandara.* Philips 6526 003; Nippon Victor SJX 1004.

Oliveros, Pauline. *I of IV.* Odyssey 3216 0160.

Pousseur, Henri. *Scambi.* Philips 835 485/86AY; Mercury SR-2-9123.

Powell, Mel. *Second Electronic Setting.* CRI S-227.

Raaijmakers, Dick. *Contrasts.* Epic BC 1118.

Schäffer, Boguslaw. *Symfonia.* Philips 6526-003.

Shibata, Minao. *Improvisation.* Philips 6526 003; Nippon Victor SJX 1004.

Varèse, Edgard. *Poème Électronique.* Columbia MS 6146; Columbia MG 31078.

Weiland, Frits. *Study in Layers and Pulses.* Composers' Voice CV 7803. (see Badings entry above).

FOR FURTHER LISTENING

Arel, Bulent. *Stereo Electronic Music No. 1.* Columbia MS-6566.   Composed in 1960, this work is stylistically similar to the more developed *Stereo Electronic Music No. 2.* The timbres of *Stereo Electronic Music No. 1* are more elemental, and the musical ideas seem to be somewhat less controlled. Nevertheless, it remains one of the stylistic and technical models for this genre of classical studio electronic music.

Badings, Henk. *Evolutions-Ballet Suite.* Epic BC 1118; Limelight 86055. *Evolutions* was realized in 1958 at the Philips studio with the help of Dick Raaijmakers. It consists of six movements: *Overture, Air, Ragtime, Intermezzo, Waltz,* and *Finale.* The music tends to concentrate on aspects of pitch and rhythm that are easily perceivable in traditional terms. While usual classical studio techniques are obviously present, so is the use of electronic keyboard instruments. The various musical and technical qualities of *Evolutions* add up to a curious sense of anachronism.

Davidovsky, Mario. *Electronic Study No. 2.* Son Nova 3.   Written in 1962, *Electronic Study No. 2* is more percussive than the later *Electronic Study No. 3,* but the same stylistic hallmarks are in evidence. Tape delay techniques are heard a great deal.

Kagel, Maurico. *Transition I.* Philips 845 485/86AY; Mercury SR2-9123. Kagel was born in Buenos Aires in 1932 but did most of his composing in Cologne. His *Transition I* was composed between 1958 and 1960. *Transition I* makes use of analogies between timbres as devices for transition between sections of the music. Specific qualities of the sound are less important than general characteristics. *Transition I* contains an impressive array of timbres for a work of this vintage.

Kreiger, Arthur. *Short Piece.* Odyssey Y34139.   *Short Piece* is striking in its directness. Sound events are almost always presented one at a time, creating a jerky monophonic stream of changing, complex timbres. This work was composed at the Columbia-Princeton Electronic Music Center in 1974 and seems to be a distillation of earlier classical studio styles.

Maxfield, Richard. *Night Music.* Odyssey 32 16 0160.   Maxfield (b. 1927, Seattle; d. 1969, Los Angeles) was a composer who liked unusual sound sources and aleatoric (chance) procedures. *Night Music* combines both. The material is frequency-modulated electronic sounds produced by an unusual interaction of an oscilloscope and a tape recorder. Out of hours of material, Maxfield selected certain sound events that evoke sounds of birds and insects. The particular ordering of events is aleatoric. The commercially recorded version of *Night Music* was realized circa 1966, although the original material dates from several years earlier.

Powell, Mel. *Events.* CRI 227 USD.   *Events* (1963) is unique among Powell's tape works. It combines electronic and voice sounds, the latter from readings by Lee Bowman, Mildred Dunnock, and Martha Scott, of Hart Crane's poem *Legend.* Whereas the *Second Electronic Setting* is a highly rationalistic and objective work, *Events* is dramatic and intuitive. Meanings exist on several levels simultaneously in *Events.* Powell has interpreted the poem by creating new juxtapositions of words using various tape manipulation techniques; he has also elaborated the ideas of the poem and its constituent words by these methods. In addition, the electronic sounds provide both a background and abstract commentary on the verbal collage.

Semegen, Daria. *Electronic Composition No. 1.* Odyssey Y34139.   Composed at the Columbia-Princeton Electronic Music Center in 1971-72, *Electronic Composition No. 1* is almost a textbook of classical studio electronic music techniques. Semegen (b. 1946) has delineated the sections of the piece by characteristics of pitch, timbre, and rhythm.

Walter, Arnold, Myron Schäffer, and Harvey Olnick. *Summer Idyll.* Folkways 33436.   Composed in 1959, this was the first work realized in the Toronto studio. It is a simple, lyrical work consisting mostly of sine tones. The structure is ABA, and the refrain is played backward. The work is unusual in that it is a collaboration by three composers.

Wilson, Olly. *Cetus.* Turnabout TV 34301.   *Cetus* was realized in 1967 at the University of Illinois. Wilson (b. 1937, St. Louis, Missouri) has chosen to deal with an electronic music primitivism using only simple timbres and basic manipulations and processings. The work has a general arch structure beginning with, and returning to, a sine wave with variable tremolo (AM).

13
ELECTRONIC MUSIC SYNTHESIZERS

THE EARLY DEVELOPMENT OF SYNTHESIZERS

The number and importance of electronic music studios increased greatly during the 1960s. By 1970, there were over four hundred studios in the United States.[1] Of course, the size and nature of these installations varied from small home studios to large university complexes. Most of these studios, however, especially those created after 1966, owed their existence to the development of the *voltage-controlled electronic music synthesizer*.

The precise definition of a synthesizer is a problem. Probably the first application of the term *synthesizer* to electronic music came in 1929 when A. Givelet and E.E. Coupleux demonstrated a device they called a synthesizer. This invention produced sound via four electronic oscillators. In this sense, *synthesizer* refers to the building of complex sounds by the addition of simple ones; this is additive synthesis.

In the late 1930s, a device called the *ANS Synthesizer* was built for the Moscow experimental music studio. This invention produced sound by

---

[1] This is according to a 1970 survey made by the College Music Society and reported in *Symposium*.

means of optical tracks. In this sense, *synthesizer* refers to creating sound by translating one form of energy into another.

The two senses of the terms *synthesizer* expressed by these early inventions are not the same. Furthermore, the technologies of both devices had previously been demonstrated without reference to the term "synthesizer." The Telharmonium used additive synthesis in 1906 and Fischinger created sound by using optical tracks in 1932. Clearly, the historical use of *synthesizer* has been subjective.

Since a precise definition of *synthesizer* cannot be based on early use, and since there has been no consensus in the interim, the definition of *synthesizer* in this book is, simply, an integrated and self-contained system for the production of electronic music. It is very important to note that this definition distinguishes by physical or design characteristics, rather than by function or use alone. An electronic music synthesizer, therefore, is easily distinguished from a classical electronic music studio, although both may be used to produce the same results. The relationship between form and function is circular, and secondary to the intent of an external agent.

The historical development of electronic music systems is due largely to the influence of technology and the uses made of it. As electronic technology moved from tubes to transistors, to integrated circuits, to microelectronics, new electronic music systems were invented. The design of new systems was often an integration or miniaturization of previous designs; sometimes a new approach to design philosophy developed. The early synthesizers of the 1960s were largely designed to integrate the functions of the classical electronic music studio. By the end of the 1960s, some synthesizers were being designed for real-time performance, a trend that became dominant. Eventually, the distinction between synthesizers and electronic keyboard instruments was blurred. As a result, one can speak of synthesizers only in very broad or quite specific terms, dealing with a certain model of a particular make. For the purposes of this book, the first course makes the most sense, and a broad division of synthesizers can be made on historical and technical bases into three general divisions: the RCA Synthesizers, voltage-controlled synthesizers, and digital synthesizers.

THE RCA SYNTHESIZERS

The first *RCA Electronic Music Synthesizer* was completed in 1955. It had been constructed by Harry Olsen and Herbert Blair to investigate the creation and control of electronic sounds.[2] Shortly thereafter, these engineers built a second and larger synthesizer, the *Mark II*, at a cost of over $250,000.

[2] For more information on the first RCA Synthesizer, see H.F. Olsen and H. Belar, "Electronic Music Synthesizer," *Journal of the Acoustical Society of America*, 27 (1955), 595; H.F. Olsen, H. Belar, and J. Timmens, "Electronic Music Synthesis," *Journal of the Acoustical Society of America*, 32 (1960), 311; *The Sounds and Music of the RCA Electronic Music Synthesizer*, RCA Victor, LM-1922.

The Mark II is a very large system, containing over 1700 tubes; it is 20 feet long and 7 feet high. The components of the Mark II (oscillators, filters, mixers, and so on) are initially controlled by the composer by means of two alpha-numeric keyboards on the front of the synthesizer. The composer determines the various aspects (pitch, envelope, timbre, dynamics, duration) of each sound, and, as these elements are specified, the synthesizer produces the desired results. Instead of using written notation, the information necessary to recreate the specified events is stored on a roll of perforated paper tape. The holes punched in this long roll of paper represent a *binary coding system*.[3] This method of information storage is similar to certain older computer systems. A piece composed in this manner could be heard through use of the paper tape to "play" the synthesizer, in a fashion analagous to a player piano. Only at that point would the completed composition be recorded on magnetic tape.

The RCA Mark II Synthesizer differs from the classical electronic music studio in three basic ways. First of all, the Mark II is a self-contained, integrated system of devices for creating electronic music. Unlike the classical studio, the Mark II does not require any physical arrangement or re-arrangement in order to function in a given way. Secondly, the Mark II precludes the need for tape manipulation. The tape recorder is necessary only for recording a "performance" of the finished work. Finally, the Mark II establishes an intermediary stage in communication between the composer and the sound he is creating. In the classical studio, a sound could be heard simply by turning on and amplifying an oscillator; the line between action and result is direct. On the Mark II, a sound must be specified before it is heard; there is an intermediate stage of translation (the language of specification) between the composer and his creation. Unquestionably, the Mark II is not a performance instrument, it is an elaboration of studio composition.

While these three qualities distinguish the Mark II from the classical studio, they also set it apart from other synthesizers as well as from computer music systems. For while all synthesizers are integrated systems, they usually do not require the use of intermediary translation common to computer music systems. These anomalies make the RCA Mark II unique.[4]

Ensembles for Synthesizer
by Milton Babbitt

The RCA Mark II Electronic Music Synthesizer has been almost the sole province of one man, Milton Babbitt (b. 1916, Philadelphia). The reasons for this lie primarily with the machine and the man. The use of the

---

[3] In computer systems, information is represented by means of a *code*, a systematic arrangement of symbols. The *binary number system* uses the symbols 0 and 1. Therefore, a *binary coding system* is one that represents information in binary numbers. For more information, see Hubert S. Howe, Jr., *Electronic Music Synthesis* (New York: W. W. Norton & Co., Inc., 1975), pp. 148-156.

[4] For further information on the RCA Mark II see Milton Babbitt, "An Introduction to the RCA Synthesizer," *Journal of Music Theory*, 8 (1964), 251-265.

Milton Babbitt, with the RCA synthesizer in the background. (Photo courtesy of Columbia-Princeton Electronic Music Center)

The RCA Synthesizer. (Photo courtesy of Columbia-Princeton Electronic Music Center)

Mark II requires great precision in the specification of sound. This degree of detail is not welcomed by most composers; it requires a great deal of time and effort. But this kind of detail and precision is exactly what interests Babbitt. He was probably the first American composer to write completely serialized music, applying the principles of twelve-tone writing to all dimensions of music capable of being notated. This led to a compositional style of great complexity, requiring exacting precision in performance. Often, Babbitt's music requires more than most performers are capable of, and inexact realizations are the result. In composing for the Mark II, Babbitt can avoid these problems, for the synthesizer allows him to specify and create exactly what he wants.

Babbitt's music is, as he says, cerebral, providing a density of information that is almost unfathomable, presenting a context that for most people is impossible to understand. But Babbitt's is a specialized music for a specialized audience. It is exactly what he wants.

Ensembles for Synthesizer (1964) is a good example of Babbitt's electronic music. In listening to *Ensembles*, the listener, if he is not well versed in serial thinking, may experience some difficulty in deciding what to listen to. Structurally, the work is not immediately characterizable. There is a brief introduction that returns at the end as a kind of coda. Babbitt says that the piece exists in two main parts, Part I ending at precisely 4'49½". However, the caesura may not be easily perceived by everyone, and, even if it were, it does not provide much information, being rather general in nature.

Regarding the microcosmic structure of *Ensembles*, the specific changes of the elements of the music are determined by serial procedures. The various "dimensions" of the music (pitch, rhythm, timbre, and so on), and their constituent "elements" are determined independently of one another, at least on a perceptual, if not a rational, level. Aurally, then, *Ensembles* appears to many listeners as a complex maze of changing sounds.

The best way to approach *Ensembles* is with an expert knowledge of serial technique and a written score of the work. This is not possible in the context of this book. The second best way to approach *Ensembles* is, curiously enough, in a manner similar to that suggested for Cage's *Williams Mix* in Chapter 4. If, without undue expectations or preconceptions, one listens to *Ensembles* simply for what one can hear, one will probably hear a great deal. Certain passages will stand out, highlighted by their pitch, timbral, or rhythmic qualities. Interestingly, after repeated listenings, one comes to "know" *Ensembles* in the sense that memorization creates expectations through recognition. Although this is not the level at which Babbitt would hear his music, it is an acceptable level of listening, and can afford the listener an honest degree of understanding and appreciation.

About *Ensembles for Synthesizer*, Babbitt has written the following:

The title refers to, among a number of properties of the composition, that most immediately manifest characteristic: the numerous and varied succession of short "ensembles" which constitute the body of the work, between what is obviously an "introduction" and its explicitly similar return as a "coda." These "ensembles," which differ timbrally, rhythmically, dynamically, registrally and durationally, are yet closely related—particularly in the pitch domain, and therefore, if less immediately, in the temporal realm—as polyphonically compounded mutations of that material of the introduction, and are associated into five large sectional groups by thematic dominances. These characteristics suggest yet another pertinence of the title, in the sense of "collection," aggregate," and "set."

Perhaps most centrally, the work exhibits those capacities of the electronic medium with respect to flexibility of pitch, dynamic, durational, and timbral succession, the ensemble coordination of such successions and—in general—the control of, and accuracy of, specifications within the world of musical time.[5]

The RCA Mark II Electronic Music Synthesizer remains an unique system. As such, it has had more of a theoretical than practical influence on electronic music. More important was the development of the *voltage-controlled synthesizer*.

VOLTAGE-CONTROLLED SYNTHESIZERS

A voltage-controlled synthesizer is an integrated system of equipment, or *hardware*, designed specifically for the creation of electronic music. The earliest voltage-controlled synthesizers, which began to appear around 1964, were actually attempts to assemble the tools and functions of the classical studio into one miniaturized package for the generation and processing of electronic sounds. Thus, with a voltage-controlled synthesizer and some tape recorders, one could have a complete electronic music studio in a relatively small space.

In "synthesizing" the classical electronic music studio, the early voltage-controlled synthesizers adopted a modular approach to design. Three general classes of *modules*, or components, were created: sound producing (oscillators, noise generators); sound processing (amplifiers, mixers, filters, reverberators, ring modulators, and so on); control sources (envelope generators, sequencers, keyboards, and so on). The most important aspect of this approach was the concept of control sources. They allowed the composer to change any aspect of sound by applying a *control voltage* in a particular way. This is similar to the way Koenig had used the Utrecht studio function generator to create control signals for his *Funktion* compositions.

[5] Babbitt, Milton. Notes from *Columbia-Princeton Electronic Music Center*. Finnadar QD 9010.

In a voltage-controlled synthesizer, the composer has several choices as to the format of the control voltage. This format is determined by the design of the specific control voltage module. Control voltages differ as to the *nature* of voltage change, which may be *continuous* or *discrete*. A continuous change in voltage would move from, say, 3 to 5 volts and include all points between the outer limits. A discrete voltage would jump from 3 to 5 volts. Control voltage formats also differ as to the *method* of their change, which can be either *manual* or *automatic*. A keyboard provides a manual method of change, while a *sequencer* changes automatically. Thus, by combining these qualities of format (continuous or discrete, manual or automatic), various kinds of control voltage sources can be created.[6] The following are some common control voltage modules found on most voltage-controlled synthesizers:

Keyboard   A keyboard usually produces discrete voltages that are manually changed. With a few exceptions, it is identical to the keyboard of an electronic organ.

Sequencer   A sequencer produces discrete voltages that are automatically changed. Sequencers can have any number of *stages* or positions, but they usually have between eight and sixteen stages.

Envelope Generator   An envelope generator produces continuous voltages that change automatically. Thus, they are capable, when connected to a *gate*, or *voltage-controlled amplifier (VCA)*, of giving a sound event a certain envelope: attack; sustain; decay. Envelope generators are sometimes called "attack generators."

Random Voltage Generator   A random voltage generator can often produce both discrete and continuous voltages that may be changed manually and/or automatically. Random voltage generators are sometimes controllable as to their degree of randomness.

Pulse Generator   A *pulse* is a special kind of control signal. Pulses are kinds of pulse waves with, usually, very short positive amplitudes; for this reason, they are sometimes called *spikes*. Pulses are usually used to *trigger*, or pulse, certain modules; in so doing, they may initiate an event, start or stop a module, or change stages of a module.

Any control voltage source can determine any aspect of sound. A keyboard, for instance, can determine pitch if it is controlling a *voltage-controlled oscillator (VCO)*. The same keyboard could determine timbre if it were controlling a filter or reverberator. The concept of the voltage-controlled

[6] Voltages can also be mixed and processed to create more complex control signals. For further information see Joel Chadabe, "The Voltage-Controlled Synthesizer," in *The Development and Practice of Electronic Music*, ed. Jon H. Appleton and Ronald C. Perera (Englewood Cliffs, NJ: Prentice-Hall, Inc., 1975), pp. 140-143 and pp. 155-167.

synthesizer is that all of the components of the system are compatible with each other, thus providing an integrated system for creating electronic music.

In using a voltage-controlled synthesizer, the composer connects the various modules in a particular arrangement. This configuration of connections is known as a *patch*. Any given patch will produce a specific aural result. For example, one might wish to control the pitch of an oscillator (VCO) by means of a keyboard, then filter and reverberate the output of the oscillator. This specific patch could be visually represented by the patch diagram shown in Figure 13-1. In this diagram, a dotted line represents a control voltage connection, while a solid line represents an audio signal connection.[7] Some voltage-controlled synthesizers require the composer to patch directly, using *patch cords* to connect modules, while other designs use a series of switches to accomplish the same results.

Voltage-controlled synthesizers differ from each other in several respects, reflecting the different design philosophies of their inventors. Some offer a truly modular approach, so that the constituent modules may be arranged in any conceivable way; others are fixed packages with permanent arrangements. Certain voltage-controlled synthesizers are designed primarily as systems for studio composition, while others adopt varying degrees of real-time performance design. The size of voltage-controlled synthesizers also varies greatly, but almost all the systems will contain the following modules or their functional equivalents:

Signal-Generating Modules   Oscillators
                               Noise Generators;
Signal-Processing Modules   Amplifiers
                               Mixers
                               Filters
                               Reverberators

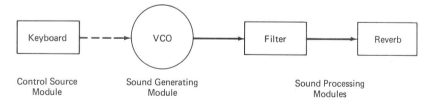

Figure 13-1   A Diagram of a Simple Patch.

[7] Patch diagrams, sometimes called *flow charts,* are not further discussed in this book. Symbols and procedures for diagramming are relatively universal, and are more important to those who use synthesizers than to listeners. Diagrams exist in profusion, although in different formats, in both Joel Chadabe, "The Voltage-Controlled Synthesizer," in *The Development and Practice of Electronic Music,* ed. Jon H. Appleton and Ronald C. Perera (Englewood Cliffs, NJ: Prentice-Hall, Inc., 1975), and in Alan Strange, *Electronic Music* (Dubuque: William C. Brown Co., Publishers, 1972).

Control Voltage Sources   Keyboards
                                 Sequencers
                                 Envelope Generators
                                 Random Voltage Sources
                                 Pulse Generators.

Many other kinds of processing and control voltage modules exist, but those listed above are employed in almost all systems.[8]

The three earliest voltage-controlled synthesizers were the *Buchla*, the *Moog*, and the *Syn-Ket*. These systems differ appreciably from each other and represent the three main design philosophies of voltage-controlled synthesizers: studio systems (Buchla); real-time performance systems (Syn-Ket); and a combination of these approaches (Moog).

THE BUCHLA SYNTHESIZER

The Buchla synthesizer was originally developed by Donald Buchla for the San Francisco Tape Music Center. The Tape Music Center was founded in 1959 by composers Morton Subotnick (b. 1933, Los Angeles) and Ramon Sender (b. 1934, Spain); they were later joined by Pauline Oliveros and Terry Riley, among others. The first attempts by Buchla to produce equipment for the Tape Music Center resulted in specific devices, rather than an integrated system. Certain prototypes of some Buchla modules existed long before an integrated synthesizer had been constructed. However, it was not until 1966 that the first Buchla synthesizer had been installed in the San Francisco Tape Music Center.

One of the most striking features of the Buchla 100-series system, as well as of most later Buchla synthesizers, is the lack of an organ keyboard. The Buchla system is not designed to be "played" in any traditional, instrumental sense; it is primarily a system for studio composition. Another characteristic of the Buchla synthesizer is its complete separation of the audio and control voltage portions of the system. Most other systems allow certain signals, such as an oscillator output, to be used as either an audio or a control voltage source.[9]

THE WORK OF MORTON SUBOTNICK

The composer most closely associated with the Buchla synthesizer has been Morton Subotnick. The reason for this is that he worked closely with Buchla as the system was being designed, and he has used Buchla-designed equip-

---

[8] Different systems display different arrangement of modules and functions. The photographs of voltage-controlled synthesizers included in this book illustrate various designs.

[9] The original Buchla synthesizer is still alive and well at Mills College, which took over the operation of the San Francisco Tape Music Center in the late 1960s. The Smithsonian is reportedly considering the system for acquisition.

ment almost exclusively since 1966. Subotnick's electronic music first gained public notice through the commercial recordings of his early works *Silver Apples of the Moon* (1967) and *The Wild Bull* (1968). *Silver Apples* uses timbres similar to classical studio electronic music: basic waveforms, filtered noise, simple modulations. The most striking material in this piece is the first section (after an introduction) of Part II (1′24″-9′27″). This is a real-time realization, showing the power of Buchla's new system. This dance-like music with its ostinatos and layered rhythms, punctuated by random bursts, became typical of Subotnick's early electronic music and one of its most imitated features.[10] The metric rhythm is Subotnick's music is the result of pulse generators triggering many events while maintaining a constant period of pulsation. Sequencers are used to create ostinato figures and the touch-sensitive "keyboard" is used for the more random punctuations.

    The Wild Bull also contains Subotnick's hallmark use of metric rhythm and repetition. More important, however, is the more fully developed sense of timbre. The initial sound in *The Wild Bull* is one of the timbral themes of the piece. Unlike the timbres of *Silver Apples*, this sound is given greater complexity in the construction of its spectra and envelope. This "Wild Bull sound" has a *complex envelope*, one which contains more than one attack and/or sustain and/or decay. In addition, this timbre is given a specific identity through development. One or two aspects of this sound are changed in each section of the piece, but the basic identity remains. Register might be higher or lower, for instance, or the overall envelope might be longer or shorter. But because enough important information remains constant, the sound is still identifiable. Thus, Subotnick creates a family of "Wild Bull sounds," analogous to a family of instruments.

    This extension and development of the concept of *klangfarben-melodie* is an important concept in electronic music. Not only can new timbres be created, but they can be extended and controlled to degrees not possible with acoustic instruments. Thus, timbres can be stated, related, and varied, just as pitch configurations or melodies were in older music. Timbre can be not only a consciously unifying factor in a work, but it can now also be the most important aspect of the piece.

    While the use of timbre is important in Subotnick's *The Wild Bull*, timbre is not the central ideal of the piece; it is developed only insofar as to create a related group of sounds. The structural and functional use of timbre is more highly developed in *Touch* (1969), perhaps Subotnick's most timbre-centered work to date.

Touch *by Morton Subotnick*

    There are two main timbres in *Touch*. The first and primary timbre is a percussive electronic sound (timbre A), somewhat akin to the sound of a marimba. The second timbre, first heard at 0′09″, is a concrete sound (timbre B), a woman's voice pronouncing the phonemes of the word

---

[10] An *ostinato* is a repeated series of sound events, a recurring pattern.

"touch": "t"; "ou"; "ch". These voice sounds are processed and manipulated so that they seldom resemble the original speech sounds. The result is that timbre B has a noise quality about it, and appears to be nonpitched in the usual sense of an identifiable fundamental. This is in contrast to timbre A which is definitely pitched.

The beginning of Part I of *Touch* is an introduction, lasting until 0'36". It is in this introduction that the listener must grasp the context of the piece if he is to understand it.[11] When timbre A is first heard, one is struck by the pitch information. Similarly, when timbre B is first presented, the rhythmic information associated with it stands out. Yet, while pitch and rhythm are musically important in *Touch*, they remain secondary, both structurally and functionally, to timbre. In *Touch*, Subotnick creates characteristic timbres that are the main themes of the work.

Structurally, *Touch* is in two parts, each part being constructed of an introduction and three sections. Table 13-1 shows the timings of the large sections of *Touch*, along with their characteristics of timbre and tempo.

Table 13-1

DIVISION	TIMING	MAIN TIMBRES	GENERAL TEMPO
Part I			
Introduction	0'00"-0'36"	A & B	Slow
Section 1	0'36"-4'58"	A & B	Fast
Section 2	4'58"-9'40"	Extensions of A; new material	Slow
Section 3	9'40"-14'41"	A & B	Fast
Coda	14'41"-14'55"	A	Slow
Part II			
Introduction	0'00"-2'40"	Extensions of A; new material	Slow
Section 1	2'40"-8'41"	Extensions of A; new material	Slow
Section 2	8'41"-12'44"	A & B[12]	Fast
Section 3	12'44"-15'34"	Extensions of A; new material	Slow

---

[11] This remains, generally, an important consideration in contemporary music. If one does not know the context of a particular work, its syntax and grammar remain mysterious, or worse, confusing.

[12] In Part II, Section 2 of *Touch*, Subotnick introduces a new word (other than "touch") into the music. This word is "sake," and is again spoken in phoneme units ("s," "a," "ke") by the female voice. The word can be almost clearly heard at 12'23". Subotnick claims that "sake" is the phonemic reversal of "touch," and is here used for contrast.

From these cursory observations, it can be seen that timbre and tempo are both used to delineate the large sections of *Touch*, and that Part II is the structural eversion of Part I.

Subotnick uses timbres in *Touch* in an extension of the practice he developed in *The Wild Bull*. Timbre A is developed a great deal from its original form. This development is accomplished by changing one or more aspects of the timbre while maintaining enough information to sustain recognition. These changes primarily occur within the qualities of envelope, spectra, and range of the sound, the basic qualities that determine timbre.[13] For instance, the decay portion of a short envelope can be lengthened to a point of continuous sound, resulting in a continuum of timbral change with regard to this one factor. The same can be done with spectra and range. At what point does a timbre become unrecognizable as to its origins? The answer really depends on how it is presented. For an example, consider Part I, section 1 of *Touch*.

Part I, section 1 of *Touch* consists of several small subsections. As is characteristic of much of Subotnick's music, these sections are spliced together back to back, without any transition. Table 13-2 shows the divisions of section 1, along with broad characteristics of timbre.

Characteristics of timbre are here considered in very broad terms. In the case of envelope, categories of short, medium, and long overall durations have been used. Spectrum is merely considered as simple, moderate, or complex. Register is low, middle, or high. But even such broadly characterized differences can prove useful for observation.

Structurally, it can be seen that the divisions of this section are partially delineated by timbral changes; this is primarily the domain of timbre A, since timbre B's characteristics remain fairly constant. In addition to timbral change, each section also has associated with it particular pitch and rhythmic qualities. For instance, a(I) is typically   , while a(II) is   plus   . These pitch and rhythmic contours do not develop, nor do they return in section 1. Therefore, while they aid in the structural delineation of the piece, they have little functional value. That lies chiefly with the timbre.

The idea of a timbral theme exists in *Touch* in much the same way as a pitch theme (melody) exists in tonal music. In tonal music, the development and use of pitch at any point is understandable only with reference to the original and ensuing presentations of the pitch material. The same can also be done with timbre, and in *Touch* this is the case. The original form of timbre A becomes the basis for a wide range of development. Some forms

---

[13] It is interesting to note that what is here being done by a synthesizer was earlier done by tape manipulation. Changes in the envelope, spectra, and range of a sound were previously accomplished primarily by cutting and splicing, and speed change. In this important sense, Subotnick uses the synthesizer in the context of studio composition.

Table 13-2   Touch, Part I, Section 1 (0'36"-4'58")

DIVISION	TIMING	TIMBRE			
		Type	Envelope	Spectrum	Register
a	0'36"-1'31"	A	short	simple	middle
a(I)	0'36"-1'31"				
a(II)	1'11"-1'31"				
b	1'31"-1'35"	B	short	complex	middle
c	1'35"-2'40"	A	short	moderate	middle & low
d	2'10"-2'26"	A	short & medium	complex	middle
e	2'26"-3'09"	A &	short & medium	complex	middle & low
		B	short	complex	middle
f	3'09"-3'45"	A &	short	simple & moderate	middle & low
		B	short	complex	middle
g	3'45"-4'58" (dovetails into section 2)	A	short & medium	complex	high & middle

of timbre A are far afield from the original, as is the case in Part I, section 1, division g. And yet, because of the previous development, these timbres can be heard as a variation of timbre A. Thus, timbres in *Touch* can be said to have functional development.

The functional use of timbre is indigenous to electronic music. Unaided by electro-acoustic means, acoustic instruments cannot produce such results.[14] The extended use of timbral themes in *Touch* is a development of *klangfarbenmelodie* unique to electronic music.[15]

Touch is a studio composition, realized with a voltage-controlled synthesizer; it is in no sense a real-time work. Essentially, the Buchla 100-series system was not designed as a performance or instrumental synthesizer. The *Syn-Ket*, on the other hand, was intentionally designed to be used in live performance.

THE SYN-KET

The Syn-Ket was built by Paolo Ketoff, an Italian sound engineer, in 1964. It is a small system that can be easily transported. There are three keyboards on the Syn-Ket, each having a two-octave span. Above the keyboards are

[14] Some composers have tried to achieve an instrumental timbral development but not with much success. Consider the opening of Penderecki's *Symphony*.

[15] A further extension of this idea is the functional use of an entire timbral continuum, beginning at one point and changing the timbre continuously until the desired result is achieved. This concept is referred to by the author as "linear timbral transformation," and is a concept totally removed from acoustical experience.

various controls in a vertical arrangement. Thus, the system is played by a performer manually changing the controls and using the keyboards. Unlike the Buchla synthesizer, the Syn-Ket does not have a modular arrangement; its layout is fixed.

It is Syn-Ket an instrument? By historical definition and intention of design, the answer is yes. Historically, all instruments are real-time performance devices, and Ketoff designed the Syn-Ket to be just that. It is also true that instruments have always had fixed, rather than modular formats. This is because one must deal with repeatable space-action-function references in order to learn to play an instrument. By these considerations, the Syn-Ket is an instrument.

Unfortunately, the conundrum is not that easily solved. As was mentioned at the beginning of this chapter, the use to which something is put may be counter to intentions of design: Oliveros and Shibata composed real-time works in the classical studio; electronic keyboard instruments were used in the Cologne and Philips studios to produce studio compositions. Since use is so variable, it is not a practical means by which to consider the nature of a synthesizer. Classification by design, then, is the only practical consideration.

There are, by design, two general kinds of synthesizers: studio synthesizers and performance synthesizers. The only relevant test is whether or not the synthesizer was designed *primarily* for real-time performance. The Buchla synthesizer (100-series) is a studio synthesizer; the Syn-Ket is a performance synthesizer. Modularity is a secondary consideration; the RCA Synthesizer is not modular, but it is a studio system. The historical influence of the studio synthesizer is the classical electronic music studio, while the historical influence for the performance synthesizer is the organ, formerly the most highly developed polyphonic instrument, in all of its many incarnations. In the realm of performance synthesizers, there are both monophonic and polyphonic instruments. But just as earlier electro-acoustic musical instruments developed toward mostly polyphonic design, so it is with performance synthesizers. While melody (monophonic) instruments exist, most newer designs are for soloist, polyphonic instruments. The overwhelming majority of performance synthesizers use organ keyboards and, after all considerations, are separable from contemporary electronic organs on only subjective bases.

Soliloquy for Syn-Ket
by John Eaton

As the first performance synthesizer, the Syn-Ket offered new performance possibilities. Some of these were first realized by John Eaton (b. 1933, Bryn Mawr, Pennsylvania). Eaton was the first composer to write extensively for the Syn-Ket, and, as a result, the instrument has usually been associated with his name. Eaton approached the Syn-Ket not merely as a keyboard device, but specifically to take advantage of electronic sounds in real-time performance. These qualities can be heard in Eaton's *Soliliquy for Syn-Ket* (1967).

Soliloquy for Syn-Ket displays several possibilities of the instrument. From the opening frequency modulation sounds with varying modulating-wave frequencies, to extended portamento, and repeating sequences of short-enveloped sounds. These effects, used in *Soliloquy*, tend to be characteristic of early synthesizer music; they use only one or two oscillators at a time, and have a definitely electronic character. Seldom are there more than two simultaneous sound events in *Soliloquy*, a result of the limited nature of the Syn-Ket.

THE MOOG SYNTHESIZER

At the same time that Buchla and Ketoff were independently designing their synthesizers, Robert A. Moog was building the Moog synthesizer in Trumansburg, New York. The first Moog synthesizers expressed a design philosophy that was different from those of both the Buchla and the Syn-Ket, and yet represented a combined approach. The Moog was designed in a modular fashion with a keyboard. Thus, it represented both studio and performance possibilities. The original and 900-series Moog systems, however, were primarily designed as studio synthesizers; this is clear from an early demonstration record of the Moog synthesizer produced in conjunction with Walter Carlos.[16] As Subotnick is associated with the Buchla system, and Eaton with the Syn-Ket, so Carlos (née Walter; now Wendy) has come to be in association with the Moog system. Most of Carlos's work, however, has been in the field of transcription, rather than original composition. Carlos's use of the Moog has defined many applications and qualities of synthesizers in popular and commercial use.

Tragoedia *by Andrew Rudin*

An example of original composition done with the Moog synthesizer is *Tragoedia* (1967-68) by Andrew Rudin (b. 1939, Newgulf, Texas). The third movement of *Tragoedia*, *Peitho*, demonstrates the use of a voltage-controlled synthesizer in conjunction with tape manipulation techniques. *Peitho (Temptation)* is in two main sections that are separated by a brief climactic section: section 1—0′00″-2′15″; climactic section—2′15″-2′35″; section 2—2′35″-4′50″; codetta—4′50″-5′00″. Section 2, as Rudin notes, is the "structural retrograde" of Section 1. There are three basic timbres in *Peitho*.

---

[16] *Moog 900-Series Electronic Music Systems Demonstration Record.* (Originally available from R.A. Moog Company, Trumansburg, New York 14886.) This record may now be something of a collector's item, but it is well worth searching out. Its contents are a fascinating and revealing document of early intentions and concepts.

Moog Synthesizer System 35 (Photo courtesy of Moog Music, Inc.)

Timbre A is a sawtooth wave, first heard at 0'00"; timbre B is a frequency modulated sound with a very short envelope, creating a nonpitched effect at 0'19"; timbre C is a square wave first heard at 0'44". These three timbres are played from the keyboard, using the control voltage output of the keyboard to determine the frequencies of the oscillators. The instantaneous change among timbres is achieved in real-time, demonstrating the synthesizer's flexibility. These three timbres repeat in a circular fashion (Table 13-3).

Table 13-3

APPEARANCE →	1	2	3	4	ETC.
Timbre ↓					
A	0'00"	1'07"	1'40"	1'57"	
B	0'19"	1'18"	1'46"	2'00"	
C	0'44"	1'29"	1'51"	2'04".	

The increasing tempo of this material is most likely the result of speed change on a variable speed tape recorder.

Two other "voices" or parts can be heard in *Peitho*. A nonenveloped, high-pitched, sinusoidal sound with vibrato is first heard, although barely discernible, at the beginning of the movement. This sound is also transposed. Another sound, short-enveloped and bell-like is quality due to ring modulation, is first heard at 1'20" and again at 1'54". This sound has an echo quality due to tape delay (feedback).

Entropical Paradise *by Douglas Leedy*

Studio synthesizers, can, of course, also be used for real-time composition. In this case, however, it is desirable to have as much equipment as possible, particularly automatic devices. *Entropical Paradise* (c. 1968) is a collection of real-time works created on the Buchla and Moog synthesizers by Douglas Leedy (b. 1938, Portland, Oregon). *Entropical Paradise* is a set of six works that Leedy calls "Sonic Environments." As such, they are part of a large body of *environmental music*, a class of compositions whose purpose is to be a background for something else. Within the classification of environmental music there are many types: There is music for meditation, music for art gallery showings, music for dining, and so forth. Environmental music is generally not intended by the composer as an object for conscious attention, and, as a result, often deals with concepts such as drones or random changes.[17]

The production of the environments of *Entropical Paradise* involved the creation of automated patches on the Buchla and Moog synthesizers. These patches were self-generating "programs" creating random results within certain specified limits. *White Landscape*, for instance, is simply a randomly recurrent series of different long-enveloped filterings of reverberated white noise, combined with another random but sparsely appearing, low-frequency reverberated sawtooth wave with slight portamento.[18]

DEVELOPMENT OF
THE VOLTAGE-CONTROLLED SYNTHESIZER

The voltage-controlled synthesizer has been an unqualified success. It is more efficient and far less costly than a classical electronic music studio. A voltage-controlled synthesizer is easier to house and use than older style equipment. As the availability of the voltage-controlled synthesizer increased, most of the major colleges and universities in the United States acquired synthesizers and established electronic music studios. Older studios had to buy the new equipment or become anachronisms.

Since the synthesizer was primarily an American phenomenon, the development and practice of electronic music grew rapidly in the United States. The demand for new systems was great. Buchla and Moog designed new systems and formed companies for the distribution of their products.[19] By the middle 1970s dozens of manufacturers had sprung up, including some in England and Japan. They offered varied designs, largely influenced by what Moog had done previously. By 1975, it was clear that voltage-controlled synthesizers were here to stay for a while, and that the main thrust of their development was toward real-time performance instruments, not studio systems.

[17] Because of the easy accessibility of music in almost any environment, *any* music could be environmental by perception.

[18] For performance instructions and a patch diagram for Leedy's *Entropical Paradise with Bird Call*, see Alan Strange, *Electronic Music* (Dubuque: William C. Brown Co., Publishers, 1972), pp. 138-143.

[19] Ketoff also designed the Syn-Ket II, but, like the original Syn-Ket, it remained largely the province of John Eaton.

ARP 2600 Synthesizer. (Photo courtesy of ARP Instruments, Inc.)

Voltage-controlled synthesizers made electronic music available to the popular music practitioner. A keyboard was familiar ground for most popular performers, and the new sounds offered by synthesizers were most welcomed. Since popular demand made synthesizer development commercially feasible, manufacturers created systems they could sell. The synthesizers that popular musicians wanted were not modular studio-oriented systems, for these were impractical to deal with as instruments. Instead, synthesizers were developed in the form and spirit of small electronic organs with prepatched "voices," combinations of oscillators, filters, and amplifiers. Presets were offered, allowing the performer to change the timbre of a voice by simply throwing a switch or pressing a button. Specialized synthesizers were developed to imitate acoustical instruments such as strings and percussion. The lines between synthesizers, electronic instruments, and electronic organs became blurred, and many types of popular music became largely electronic.

By 1980, the modular, studio voltage-controlled synthesizer was receiving little consideration. Certain manufacturers, particularly Buchla and Peter Zinovieff, had designed new large studio systems, but very few were sold. In 1980, the synthesizers most used, listed by manufacturer, were those shown in Table 13-4.[20]

---

[20] "Billboard Studio Equipment Survey," in *Billboard 1979-1980 International Recording Equipment and Studio Directory*. Reprinted by permission.

Roland 100M Electronic Music System. (Photo courtesy of Roland Corp., U.S.)

Korg PS-3100 Synthesizer. (Photo courtesy of Unicord/Korg)

Table 13.4

SYNTHESIZER	SURVEYED PERCENTAGES OF USE
ARP	39%
Moog Norlin	25%
Korg/Unicord	5%
Oberheim	5%
Roland	4%
EML	4%
Sequential Circuit	2%
Cat	1%
Other (each less than 1%)	15%

While ARP, Moog Norlin, Oberheim, and Roland have offered some modular, studio systems, these are a small percentage of what is sold and used. Most of the equipment surveyed is instrumental in design; most of it is used by popular musicians or is housed in commercial recording studios.

DIGITAL SYNTHESIZERS

In 1972, composer Jon Appleton (b. 1939, Los Angeles) began working with engineers Sydney Alonso and Cameron Jones to develop a *digital synthesizer*. The result of this collaboration was the *Dartmouth Digital Synthesizer*.

The voltage-controlled synthesizer is an *analog* system, while the Dartmouth synthesizer is a *digital* system. In a very general sense, the difference between the designations *analog* and *digital* is the way they *quantify*, or express quantities. *Analog quantification* is done on a continuous scale, whereas *digital quantification* is done on a scale of discrete, evenly spaced steps. These differences can be easily understood by comparing the traditional, round-faced clocks with the newer digital clocks. Traditional clocks are analog devices, using a continuous scale capable of representing not only, say, ten o'clock and one minute past ten o'clock, but also all points between these. Digital clocks use a discrete scale that counts only by step such as from 10:00 to 10:01, excluding all points between steps.

In an *analog synthesizer*, *quantities* are *measured* by *representation*. For instance, suppose that one wishes to produce the frequency of 442 Hz on an oscillator of a voltage-controlled synthesizer. The output of any voltage source required to produce 442 Hz is, say, 5.025 volts. "5.025 volts" is an analog quantification, "5.025" being a measurement, and "volts" being a representation of something, in this case electrical force. 5.025 volts is thus analogous to 442 Hz. In another application, a different patch, 5.025 volts could be analogous to a certain dynamic, tempo, timbre, and so forth.

It is possible to create a *hybrid electronic music system* by using digital technology, such as a computer, to determine the control voltages needed to operate an analog synthesizer. In digital systems, *quantities* are *counted* by *numbers.* Suppose that the digital quantification needed to produce 442 Hz is 10. In the hybrid system, the hypothetical digital quantification of 10 would be changed to the hypothetical analog quantification of 5.025 volts by a *digital to analog convertor (DAC).*

A *digital synthesizer* is one that uses digital technology, as opposed to an analog synthesizer, or the hybrid system that uses digital control of analog equipment. The difference between a digital synthesizer and a computer music system is, in practice, not entirely clear. Historically, however, a difference can be inferred by design intention. Just as the analog voltage-controlled synthesizer was first developed to amalgamate the classical studio, so the digital synthesizer was originally seen as a technological and functional improvement on modular analog systems. Digital synthesizers provide the functions of analog systems without the actual instrumentation. Thus, a *digital oscillator* is not, strictly speaking, a piece of equipment, but rather a digital simulation of an analog oscillator. This is historically different from a computer music system, in use of which a composer had to specify all of the required information before a sound was generated. A digital oscillator is immediately available for use, as is an analog oscillator.

Digital electronics are superior to analog in two ways: precision is greater, and operational programs may be stored. For example, the precision and stability of a digital oscillator is superior to that of an analog oscillator.

The Dartmouth Digital Synthesizer is a studio system formed by the combined use of several pieces of equipment. An alpha-numeric keyboard is

Synclavier II. (Photo courtesy of New England Digital Corp.)

used to communicate with a computer and visual representations of the information created is displayed on a video monitor. This information can also be digitally recorded for future use. Thus, the re-creation of patches, a problem on analog systems, is easily accomplished. The Dartmouth Digital Synthesizer provides the *hardware* (physical machinery) of the computer music studio with the *software* (programming, the instructions that cause the system to function) of a voltage-controlled synthesizer.

The Dartmouth Digital Synthesizer broke new ground in electronic music studio design, but it was not practical from the standpoints of performer orientation or portability. Appleton, Alonso, and Jones designed the *Synclavier* in 1976 to improve these aspects of digital synthesis. The Synclavier was the first commercially distributed digital synthesizer. While the software and hardware of the Synclavier are similar to that of the Dartmouth Digital Synthesizer, the control of the system is drastically different. The Synclavier has an organ keyboard attached to a vertical control panel; a second package contains the computer and dish drive. The two parts of the Synclavier can be easily connected or disconnected and are relatively small in size, affording portability. The most striking thing about the Synclavier is that it can easily be used as a real-time performance instrument as well as a studio synthesizer. The Synclavier is played from the keyboard and can be programmed by using the same keyboard in conjunction with a few operationally simple controls.

About fifty Synclaviers were built during the latter half of the 1970s, but Alonso and Jones were still not satisfied with the system. In terms of the commercial realities of human engineering, what was needed, they felt, was improved programming and a clearly instrumental package. This they provided in the Synclavier II, unveiled in 1980. The Synclavier II is quite compact and easily portable. It consists of a five-octave keyboard with a vertical control panel and foot pedal(s). Some of the features of the Synclavier II are: over 64 preprogrammed voices; up to 128 programmable voices; a sixteen-track digital memory recorder using disketts; velocity-sensing keyboard; a large array of special timbral modification effects; outputs compatible with most analog systems. Like the original Synclavier, the Synclavier II must be connected to a "control unit," a separate, but quite small, computer.

It seems fair to say that the Synclavier II is primarily designed as a performance instrument. This is also true of the *Con Brio ADS 200* digital music synthesizer, which consists of a single package containing two keyboards, a video monitor, digital recorder, and control panel. Other systems, such as the *Fairlight Computer Music Instrument*, the *Crumar General Development System*, and the *Alpha Syntauri* system are similar to the Dartmouth Digital Synthesizer except they have organ as well as alphanumeric keyboards. Each of these digital systems contains features unique to itself. The Fairlight, for instance, allows the composer to literally draw a waveform on the video monitor by use of a *light-pen* and instantaneously

Con Brio ADS 200 Digital Music Synthesizer. (Photo courtesy of Con Brio Digital Music Synthesizers)

Fairlight Computer Music Instrument. (Photo courtesy of Fairlight Instruments U.S.A.)

Alpha Syntauri Electronic Music System. (Photo courtesy of Syntauri Corporation)

hear the result. The Alpha Syntauri system is designed for use with the Apple II computer, affording digital synthesis at a remarkably low cost.

Working with a digital synthesizer can solve several problems for the composer of electronic music. Patches and compositional information can be recorded for later use, providing exact retrievability. Most, if not all, of a composition can be realized in real-time, thus saving generations of tape recording; in fact, the work may not have to be tape recorded at all, since it can be reproduced via the synthesizer countless times. Another possibility is the easier production of complex timbres that, like acoustical sounds, have time-variant qualities.[21]

Georganna's Farewell *by Jon Appleton*

One of the earliest works composed on a digital synthesizer is Jon Appleton's *Georganna's Farewell* (1975), realized on the Dartmouth Digital Synthesizer. *Georganna's Farewell* is a sectional work based on traditional pitch structures. The work begins with a series of large, vertical, diatonic chords in the minor mode. These chords clearly establish a tonic-dominant

---

[21] Many composers and listeners have objected to the periodic, "steady-state" quality of the sounds produced by analog oscillators. It has been said that they create patently "electronic" timbres lacking the normally occurring complex and random changes found in the spectra of acoustic sounds. One of the tenets of digital synthesis has been that digital synthesis allows far better possibilities of creating complex, more natural timbres than analog systems can. This is theoretically true.

relationship. The many small sectons, or episodes, that follow deal with new ways of elaborating the chords, such as arpeggiation, or new tunings other than diatonic. Sometimes both manner of presentation and tuning characterize a section. The material from the first section reappears three times in the work, and so creates a kind of refrain. A cursory division of *Georganna's Farewell* is given in Table 13-5.

The constant changing of tunings and gestures of pitch presentation give *Georganna's Farewell* an unusual sense of elastic plasticity: a stretching and distending of musical materials that periodically return to their original form.

Technically, *Georganna's Farewell* displays some of the possibilities of digital synthesis. The chords of the refrain would be very difficult and time-consuming to realize by classical studio technique, or even on most analog synthesizers. The changes that occur between sections of the piece would require a complete repatching of an analog system and also necessitate separate tape recordings to be spliced or mixed with other sections. Using the Dartmouth Digital Synthesizer, however, the programming changes made during the act of composition are perfectly recalled by the system so that the entire composition can be realized in real-time.

Certain sections of *Georganna's Farewell*, particularly the refrain, have a keyboard performance quality. The Dartmouth Digital Synthesizer, however, is not a performance system and so, while the music could be realized in real-time, it could not be performed or played in the instrumental sense. It is quite easy to equate the terms *compose*, *realize*, and *perform* when speaking of a studio composition. *Georganna's Farewell* is a studio composition with the difference that it can be realized in real-time. But, like any studio composition, it cannot be repeatedly performed in real-time.

Table 13-5

SECTION	TIMING	CHARACTERISTICS
Refrain	0'00"-0'24"	Vertical, diatonic chords; minor mode
A	0'24"-1'08"	New tuning; alternated broken chords
B	1'08"-1'29"	Descending arpeggios
Refrain	1'29"-1'48"	
C	1'48"-2'04"	Vertical chords; new tuning
D	2'04"-2'16"	Ascending arpeggios (overlapping)
E	2'16"-2'31"	Ascending arpeggios; increased tempo (overlapping)
F	2'31"-3'00"	Reversal of envelope shapes
G	3'00"-3'15"	Ascending and descending arpeggios
Refrain	3'15"-3'30"	
H	3'30"-4'05"	Vertical chords; new tuning
I	4'05"-4'32"	Ascending arpeggios; decreased tempo
J	4'32"-5'07"	Predominantly descending arpeggios; decreased tempo
K	5'07"-5'30"	Predominantly ascending arpeggios; increased tempo
Refrain	5'30"-6'10"	

The keyboard performance characteristics heard in parts of *Georganna's Farewell* are more fully developed in some of Appleton's more recent works such as *In Deserto* (1977) and *Syntrophia* (1977), both composed on the Synclavier. Although the keyboard control of the Synclavier does not necessarily have to have a traditional keyboard performance correspondence to the music, it often does in Appleton's most recent music. This is partly because these works are designed for a live performance, although only some of the music is played in real-time, while other parts are realized from digital memory. In this regard, these compositions are live/electronic music and the Synclavier is a system for, simultaneously, the recording, reproducing, and performance of music.

It is at this point that traditional, historically derived terminology begins to fail. Perhaps the term "synthesizer" has outlived its usefulness and might better be replaced by the words "electronic music system." There are, then, studio electronic music systems and performance systems; analog systems and digital systems. And there are, or will be, all possible combinations of these. As yet, there is no final analysis, or synthesis.

DISCOGRAPHY

Appleton, Jon. *Georganna's Farewell*. Folkways FTS 33442.

———. *In Deserto*. Folkways 33445.

———. *Syntrophia*. Folkways 33445.

Babbitt, Milton. *Ensembles for Synthesizer*. Columbia MS-7051; Finnadar QD 9010.

Eaton, John. *Soliloquy for Syn-Ket*. Decca DL 710165.

Leedy, Douglas. *Entropical Paradise*. Seraphim 6060.

Rudin, Andrew. *Tragoedia*. Nonesuch 71198.

Subotnick, Morton. *Silver Apples of the Moon*. Nonesuch 71174.

———. *Touch*. Columbia MS-7316.

———. *The Wild Bull*. Nonesuch 71208.

FOR FURTHER LISTENING

Babbitt, Milton. *Composition for Synthesizer*. Columbia MS-6566. Composed in 1964 on the RCA Mark II, *Composition for Synthesizer* is another example of Babbitt's sophisticated and complex serial style.

Budd, Harold. *Oak of the Golden Dream*. Advance 16. Harold Budd (b. 1936, Los Angeles) has been referred to as a "minimalist" composer, although he does not particularly fancy that description. *Oak of the Golden Dream* (1970) is one of Budd's few electronic works and was composed on the Buchla 100-series system. It consists of a drone over which a melody is improvised. It could be performed in real-time; however, this recording was not so done.

The Nonesuch Guide to Electronic Music. Nonesuch HC-73018.   Compiled in 1968 by Paul Beaver and Bernard Krause, this set was intended to guide the novice through the maze of electronic music. It is now something of an historical curiosity.

Smiley, Pril. *Kolyosa.* CRI S-268.   Smiley has made an analogy between wheels (*kolyosa* in Russian) and the sequencer of the Buchla synthesizer. Since the sequencer is used here to control pitch, it is capable of producing a repetitive, hence circular, pattern; it can produce a "wheel" of sound. Pulsing the sequencer at various rates can produce everything from repeated pitch sequences (slow pulse rate) to various kinds of frequency modulation timbres (fast pulse rate). The result is a fascinating flow of spinning sounds, demonstrating the perceptual continuum between pitch and timbre. *Koloysa* was composed in 1970 at the Columbia-Princeton Electronic Music Center.

The Sounds and Music of the RCA Electronic Music Synthesizer. RCA Victor LM-1922.   This record is definitely a collector's item and is worth trying to find. Side one contains a lecture-demonstration on the RCA Synthesizer and the properties of sound. Side two is devoted to musical transcriptions. Recorded in 1955, this disc contains fascinating, if naive, versions of *Blue Skies, Home, Sweet Home*, and, of course, some Bach. It also has one of the earliest recorded experiments in voice synthesis.

Subotnick, Morton. *Until Spring.* Odyssey Y 34158.   For a detailed discussion of this work see the interview with Morton Subotnick in Part III.

Wuorinen, Charles. *Time's Encomium.* Nonesuch 71225.   Wuorinen (b. 1938, New York City) used the RCA Mark II to compose the original material for this piece. Then he processed the results in one of the analog studios of the Columbia-Princeton Electronic Music Center, using, primarily, Buchla equipment. *Time's Encomium* (1968-69) is a serial work.

14
COMPUTER MUSIC

THE DEFINITION OF COMPUTER MUSIC

The definition of computer music is a continuing problem. According to composer Joel Chadabe, "By the term *computer music*, I mean music that is produced by a hardware and software system that importantly includes a computer, but may also include other analog or digital synthesis equipment."[1] This is a broad definition, and one that is increasingly popular. For the purposes of this book, however, Chadabe's definition is too inclusive, for it would include not only hybrid electronic music systems but computer-generated scores for instruments as well.

Until the late 1970s, the definition of computer music was rather clear. With the exception of computer-generated scores, computer music usually meant a type of studio-composed, electronic music in which the sound material was generated by a computer. The continuing development and increasing availability of digital computers, along with the incorporation

[1] Chadabe, Joel, "Some Reflections on the Nature of the Landscape within which Computer Music Systems Are Designed," *Computer Music Journal*, 1, no. 3 (June 1977), 5.

of instrumental design philosophies, has expanded the possible application of the term "computer music" as Chadabe has noted. However, to equate the performer of a digital music instrument with a composer in a computer music studio creates certain philosophical problems. For this reason, the definition of computer music used here is the older and continuingly important one of studio-composed electronic music in which the sound material is generated by a computer.

THE COMPUTER MUSIC STUDIO

The computer music studio developed from traditional computer use and technology combined with the practices that evolved in the classical electronic music studio.[2] In the most general sense, the use of a computer music facility would involve the following steps:

1. The composer prepares and sends instructions to the computer by means of a *program*;
2. The instructions are converted to numbers;
3. The stipulated functions are performed by the computer;
4. The resulting information is converted to a voltage by a digital-to-analog converter;
5. The voltage drives a loud speaker and sound is created.

This simplified process is illustrated in Figure 14-1. While the process is here related as a continuous procedure, such is not always the case. Even though real-time computer music is possible, many computer music facilities do not have real-time capabilities. Usually, there is a delay between the time when a composer prepares his score and when he or she hears the music. This delay can be anywhere from a few hours to several days, depending upon the nature of the computer installation.

The only part of the computer music process of necessary concern to the composer is the initial input stage: the *program*. The program is a set of instructions to the computer, and is written in one of several special languages. There are various computer music programs such as MUSIGOL, MUSIC IV, MUSIC V, TEMPO, PERFORM, and MUSIC 360. All of these programs allow the composer to create a score in a language comprehensible

---

[2] Previous chapters of this book have included technical information pertinent to the understanding of various aspects of electro-acoustic music, especially timbre. Since the technical aspects of digitally synthesized sound are not necessarily relevant to a comprehension of the sound itself, no technical discussion of digital synthesis is presented in this book. As an example, the definition of a sine wave should be clear from previous chapters, and an explanation of how a sine wave is digitally synthesized will not add any information necessary for comprehending that sound. For further information on computer music and digital synthesis, see the bibliography at the back of this volume.

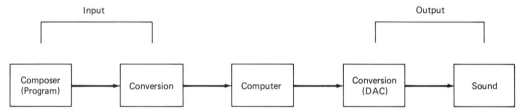

Figure 14-1   The Process of Using a Computer Music Studio.

to the computer system.[3] While these programs make available certain functions to the composer, he must usually specify the particular nature of the sounds he wishes to use and the particular manner in which they occur. The natures, or descriptions, of the sounds used in computer music are sometimes referred to as "instruments" that, collectively, constitute an "orchestra." The specification of the "orchestra" within the computer music program is called a *subprogram*, since it is secondary to and dependent upon the main program. The manner in which the sounds occur is represented by a score; this is analogous to a traditional music score, but, of course, in a different format. The various computer music programs differ in several regards, primarily in the nature of the simulation of sound and the more conceptual aspects of the compositional process. In order to use a computer music system, a composer must first learn a particular program and, to some extent, the language in which it is written. This is a problem for some composers since it necessitates a new and intermediary stage of translation between the composer and the music.[4] Furthermore, the degree of specification required by a particular program may be quite beyond the knowledge or concern of some composers. It is one thing to use a certain process and quite another to specify the results of that process.

There are thus two major differences between composing in the computer music studio and using other approaches to electro-acoustic music:

1. An intermediary and translational step (the program) exists between the composer and his score for the music;
2. The analytical details of a sound event must be understood before that event can be synthesized.

In comparison with other approaches to electro-acoustic music, the computer music studio has attracted fewer adherents than any other means

---

[3] Information is usually entered into the computer by means of a *console*, which is usually, but not always, an alpha-numeric keyboard. Common input media include such forms as cards, paper tapes, magnetic tapes, and magnetic discs. For more information on input and output methods, see Abraham Marcus and John D. Lenk, *Computers for Technicians* (Englewood Cliffs, NJ: Prentice-Hall, Inc. 1973), pp. 228-258.

[4] This is similar to the operation of the RCA Mark II as discussed in Part III, Chapter 5.

of production. The reasons for this are the great costs of building and maintaining a large computer music facility, and, perhaps more important, the scarcity of composers who are interested in this compositional approach. Both of these factors are rapidly changing.

EARLY COMPUTER MUSIC

Max Mathews and Bell Labs

The suggestion that computers might be suitable for the production of music came as early as 1843. Lady Ada Lovelace, referring to Charles Babbage's *Analytical Engine,* a precursor of the modern computer, supposed that the engine could be used for making music, if only the necessary information could be understood and properly expressed. But it was not until 1957 that computer-generated music became a reality at the Bell Telephone Laboratories in Murray Hill, New Jersey.[5] The pioneering father of computer-generated sound is Max Mathews. Mathews, an engineer at Bell Labs, began working on the computer generation of music and speech sounds in the late 1950s. Together with John Pierce and Joan Miller, Mathews has written several computer music programs. Almost all subsequent development of computer music is based upon this early work.

Mathews created computer music programs, such as MUSIC IV and MUSIC V, which allow the composer to deal with the computer by means of simulating analog synthesizer modules and functions. The programming concepts of MUSIC IV and MUSIC V allow the composer to use the functions of *unit generators,* subprograms that perform operations similar to analog equipment such as oscillators, filters, reverberators, and so on. These unit generators can then be linked together in a manner conceptually akin to patching an analog synthesizer. Thus, it is not necessary for the composer to specify the basic nature of the "equipment," for he is able to use what is available in the program.

While this approach allows the composer freedom from computation, it also binds him to the limitations of the program. The basic problem in generating sound with computers is the same problem faced by users of the RCA Mark II: A sound must be specified before it can be realized. On an analog synthesizer, the composer can easily experiment with patch variations in order to discover new sound possibilities. In computer music, however, nothing can be realized until it is completely specified. This means that a desired sound must be analytically comprehended before it can be produced. Digital synthesis of sound offers the possibility of creating literally any

[5] For a discussion of the historical background of computer music, see Edmund A. Bowels, "Musicke's Handmaiden: Or Technology in the Service of the Arts," in *The Computer and Music,* ed. Harry B. Lincoln (Ithaca: Cornell University Press, 1970).

sound event, but the difference between this possibility and any given reality depends largely on the quality of the program used and the skill of the composer using it.

The early experiments at Bell Labs aimed at simple transcriptions and primitive voice synthesis.[6] Like the early experiments with the RCA Mark II, these works have a naive quality. Transcriptions of tunes such as *Frère Jacques* are fascinating in an historical context, but are obviously experimental, lacking timbral complexity and sounding rather flat. The voice synthesis in *A Bicycle Built for Two*, made famous by Stanley Kubrick's film *2001*, is captivating, but hardly realistic. It was clear from these experiments that improvements were necessary, not only in the machinery, but especially in the programs for both the analysis and synthesis of sound.

Stochastic Quartet *by James Tenney*

One of the first composers to do extensive work at Bell Labs was James Tenney, (b. 1934, Silver City, New Mexico). Tenney, originally an electrical engineer, worked at Bell Labs between 1962 and 1968, and composed several computer music compositions. Tenney's work *Stochastic Quartet* (1963) demonstrates his interest in computer-generated scores as well as computer-generated sound. *Stochastic Quartet* exists in two versions: First, as *Stochastic String Quartet* for acoustic instruments, and as *Stochastic Quartet*, a computer realization of the same score. Tenney devised computer programs to aid in the compositional selection of musical elements for *Stochastic Quartet*.[7] These programs generated random and aleatoric sequences of values that were used to control pitch, envelope, dynamics, and so forth. To the extent that these values were broadly controlled or predicted, the work is stochastic. Tenney then used this computer-generated information to construct a traditional score for a string quartet.

Tenney also used the facilities at Bell Labs to realize a computer-synthesized version of *Stochastic Quartet*. He made no attempt to imitate the sounds of a string quartet in his computer realization. Indeed, at the time, such a feat would have been quite formidable since the analytical knowledge of the complex sounds of the string instruments was very limited. The actual timbres that Tenney used for *Stochastic Quartet* were those within the available range of the program MUSIC IV. This, like other early computer music programs, was based on the concept of additive synthesis of harmonic partials. This process is not appreciably different from the approach taken by Thaddeus Cahill or Laurens Hammond, even though the number of partials is not, theoretically, as limited. Furthermore, while

[6] Several of these experiments are recorded on Decca DL 79103.

[7] As mentioned in Chapter 12, much work on the use of computers for generating instrumental scores was done at the University of Illinois during the late 1950s and throughout the 1960s. This work is well documented in Lejaren Hiller, "Music Composed with Computers—A Historical Survey," in *The Computer and Music*, ed. Harry B. Lincoln (Ithaca: Cornell University Press, 1970).

the amplitudes of the various partials could be individually controlled, they often appear in fixed relationships, and little attempt was made to create truly complex envelopes. The timbral possibilities within such a situation are necessarily limited. As a result, the timbres in *Stochastic Quartet* are not very complex and sound somewhat like a quartet of Ondes Martenots.

Mutations I *by Jean-Claude Risset*

Jean-Claude Risset (b. 1938, Puy, France) is another composer who worked at Bell Labs during the 1960s. Risset is one of the few composers of electronic music with a firm background in both music and the hard sciences. He was also one of the first composers to recognize some important problems of computer music: ". . . the computer makes it possible to produce any sound whatsoever that can be described numerically, but then it is not always possible to numerically describe certain sounds, even though they are very familiar."[8] He also saw a solution to the problem: "So, in order to profit from the immense sound resources offered by the computer, it becomes necessary to develop a psychoacoustical science, involving a knowledge of the correlations between the physical parameters, and the perceptible characteristics, of sound."[9]

Risset's own compositions reveal the results of his considerations. He makes use, not only of harmonic partials, but also *inharmonic partials*, partials that are not integral multiples of a fundamental frequency. Although these partials had been used previously as a result of certain frequency modulation processes, they had been dealt with as accidental results, rather than as consciously constructed elements of timbre. Risset often varies the amplitudes of each partial within the additive structure. This creates very complex envelopes. Another principle of complex timbral construction used by Risset involves treating these frequency and amplitude constituents in a nonperiodic, or nonrepetitive manner. By these and other procedures, Risset is able to create what he calls "lively" sounds: timbres that simulate the complexity of acoustical sounds.

These qualities are present in Risset's work *Mutations I*, written at Bell Labs in 1969 using a version of MUSIC V. *Mutations I* is a rather sectional piece that nevertheless remains unified because of Risset's method of relating pitch and timbre. An example of this technique can be heard at the beginning of the piece. The initial sequence of five pitches (0'00"-0'02") uses a complex and percussive timbre. As these pitches decay, however, a second series of envelopes on the same pitches begins to crescendo (0'01"-0'04"). This second statement of these five pitches thus forms a vertical chord, contrasting with the original horizontal, melodic presentation. At 0'04", a third

---

[8] Jean-Claude Risset, "Synthesis of Sounds by Computer and Problems Concerning Timbre," in *Music and Technology* (Paris: La Revue Musicale, 1971), p. 123. Quoted by permission of UNESCO and the author.
[9] Ibid.

presentation of the same five pitches is heard. This time the result is a gong-like sound created by a vertical presentation of the five pitches articulated by a single envelope. This is a form of additive synthesis using only sine waves. However, since these five pitches are not in the harmonic series, they are inharmonic partials; heard in this simultaneous fashion, they form a new timbre. So, treating the same five pitches in three different ways, Risset relates melody (first statement), harmony (second statement), and timbre (third statement) in the beginning of *Mutations I.*[10]

THE PRINCETON STUDIO

Works by J.K. Randall, Barry Vercoe, and Charles Dodge

In 1964, the work of Mathews at Bell Labs was extended to Princeton University by Hubert Howe and Godfrey Winham (b. 1934, London; d. 1975, Princeton). Howe and Winham established computer music facilities at Princeton, now known as the Godfrey Winham Laboratory, and wrote MUSIC IVB, a variation of the MUSIC IV program.

J.K. Randall (b. 1929, Cleveland) composed one of the earliest works to come out of the Princeton facility. *Quartets in Pairs* (1964), Randall's first piece of computer music, is a short but concentrated work. As in much of Randall's music, a pointillistic quality is created by complex relationships between the pitch and durational aspects of the music. The intricacies of this compositional approach moved Randall to consider computer-generated sound instead of instrumental performance. Not only would the temporal aspects of *Quartets in Pairs* provide performers with a difficult problem, but the wide range of pitches called for by Randall's score is beyond the limits of most acoustical instruments. By using a computer to realize *Quartets in Pairs*, Randall was able to create "instruments" capable of performing the work.

Barry Vercoe (b. 1937, Wellington, New Zealand) began composing computer music at the Princeton facilities in 1968. Vercoe developed a new computer music program in 1969: MUSIC 360. MUSIC 360 is a high-speed program, allowing faster results than older computer music programs. It has proven to be a popular approach and is used at over forty universities in the United States and Europe.

One of the first compositions made with the MUSIC 360 program was Vercoe's *Synthesism* (1969). In *Synthesism*, Vercoe created a fairly large "orchestra" of electronic sounds, ranging from sinusoidal to noise

[10] *Mutations I* is discussed in greater detail in the interview with Jean-Claude Risset in Part III. A graphic representation of the beginning of *Mutations I* (0′00″-0′15″) is on page 197.

timbres. These timbres are randomly varied throughout the piece. Like Randall's *Quartets in Pairs*, Vercoe's *Synthesism* deals primarily with related variations of pitch and duration.Vercoe uses a sixteen-unit set for controlling pitch, duration, and envelope. It is this equal-tempered sixteen-note division of the octave that gives *Synthesism* its slightly out-of-tune character.

Vercoe's *Synthesism* is an excellent example of a composition indigenous to the computer music studio. It is impossible, in any practical sense, to write for acoustic instruments using scale and time divisions based on the number 16. Furthermore, while *Synthesism* could have conceivably been composed using the classical electronic music studio or an analog synthesizer, it would have required an inordinately long time to realize. There is no question that the computer allows composers the best method of realizing complicated procedures and translating involved processes into sound. An extreme example of such translation is offered by *Earth's Magnetic Field* (1970) by Charles Dodge (b. 1942, Ames, Iowa).

Earth's Magnetic Field is, in part, a translation into sound of a totally unrelated medium. This medium is a Bartels diagram, representing measurements of change of the earth's magnetic activity, and named after its inventor, Julius Bartels. A Bartels diagram represents the change in magnetic activity by means of a graphic representation not unlike traditional music notation. For this reason, they are often referred to as *Bartels' musical diagrams*. Dodge capitalized on the two basic similarities of the notations: the horizontal representation of time, and the vertical repesentation of degree. Dodge interpreted the measurements of magnetic change for the year 1961, translating this information into a system for determining the pitch, duration, tempo, and register of the music. The timbres seem to have been determined independently of the other musical elements.

Earth's Magnetic Field is in two parts. Part One is a monophonic realization of Dodge's process, using a diatonic (seven pitch) division of the octave, so that Part One has the tonal characteristics of the major mode. Dodge uses three distinct timbres in Part One. Timbre A is used from 0'00" to 2'00" and resembles a muted tuba having no reverberation. Timbre B lasts from 2'00" to 4'00" and is far more complex, containing a larger overtone structure and complex envelopes. Even though the music is monophonic, the overlapping of the envelopes and use of long reverberation times creates a pleasantly acoustical quality in Timbre B. As in an acoustical situation, each sound event has its own independent envelope. This aspect becomes very important in Timbre C, which lasts from 4'00" to 14'04". Timbre C is similar in overtone structure to Timbre B, but envelopes and reverberation times vary independently for particular events or groups of events.

Part Two of *Earth's Magnetic Field* uses Timbre C throughout, continuing the practice of varying complex envelopes. This part differs from the first in that it is polyphonic and utilizes the chromatic scale. As a result, the music is more complex and lacks the tonal quality of Part One.

Speech Songs *by Charles Dodge*

Dodge is perhaps best known for his work with synthesized voice sounds, which be began in 1971 at Bell Labs. In Dodge's process, the text to be used for a composition is spoken by a human performer and recorded digitally. The digitized speech information is analyzed by various special programs. The resulting information can then be used to re-create the speech sounds. This is an example of how the computer can be used to analyze, as well as synthesize, a sound. Through such procedures, a great deal of information can be learned about the nature of sound.

Dodge does not stop at simply re-creating the original speech; he treats the analyzed information as a basis for altering the final synthesized sound. For instance, the pitch contour of the original speech can be changed into a new form more closely resembling a melodic configuration. Durational aspects of the sound that affect both rhythm and the timbre of the speech can be altered. Thus, the resulting synthesized speech can be a considerable extension of the human voice. Dodge's synthesized speech music is a unique type of electronic music: computerized text-sound composition.

The main qualities of Dodge's compositions for synthesized voice can be heard in the third and fourth *Speech Songs* (1973). This set of four pieces is based on short poems by Mark Strand. *Song #3: A man sitting in the cafeteria*, presents a monophonic setting in which the original voice recording is not drastically altered in the process of synthesis. By comparison, *Song #4: The days are ahead*, presents a polyphonic setting of the text with extensive alteration of the pitch material. An example of this can be heard at 0'14" when a chorus of synthesized voices performs an elaborate and breathless portamento.

FURTHER APPLICATIONS OF DIGITAL TECHNOLOGY TO ELECTRO-ACOUSTIC MUSIC

The continuing research in computer music during the 1970s has led to more sophisticated techniques, as well as to a better understanding of the qualities of sound itself. Some of the most important work in these areas has been done by John Chowning, director of the Stanford Center for Computer Research in Music and Acoustics. Chowning has thoroughly investigated the possibilities of frequency modulation and has developed complex programs for simulating the movement of sound in space.[11]

[11] For information on Chowning's work, see John M. Chowning, "The Simulation of Moving Sound Sources," *Journal of the Audio Engineering Society*, vol. 20, no. 6 (9171); John M. Chowning, "The Synthesis of Complex Audio Spectra by Means of Frequency Modulation," *Journal of the Audio Engineering Society*, vol. 21, no. 7 (1973); John M. Chowning, John M. Grey, James A. Moorer, Loren Rush, *Computer Simulation of Music Instrument Tones in Reverberant Spaces*, Department of Music, Stanford University, Technical Report STAN-M-1, 1975.

The work of people like John Chowning and Max Mathews is not important merely for its relationship to present and past compositions, but for future knowledge and applications as well. The design of the Synclavier is partially dependent on Chowning's research into frequency modulation, for example. One of the newer centers for computer music, at the Institute de Recherche et Coordination Acoustique/Musique (IRCAM), combines the work done at Bell Labs and Stanford University, in order to better deal with both analysis and synthesis of sound.[12]

Continuing advances in both hardware and software have enabled computer music to develop beyond the studio-based procedures discussed in this chapter. Digital synthesizers and computer music instruments share the same technology with the computer music studio. As suggested by James A. Moorer, there are essentially three types of approaches to computer music.[13] The first type, characterized by the work of Mathews, Randall, and Vercoe, is *direct synthesis*, in which a computer music program is used to produce sounds as specified by the composer. The second type of approach, represented by Dodge's synthesized speech music, is *analysis-based synthesis*, where natural sounds are first analyzed by the computer and then serve as a basis for composition. The third type is *concrète computer music*, in which acoustic sounds are digitally recorded and then changed by the computer, much in the same way as they are changed by tape manipulation techniques in musique concrète. All of these approaches to computer music composition may or may not be accomplished in real-time, depending on the particular circumstances of a given system.

Recent designs in both pure digital and hybrid analog/digital electronic music systems have tended to emphasize the performance possibilities of new developments. A few, such as the digital systems by Peter Samson and Buchla's 300-series and 500-series systems, are designed for studio applications but with improved real-time capabilities. Nevertheless, the importance of the large computer music facilities is greater than ever, not only for today's compositions, but for the discoveries of tomorrow's research.

DISCOGRAPHY

Dodge, Charles. *Earth's Magnetic Field*. Nonesuch 71250.

———. *Speech Songs*. CRI SD 348.

Randall, James K. *Quartets in Pairs*. Nonesuch 71245.

Risset, Jean-Claude. *Mutations I*. Collection INA-GRM, AM 564-09, (Distributed by Harmonia Mundi, P.O. Box 3087, Long Island City, NY 11103); Turnabout 34427.

[12] John K. Gardner, Brian Harvey, James R. Lawson, Jean-Claude Risset, *Computer Facilities for Music at IRCAM, as of October 1977*, Rapports IRCAM, 3/78.

[13] James A. Moorer, "Signal Processing Aspects of Computer Music—A Survey," *Computer Music Journal*, vol. 1, no. 1 (February 1977).

Tenney, James. *Stochastic Quartet.* Decca 710180.

Vercoe, Barry. *Synthesism.* Nonesuch 71245.

FOR FURTHER LISTENING

Boretz, Benjamin. *Group Variations.* CRI SD 300.   Boretz (b. 1934, Brooklyn) composed this work at the Princeton University Computer Center between 1969 and 1973. *Group Variations* is composed as a series of interlocking and continuous sections that concentrate on pitch and rhythmic structures. Timbre is primarily used for delineating voices and characterizing sections. The result is a complex, polyphonic, often contrapuntal work that seems to be always moving to and from something else.

Dodge, Charles. *In Celebration; The Story of Our Lives.* CRI SD 348.   *In Celebration* (1975) and *The Story of Our Lives* (1974) are synthesized speech music. They are longer and more complex than *Speech Songs*, displaying greater variation of the original speech. Both works were composed at Columbia University.

Hoffman, Richard. *In Memoriam Patris.* CRI SD 393.   *In Memoriam Patris* (1976) was realized at the MIT Experimental Electronic Music Studio. Hoffman (b. 1925, Vienna) uses a very limited range (one-and-a-half octaves) and a few pitches (a hexachord and its combinatorial inversion) in a "quasi-random" fashion. Even though the work is aleatoric, its imposed limitations of material create a statistical consistency. The programmatic aspect of the title aligns death with the organ and bell timbres used in the work.

Slawson, Wayne. *Wishful Thinking About Winter.* Decca 710180. Slawson composed this work in 1967 at MIT. *Wishful Thinking About Winter* was realized using computer music programs designed by Slawson and discussed by him in "A Speech-Oriented Synthesizer of Computer Music," *Journal of Music Theory*, 13, no. 1 (1969), 94-127. The basis for the composition is a haiku by the 16th-century Japanese poet Basho. The piece consists of three short sections. The first (0'00"-1'00") presents the poem in Japanese in a highly stylized manner. The second section (1'00"-1'40") uses both Japanese and English speech sounds. The final section (1'40"-3'55") uses similar synthesized voice sounds with a prerecorded, humanly spoken English version of the poem.

Ussachevsky, Vladimir. *Computer Piece No. 1.* CRI SD 268.   Ussachevsky composed this piece in 1968 with the assistance of Risset and F.R. Moore. Computer generated sound realized at Bell Labs was manipulated and processed in the Columbia-Princeton Electronic Music Center. Thus, the computer serves only as a sound source for classical studio procedures.

15
LIVE/ELECTRONIC MUSIC

TYPES OF LIVE/ELECTRONIC MUSIC

The basic topics of the previous chapters in this book have been arranged around the means of production of electro-acoustic music and the techniques involved in these approaches. Live/electronic music, however, does not involve any particular method of production or any specific technical approach. It exists as an identifiable, if very inclusive, category because it combines, in any way possible, aspects of live, real-time performance with the electronic production and alteration of sound.

Live/electronic music is a very broad genre. It does not involve any basic techniques of electronic music not already discussed in this book. However, it does use the various aspects of real-time performance that are more a part of the traditional world of performance music than they are of electro-acoustic music. Indeed, as has been discussed in the chapter on electro-acoustic musical instruments, electronic music began with such instruments, and this area continues to be an important one; perhaps, by sheer numbers of participants, it is the most important area of electro-acoustic music. But the instrumental, real-time performance aspect of this music makes it, from most composers' points of view, little different from traditional instrumental performance music, and very different from studio-composed electro-acoustic music. This is at least partially true for all areas of live/electronic music.

These differences are shown in Figure 15-1, which visually represents the basic necessary steps involved in the various approaches to electro-acoustic music from the composer's perspective.[1] Live/electronic music involves either one of the real-time performance situations described, or a combination of one or both of these with any of the studio composition approaches.

There are two general classes of live/electronic music. One type uses prerecorded electronic signals in combination with real-time performance. The prerecorded material may be used as part of the music, as is usually the case, or as control signals for altering the live material. The first general category would include such combinations as music for performers and tape, and music for real-time performance altered by prerecorded control signals.

The other general type of live/electronic music uses real-time produc-tion and performance of electronic sounds, often simply called live elec-

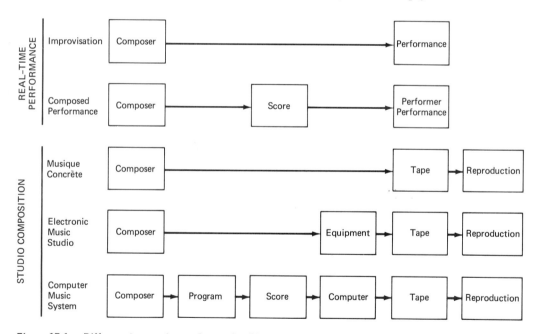

Figure 15-1 Different Approaches to Comparing Electro-Acoustic Music.

[1] Other steps could be added to each approach illustrated in Figure 15-1. A "score," for instance, could be included in the musique concrète or electronic music studio approaches, but they are not necessary; in fact, most concrète and electronic works do not have scores. Figure 15-1 compares only the most basic and necessary steps of these different approaches to composition.

tronics. Like prerecorded electronics, live electronics can be used either as part of the music or as control signals. In the former situation, the live electronics could be a solo or group performance of electronic instruments, or live electronics combined with acoustic instruments.

There are many possible combinations and extensions of the basic types of live/electronic music. So many, in fact, that an entire book could easily be written on this topic alone. Many aspects of live/electronic music center around performance practice, and much of the literature is popular and transitory in nature. For all of these reasons, the subject of live/electronic music is given only a cursory discussion in this book.

MUSIC FOR TAPE AND PERFORMERS

The use of prerecorded electronic material is more closely related to studio composition than is the use of live electronics. This is because the prerecorded electronic material can be put together in a studio using any desired studio approach. This type of live/electronic music is a combination of the composed performance and any of the studio approaches shown in Figure 15-1. Since this genre of live/electronic music involves a combination of approaches, the greatest problem facing the composer in this situation is that of how to combine the prerecorded and live elements.

Imaginary Landscape No. 1 *by John Cage*

The earliest work dealing with these problems was the *Imaginary Landscape No. 1*, by John Cage. Composed in 1939, *Imaginary Landscape No. 1* combines a piano and chinese cymbal with two variable speed phonograph turntables. Turntable one uses Victor Frequency Record 84522B and Victor Constant Note Record No. 24; turntable two uses Victor Frequency Record 84522A. These records contain sine tones at different pitches. Both turntables have performers who change the speed of the turntable, thus changing the pitch as indicated in the score. This score also includes the parts for piano and cymbal. *Imaginary Landscape No. 1* was written for radio broadcast, and thus used a fifth "performer" who determined the dynamics in the broadcast studio control room.

Cage did not generate the electronic sounds used in *Imaginary Landscape No. 1*, but he did compose the manner in which they would be used. He had two performers change the speed of the turntables, thereby making the turntables and their associated records into instruments. The problem of combining live and prerecorded material was easily solved by using the prerecorded material as if it were being produced in real-time; in more recent times, an electronic oscillator could serve the same purpose as the variable speed phonograph and sine wave record combinations. This approach to combining live and prerecorded sound remains unusual.

Déserts *by Edgard Varése*

One of the earliest works for instrumental performers and tape is Edgard Varése's *Déserts* (1949-1954; tape revised by Bulent Arel in 1961). *Déserts* is written for a wind and percussion orchestra (flute, piccolo, clarinet, horn, trumpet, trombone, tuba, piano, percussion) and two monophonic tapes each played through a separate speaker on either side of the performers. Varése began *Déserts* in 1949, dealing primarily with the instrumental parts. The tape parts were not completed until 1954 and were largely composed in the Paris studio.

Varése's method of solving the problem of coordinating live and recorded materials was to simply avoid it. Thus, *Déserts* alternates between the five sections of live orchestra and the three sections of prerecorded tape. Varése did try to achieve some integration by using sections of the instrumental music on the tapes. The effect of the work, however, is an isolation of the instrumental music from the tape music. The tapes contain predominantly concrète, but some electronic sounds. The construction of both the tape and instrumental music is sectional, and, like *Poème Électronique*, reveals Varése's notion of "organized sound." As in most of Varése's music, an interest in rhythm and timbre is foremost.

Musica su Due Dimensioni *by Bruno Maderna*

Probably the first completed work for live performer and tape was Bruno Moderna's *Musica su Due Dimensioni* (1952) for flute and tape.[2] Maderna uses the flute and tape simultaneously. The flute begins the work and then, directed by a cue from a written score, an operator starts the tape recorder at a certain point. The operator starts and stops the machine at designated points throughout the piece. This solves the problem of combining live and prerecorded material by having an operator control the tape at given intervals.

Musica su Due Dimensioni solves the problems of coordination of tape and performer in several ways. First, there is only one performer, avoiding a compounding of the problem of coordination created by using several performers. Second, the relationship between the flute and tape is somewhat relative; the flutist must follow the tape to a degree, but the coordination is not precise. Third, the flute does have solo passages, so the performer is not always locked into the curious position of being a soloist who must follow the accompaniment.

The tape for *Musica su Due Dimensioni* consists of concrète and electronic sounds, and the sound material is rather elaborately processed for that time. The tape music creates a diversified but consistently effective background for the solo flute.

[2] Unfortunately, there is no commercial recording of this work. The description here refers to the 1958 revision of the piece.

Capriccio *by Henk Badings*

One of the first live/electronic works for tape and instrument that uses a continuously playing tape is *Capriccio for Violin and Two Sound Tracks* by Henk Badings. Composed in 1952, *Capriccio* is quite a remarkable work for that time. It is perhaps the first such piece that requires no activity of the tape recorder operator, save the initial start and the final stop. *Capriccio* is really a miniature violin concerto with an introduction (0'00"-0'32"), first (0'32"-2'49"), second (2'49"-5'16"), and third (5'16"-7'25") movements. The introduction is for solo tape and serves the function not only of setting the mood of the piece, but also of delineating the tempo for the violinist. Throughout the work, Badings has provided clear visual and aural cues for the performer so that even though the violinist must follow the tape part, coordination is easily accomplished. Since the music is essentially tonal (there are some unusual temperaments) and the rhythm is basically metric, Badings was able to notate most of the tape part as a piano score. This allows for easy reference by the performer as well as practical rehearsal away from the tape.

Badings composed the *Capriccio* in the Philips studio, and undoutedly made use of the electronic keyboard instruments in realizing the tape part. However, certain tape manipulation techniques, especially cutting and splicing, and speed change, are also apparent.

The early live/electronic works for tape and performers so far discussed display the four possibilities of combining live and recorded materials: (1) The recorded sound may be constantly controlled by a "performer" of the playback equipment (Cage's *Imaginary Landscape No. 1*); (2) the recorded sound may be alternated with the live performers, avoiding simultaneity (Varése's *Déserts*); (3) the recorded sound may be started and stopped by an operator of the playback equipment at specified points (Maderna's *Musica su Due Dimensioni*); (4) the recorded sound may exist continuously from the beginning to the end of a work (Badings's *Capriccio*). The third and fourth methods of combining have proven to be the most popular with composers working in this area of live/electronic music. The reasons for this stem from the fact that most composers writing pieces for live and recorded sound combinations are primarily concerned with studio composition. Since the first method *(Imaginary Landscape No. 1)* involves a kind of live performance of the recorded material, the intent is strangely antithetical to the medium. The second method of combination *(Déserts)* offers little interest, since it avoids all possibilities of simultaneous combinations.

Synchronisms *by Mario Davidovsky*

Many works for tape and performers do not include complete notations of the prerecorded electronic music. In this case, only limited notations are used along with timings to allow the performers to coordinate. Under such circumstances, the performers must memorize the electronic music and use a timing device, such as a stopwatch. This is the case in the *Synchronisms* of Mario Davidovsky.

The *Synchronisms* are a series of works for various instruments and prerecorded electronic sounds. The early *Synchronisms, No. 1 for Flute* (1963), *No. 2 for Flute, Clarinet, Violin and Cello* (1964), and *No. 3 for Cello* (1964-65), require the operator of the tape deck to start and stop the machine at certain points as specified in the score. In these works, the instruments begin the piece, and are later joined by the recorded sound. Thus, the initial synchronization of each combined appearance is the responsibility of the tape operator. As an aid to the performers, Davidovksy includes occasional representational notations of the electronic music in the score. The result of these practices is a blend of precise and relative coordination. The remarkable unified quality of the music is the result of the dominance of Davidovsky's style in both the instrumental and electronic parts. Davidovsky's personal percussionistic pointillism is evident in both the live and prerecorded music so that both mediums express the same kinds of musical thought.

Davidovsky's later *Synchronisms, No. 5 for Percussion Ensemble* (1969), and *No. 6 for Piano* (1970), are even more successful in combining live and prerecorded sounds. This is chiefly because the sounds of percussion instruments, including piano, more closely resemble the basic electronic timbres favored by Davidovsky. Unlike the earlier *Synchronisms*, the tape is allowed to run continuously after its initiation. However, the instruments still begin these works. The result of the continuous tape is a less sectionalized music.

Kontakte *by Karlheinz Stockhausen*

One of the most extensive essays in the genre of music for tape and instruments is Stockhausen's *Kontakte (Contact)* (1960) for piano, percussion, and electronic sounds.[3] A rather long work (ca. 45′), *Kontakte* is remarkable for the virtuosity of its instrumental writing as well as its electronic music. The work exists as a series of sections, or "moments" as Stockhausen calls them, that are individually characteristic, primarily due to their timbres, pitch configurations, tempi, and density of events. These musical elements form kinds of Gestalts that are unique to each section of the work. The music is not, however, linearly kinetic, progressing from beginning to middle to end. Rather, the sound exists as a "permanent present" moving from one section to another without transition.

The score for *Kontakte* is quite complete. The piano and percussion parts are written in conventional twentieth-century notation, but the electronic music is notated graphically. Stockhausen has represented, simultane-

---

[3] Stockhausen has also released just the tape part of *Kontakte* as a separate version of the work.

ously, the most aurally obvious elements of the sound (pitch changes, direction, tempo, dynamics) with the nature of the timbre. The graphic notation of *Kontakte* visually represents the music in the same Gestalt manner in which one perceives the sound. When one looks at the score and simultaneously hears the associated music, a visual-aural correspondence is intuitively comprehended. In addition, Stockhausen provides extremely precise timings that allow for very exact coordination.

Although *Kontakte* is effective as a recorded or aural experience, it is even more interesting as a live/electronic performance situation. This is due to the great virtuosity required of the performers, which, combined with the large array of percussion instruments, introduces an element of theater. There are some live/electronic works for tape and performers that rely more heavily on the theatricality of the event. Such a work is *Animus II* by Jacob Druckman (b. 1928, Philadelphia).

Animus II *by Jacob Druckman*

Animus II (1967-68) is written for soprano, two percussionists, and a tape that uses both concrète (vocal) and electronic sounds. As a purely aural experience, *Animus II* lacks some of the most important qualities of a live performance. This is unfortunate, since these performance elements are some of the most important aspects of the work. The visual quality of the work conveys a sensuality and variation of ritual that are not apparent in an audio recording. Also, the tape part of *Animus II*, which plays a secondary, usually background role in the live performance, becomes disproportionately more important in the recorded version. This is because the delineation of elements accomplished by association of sight and sound is lacking in the sound alone.

The Wolfman *by Robert Ashley*

The loss of the visual aspect is even more important in the case of *The Wolfman* (1967) by Robert Ashley (b. 1930, Ann Arbor, Michigan). *The Wolfman* is written for voice and tape, and presents a parody of night-club singers in a rather striking manner. The vocalist improvisationally performs variations of nonverbal sounds into a microphone. The singer must place the microphone quite close to the mouth and the amplification of the singer must be very loud, often loud enough to produce feedback. The tape is a mixture of concrète and electronic sounds, and must be reproduced on separate speakers at high volumes.[4]

In a live performance situation, *The Wolfman* can be quite devastating, combining parody, social comment, and, on occasion, physical pain. Recordings of performances, however, do not adequately portray the theatri-

[4] There are two possible tapes for *The Wolfman: The Wolfman* (6′) and *The 4th of July* (18′). Both are provided by Ashley. See Robert Ashley, "The Wolfman," in *Source, music of the avant garde*, no. 4, pp. 5-6.

cality and implied meanings of the work. For works like *Animus II* and *The Wolfman*, recorded versions are incomplete representations of the composers intentions.

Collages *by Roberto Gerhard*

Most live/electronic works for tape and instruments are for soloists or small ensembles of performers. This is because the difficulty of combination and coordination increases with the number of performers; it is also because the economics of late twentieth-century art music make large ensembles rarely feasible. For these reasons, few works for orchestra and tape have been composed. One of the most successful of this small group of works is *Collages* (1960) by Roberto Gerhard (b. 1896, Valls, Catalonia, Spain; d. 1970, Cambridge, England). Timbre and rhythm are the most important elements of *Collages;* pitch is relegated to a secondary position. Gerhard presents the instrumental sounds as timbral components, both singly and in various combinations. This he does by having instruments sound one or two note statements, often of long duration, or else by presenting short, often repetitious, easily perceived pitch combinations. The electronic sounds on tape are generally amorphous and are distinguished by broad characteristics; in certain respects, they are not unlike the "Gestalt sounds" used by Stockhausen in *Kontakte*, although they are by no means as technically complex. The tape in *Collages* appears intermittently, requiring an operator to start and stop it several times.[5]

Times Five *by Earle Brown*

Another type of live/electronic music for live performers and pre-recorded sound has performers prepare the recorded material. In this case, a prescribed recording is made by the performers, usually before the public performance, or else a tape is supplied by the composer along with the score. This type of live/electronic music allows the performers to play simultaneously with recordings of themselves or other performers.

One example of this genre is *Times Five* (1963) by Earle Brown (b. 1926, Lunenberg, Massachusetts). The title of the work refers to the fact that there are five live instruments: flute, trombone, harp, violin, and cello; five basic sound sources: four loud speakers and the instrumental group; and that the piece is written in five sections. The tape for *Times Five* consists entirely of concrète, instrumental sounds. Much of the original material for the tape was derived from a recording of an eleven-piece orchestra playing material specified by Brown. In sections one and three, the tape part consists largely of sounds made by Brown himself playing such instruments as piano. celesta, harp, bass, vibraphone, and marimba. The final version of the tape

---

[5] Gerhard had a program for *Collages*, most of which escapes your author. The program can be found in the liner notes of Angel S-36558.

contain both manipulated (spliced, transposed, superimposed), as well as unmanipulated, sound.

The instrumental material in *Times Five* is an example of a compositional approach that Brown calls "open form." This means that individual instrumental events are noted in a flexible context, not specifically formed. In order to achieve this end, Brown has devised notations that are either modifications of traditional practice or graphic representations of the more "noise-like" sounds. The notational systems, and Brown's accompanying directions to the score, allow the conductor a limited freedom to explore the instrumental environment Brown has created in relation to the fixed tape. Thus, while remaining sufficiently characteristic, each performance of an open form work is unique, and the conductor also shares in the creative aspect of making compositional choices.

While the open form concept characterizes much of Brown's work since the early 1950s, *Time Five* is the first of many works to explore combinations of open and what in this context must be called "closed" forms. The tape in *Times Five*, although partially the result of improvisation, remains absolutely fixed and unchanging in its final, composed form. As such, it is, philosophically, diametrically contrasting to the live performance. The tape forms, according to Brown, an "unchanging ground" with which the live performers interact.

Violin Phase *by Steve Reich*

Another example of this genre, composed in a spirit different from Brown's, is Steve Reich's *Violin Phase* (1967). *Violin Phase* sounds deceptively simple; in fact, it is a difficult work requiring a virtuosic performance. *Violin Phase*, for violin and tape, requires the performer to play against recordings of the same material that were made prior to the performance. These recordings use three channels of a four-channel tape. As with Reich's other music, *Violin Phase* is phase music made up of phasing loops. In this case, the loop is a three-measure motive in 4/4 meter; the total loop has ten notes performed in twelve beats. The violinist first records the figure on channel 3 of the tape recorder. Then the same figure is recorded on channel 2, only this time it is four beats behind channel 3, or 120 degrees out of phase. The figure is then recorded on channel 1, eight beats, or 240 degrees, behind channel 3. This tape, with three recorded channels, is then made into a loop equal in length to one performance of the original figure, a total of twelve beats.

In a performance of *Violin Phase*, the violinist plays against previously made recordings.[6] Channel 1 of the tape loop begins the piece. Then, after 30″, the violinist joins in, playing exactly in phase with the tape. Very gradually, the performer is to go out of phase with the recording until the

---

[6] The timings given here correspond to the recording by Paul Zukofsky on Columbia MS 7265.

performer is four beats out of phase with channel 1. At this point, 4′55″, the performer makes a decrescendo, and channel 2 of the loop fades in; the performer and channel 2 are now in phase with each other. Both channels 1 and 2 of the tape loop play simultaneously for a while, and the violinist improvises on figures arriving from the combination of these two channels. At 9′00″, the performer begins playing the original figure, this time in phase with channel 2. Again, there is a gradual shift of phase with the tape loop on channel 2 until the performer is four beats out of phase with channel 2; the violinist is then in phase with channel 3. At this point, 14′35″, the performer again decrescendos as channel 3 fades in. Combination figures are again performed until 22′55″, when the violinist ceases to play. From this point to the end of the work, only the combined tape loops are heard.

The coordination problems of the gradual phasing in *Violin Phase* require that the violinist do a great deal of practicing. Even in less demanding works for tape and performers, a great amount of rehearsal time is necessary in order for the performers to memorize the tape and coordinate cues. Some composers have tried to ease this situation by providing prerecorded aids or instructions to the performers. In this situation, one of the channels of the prerecorded tape is routed to the performer(s) through headsets. This "co-ordination track" is not heard by the audience. An early example of this type of composition is *Desert Ambulance* (1964) by Ramon Sender for amplified accordion, tape, and projections. The coordination track of the tape contains reference pitches, timing cues, and spoken instructions for the performer.[7] Another procedure is to provide for the performer a metro-nome tape, or *click track*, to ensure proper tempo and synchronization with the prerecorded tape.

USES OF CONTROL TRACKS
IN LIVE/ELECTRONIC MUSIC

Live/electronic music for performers and audible prerecorded sounds has enjoyed great popularity with many composers. As a result, there is a large group of works composed in this genre. This is not the case with live/elec-tronic music for performers and prerecorded control signals. In this type of live/electronic music, the prerecorded signals are not meant to be heard by either the audience or the performers, but rather the signals are used to pro-cess, in real-time, the sounds produced by the live performers.

Recorded control signals, also called *control tracks*, are not recent innovations; they were used in the reproduction of Varèse's *Poème Élec-tronique*, and in the studio composition of Koenig's *Funktion* series, as well as in other pieces written before 1970. The use of control tracks in live/electronic music, however, is something of a rarity. Undoubtedly, one of the

[7] *Desert Ambulance* was originally composed for Pauline Oliveros.

reasons for its rarity is the difficulty of coordinating a live performer with an inflexible control that is inaudible.

Morton Subotnick is almost the only composer to have dealt with this area of live/electronic music. In his composition *After the Butterfly* (1979), for trumpet, clarinets, trombone, cello, percussion, and *ghost tape*, the ghost tape is a control track containing signals used to process the real-time instrumental sounds. For example, in the case of amplitude modulation the instrumental sound would serve as the carrier, and the control signal would be the modulator.

Subotnick has facilitated coordination in *After the Butterfly* by providing exact timings in the score and by using a conductor. Subotnick has also created musical cues by having periods of unprocessed sound. For instance, when, on a long-held note, the sound of the trumpet changes from a modulated timbre to a normal timbre, an aural or musical cue is apparent to all of the performers. This type of live/electronic music provides an area for future investigation. It will undoubtedly become more popular given the increased application of digital technology, especially real-time concrete computer music facilities.

REAL-TIME LIVE/ELECTRONIC MUSIC

The second general type of live/electronic music, involving applications of live or real-time electronic sound production and modification, is a vast area of contemporary musical practice ranging from solo electric guitar to real-time computer music performance. Much of this area has been discussed in previous chapters: electro-acoustic instruments in Chapter 9; classical studio real-time realization in Chapter 12; real-time performance with synthesizers, both analog and digital, in Chapter 13; possible real-time applications of computer music systems in Chapter 14.

To a great extent, real-time live/electronic music is a performance medium, often joining the separate worlds of art music and popular music, particularly certain kinds of jazz. Since the middle 1950s, several live/electronic performance groups have appeared and disappeared (and in some cases reappeared). The ONCE Group, The Sonic Arts Union, Mother Mallard's Portable Masterpiece Co., Gruppo di Improvisationen Nuovo Consonanza, FLUXUS, Music Elettronica Viva, AMM, The Gentle Fire, Naked Software, PULSAR, Teletopa, AMRA ARMA, and The Negative Band are but some of the live/electronic performance groups that come and go. While some of these groups perform composed works, usually written by members of the group, many bands play improvised music primarily.[8]

---

[8] For further information on live/electronic performance groups, see Gordon Mumma, "Live-Electronic Music," in *The Development and Practice of Electronic Music*, ed. Jon H. Appleton and Ronald C. Perera (Englewood Cliffs, NJ: Prentice-Hall, Inc., 1975), pp. 315-318, and David Ernst, *The Evolution of Electronic Music* (New York: Schirmer Books, 1977) pp. 176-187.

Cartridge Music by John Cage

Composed works for live/electronic performance are usually for some type of electronic instruments. However, this is not the case with Cage's *Cartridge Music* (1960). *Cartridge Music* is really not a composition in the traditional sense, rather it is a composed set of instructions for assembling a particular kind of performance. Cage provides the performers (from two to twenty people) with printed materials for generating a performance score by chance procedures. Cage thus broadly determines the process by which events happen, but not the specific results. In this way, the composition is indeterminate of performance. Cage did, however, additionally prescribe the type of sounds to be used in *Cartridge Music:* phonograph cartridges, with various objects inserted where the styli fit, and contact microphones are all scraped, rubbed, hit, and so on against various objects or used to amplify unusual sounds. This results in an ensemble of primarily noise sounds that are played by the performers according to their scores. The result is a rather cacophonous mix of sounds. Like Ashley's *The Wolfman*, *Cartridge Music* is very performance-oriented, and is most effectively experienced in a performance situation.

Reconnaissance by Donald Erb

Combining live performers of both acoustic and electronic instruments solves some of the coordination problems of real-time and recorded performance combinations. In this case, the group need only concern itself with usual performance considerations. An example of this type of work is *Reconnaissance* (1967) by Donald Erb (b. 1927, Youngstown, Ohio). *Reconnaissance* is for six performers, playing violin, bass, piano, percussion, Moog synthesizer, and Moog polyphonic instrument. Erb's intention is that the Moog inventions should appear simply as instruments in combination with other instruments. As a result, *Reconnaissance* is primarily an instrumental composition.

Echoes by Joel Chadabe

Electronic devices are often used to process and modify acoustic and electronic sounds in real-time. Such things as reverberators and filters are commonly associated with instruments and amplification systems. A more interesting use of this concept is presented in *Echoes* by Joel Chadabe (b. 1938, New York City). *Echoes* is for a solo performer (a percussionist, in the commercially recorded version on Folkways Records) and a digital control voltage generator called *Daisy*.[9] In a performance of *Echoes*, Daisy generates the information that locates the sound by distributing it among

---

[9] For more information on *Daisy*, see Joel Chadabe, "The Voltage-Controlled Synthesizer," in *The Development and Practice of Electronic Music*, ed. Jon H. Appleton and Ronald C. Perera (Englewood Cliffs, NJ: Prentice-Hall, Inc., 1975) pp. 174-176.

the loudspeakers ringing the performance space. Daisy also can determine changes in pitch and timbre as well as create slightly delayed playback, or echoes. The particular technology of Daisy allows for interaction between the performer and the processing system. The reason for this is that the output of Daisy is constantly changing, according to Chadabe's design, and the performer must react to the changes. For this reason, each performance of *Echoes* is unique.

A more usual approach to the real-time control and processing of acoustic and electronic sounds can be found in several works of Stockhausen, most notably *Mikrophonie I* (1964), *Mixtur* (1964), and *Mikrophonie II* (1965). In these works, instruments are processed and modified in real-time by having an operator, in these works it is usually Stockhausen, control devices such as filters, ring modulators, and amplifiers, thus modifying the sound. This approach is different from that taken in *Echoes* because it lacks the spontaneous interactions between performer and processor. The operator of the processing equipment is another performer, analogous to an engineer in a recording studio. This approach is conceptually similar to, although technically quite different from, Subotnick's ghost tapes.

Cybersonic Cantilevers *by Gordon Mumma*

There are some works of live/electronic music that resist easy classification. They combine elements in such ways and produce results of such natures that they must be individually considered. This applies to *Cybersonic Cantilevers* (1975), by Gordon Mumma (b. 1935, Framingham, Massachusetts). *Cybersonic Cantilevers* involves the use of both live and recorded sounds. There are no performers as such; there are participants. The participants are members of the audience who are invited to bring any sound, live or recorded, to a control station. There are several control stations, each having a microphone, oscilloscope, and stereophonic headphones. The control stations are connected to a central processing system. (The physical displacement of the control stations in *Cybersonic Cantilevers*, as well as the location of the processing system, depends on the particular space of a given performance; a large area is normally required.) The processing system for *Cybersonic Cantilevers* consists of electronics designed by Mumma for the purpose of transforming the input of the participants. The transformed material is simultaneously recorded and sent back to the participants through the headphones as well as broadcast over loudspeakers at various points. The recorded transformations could be recycled as primary sounds at a later time.

Cybersonic Cantilevers is neither a composition nor a performance in the traditional senses of those terms; *Cybersonic Cantilevers* is a process, made possible by electronics, for the transforming of sounds, and the interaction of the people that make the sounds both with each other and with the processing system.[10]

Several composers who are interested in live/electronic music have also dealt with combinations of other media and art forms with sound. The other media are usually film or aspects of theater, but they may be literally anything from hot air balloons to lasers. Imagination is limitless. Such works have been variously referred to as *multimedia, intermedia,* and *light-sound composition.* The audio portions of some of these works have been recorded, such as *HPSCHD* (1967-69), by Cage and Hiller, or *L's G.A.* (1968), by Salvatore Martirano (b. 1927, Yonkers, New York). Such recordings, however, can only convey a portion of these works.

The notion of combining different arts is, of course, rather ancient. What made the so-called multimedia works recognizably different was their combined use of electronic technologies. In this sense, these works can be seen to be offspring of the Technology-As-Art movement of the 1960s. In any event, these works concern themselves with elements that lie outside the range of this book.[11]

DISCOGRAPHY

Ashley, Robert. *The Wolfman.* Record included in *Source, music of the avant garde,* no. 4.

Badings, Henk. *Capriccio for Violin and Two Sound Tracks.* Epic BC 1118; Limelight 86055.

Brown, Earle. *Times Five.* BAM LD 072; CRI SD-330.

Cage, John. *Cartridge Music.* Mainstream 5015; DGG 137 009.

——. *Imaginary Landscape No. 1.* Avakian 1.

Cage, John and Lejaren Hiller. *HPSCHD.* Nonesuch H-71224.

Chadabe, Joel. *Echoes.* Folkways FTS 33904.

Davidovsky, Mario. *Synchronism No. 1.* CRI SD-204; Nonesuch 71289.

——. *Synchronism No. 2.* CRI SD-204.

——. *Synchronism No. 3.* CRI SD-204.

——. *Synchronism No. 5.* CRI SD-268.

[10] For a much more complete discussion of *Cybersonic Cantilevers,* as well as the work and ideas of Gordon Mumma, see the interview with Gordon Mumma in Part III.

[11] For more information on "multimedia," see David Cope, *New Directions in Music* (Dubuque: William C. Brown Co., Publishers, 1971), pp. 55-68, and Gordon Mumma, "Live-Electronic Music," in *The Development and Practice of Electronic Music,* ed. Jon H. Appleton and Ronald C. Perera (Englewood Cliffs, NJ: Prentice-Hall, Inc., 1975), pp. 326-335.

———. *Synchronism No. 6*. Turnabout 34487.

Druckman, Jacob. *Animus II*. CRI SD-255.

Erb, Donald. *Reconnaissance*. Nonesuch H-71223.

Gerhard, Roberto. *Collages*. Angel S-36558.

Martirano, Salvatore. *L's G.A.* Polydor 245001.

Mumma, Gordon. *Cybersonic Cantilevers*. Folkways FTS 33904.

Reich, Steve. *Violin Phase*. Columbia MS-7265.

Stockhausen, Karlheinz. *Kontakte*. Candide 31022; Vox 678011; Wergo 60009; (tape alone DGG 138811).

———. *Mikrophonie I*. Columbia MS-7355; CBS 32-11-044.

———. *Mikrophonie II*. Columbia MS-7355; CBS 32-11-044.

———. *Mixtur*. DGG 137 012.

Subotnick, Morton. *After the Butterfly*. Nonesuch N-78001.

Varèse, Edgard. *Déserts*. Columbia MS-6362; Angel S-36786; CRI SD-268.

FOR FURTHER LISTENING

Ashforth, Alden. *Sailing to Byzantium*. Orion ORS 74164.   Composed in 1973, this work is for tape and electronic organ. Ashforth uses a wide variety of concrète and electronic sounds to dramatically interpret Yeats's poem.

Brown, Earle. *Four Systems—for Four Amplified Cymbals*. Columbia MS 7139.   The score for *Four* Systems is one of Brown's graphic scores. The four cymbals are amplified and the volume is controlled by the performer. Timbral modification occurs from mixing and feedback.

Druckman, Jacob. *synapse→ VALENTINE*. Nonesuch H-71253.   This work, composed in 1970, is in two parts. The first part *(synapse→)* is for solo electronic tape and was composed at the Columbia-Princeton Electronic Music Center using Buchla 100-series equipment. The second part *(VALENTINE)* is for solo contrabass. This is a rather unusual arrangement, since it completely separates the electronic and instrumental elements as Varèse did in *Deserts*.

Hampton, Calvin. *Catch-up*. Odyssey 32 16 0162.   This work by Hampton (b. 1938) is for two pianos and prerecorded tape. The music consists of two sets of piano material, one live, one prerecorded. Both sets of material use four five-measure phrases referred to as A, B, C, and D. The live material also uses a fifth five-measure phrase, E, that does not appear in the prerecorded version. Both live and prerecorded sets of material are organized into repeating groups. It requires twenty sections to be performed before both the live (five-section) and prerecorded (four-section) material catch up with each other. The pianos used here are tuned in quarter-tones.

Ichyanagi, Toshi. *Extended Voices.* Odyssey 32 16 0156.   Ichyanagi wrote *Extended Voices* for live vocalists, slide whistles, electronic processing equipment (available on Buchla and Moog synthesizers), and prerecorded electronic tape. The work investigates different possibilities of transformations of voice and voice-related sounds.

Lucier, Alvin. *North American Time Capsule.* Odyssey 32 16 0155.   Composed in 1967, this work uses live voices processed in real-time by the Sylvania Electronic Systems Vocoder. The Vocoder is used to transform the improvised vocal material.

Luening, Otto and Vladimir Ussachevsky. *Concerted Piece for Tape Recorder and Orchestra.*   This is a two-part work written in 1960. The first part is by Luening and is characterized by a great deal of separation (by alternation) of the concrète tape and the live orchestra. The second part, by Ussachevsky, uses electronic sounds as well as concrète material and creates more interplay between live and prerecorded material.

Marshall, Ingram. *The Fragility Cycles.* IBU-101. (Available from IBU Records, 504 Cole St., San Francisco, CA 94117.)   *The Fragility Cycles* is a series of works that deals primarily with what Marshall calls "continuous improvisation." The first section, *Crises Upon the Mountains* ($0'00''$-$7'00''$), is a combination of prerecorded concrète material and live vocal sounds processed in real-time.

The remainder of side one of *The Fragility Cycles* consists of different versions of *Gambuh*, a continuing series of works for the Balinese bamboo flute called a *gambuh* and live electronics. (Marshall has collectively titled this music *Gambuh I.*) In these works Marshall plays the gambuh and simultaneously uses live electronics to both support and process the instrumental solo. In addition, tape recorders are used to provide tape delay effects.

In composing *The Fragility Cycles*, Marshall deals with two principal concerns: the interaction between acoustic and electronic sound sources and the blending of taped and live sound material.

Moss, Lawrence. *Auditions.* CRI SD-318.   Moss (b. 1927, Los Angeles) composed *Auditions* in 1973 for wind quintet and prerecorded tape. The music cleverly mixes abstract phrases with familiar quotations. The tape uses concrète and electronic sounds to effectively enlarge the ensemble.

Randall, J.K. *Lyric Variations for Violin and Computer.* Composed in 1968, *Lyric Variations* uses a computer-generated metronome track to coordinate the violin and tape.

Subotnick, Morton. *Laminations* Turnabout TV S 34428.   This is a large work for tape and orchestra, written between 1966 and 1969. The tape part for *Laminations* is identical to Part I of *Silver Apples of the Moon*. The tape plays continuously in this work, and coordination with the large orchestra is achieved by using exact timings for the conductor and careful, but fairly conventional, notation in the written score.

LIVE/ELECTRONIC PERFORMANCE ENSEMBLES

AMM.   *AMM Music*. Elektra (England) EUKS 7256.

——.   *Live Electronic Music Improvised*. Mainstream MS 5002.

Gruppo de Improvisazione Nuova Consionanza.   RCA Italiana MILDS 20273; DGG 643541.

Musica Elettronica Viva.   *Live Electronic Music Improvised*. Mainstream MS 5002.

——.   *The Sound Pool*. BYG 529 326. (Promodisc, 20 Rue Louis-Philippe, 92 Neuilly-sur-Seine, France).

Nuova Consonanza.   *Improvisationen (1969)*. DGG 137007.

——.   *Improvisationen*. RCA Italiana MILDS 20243.

Sonic Arts Union.   *Music for the Venezia Space Theater* by Gordon Mumma. Advance FGR-5.

VORTEX.   Folkways FX 6301.

PART III

The Art of Electro-Acoustic Music: Interviews with Composers

16

INTERVIEW WITH LUCIANO BERIO

Thema: Omaggio a Joyce

Schrader: Why did you select this particular Joyce text for *Thema*?

Berio: In the years 1957 and 1958, I was studying onomatopoeia in poetry with Umberto Eco. Among the texts that we were studying were several by Joyce. The beginning of the eleventh chapter of *Ulysses* is, in a way, an homage to onomatopoeia, and can be regarded as poetry. The entire chapter, *Sirens*, is actually an homage to music and, more specifically, to the idea of a *Fuga per canonem*. In fact, the beginning is a concentrated, emblematic exposition of the themes [that] will be developed in the chapter. In this exposition, Joyce transforms language into musical events not only by making reference to specific procedures of musical performance, such as glissandi and trills, but also by dealing with a fact fundamental to poetry and music: Any change on the level of expression is a change on the level of meaning. I was fascinated by the very intense and rich network of meanings in that chapter and by the relation between that exposition and its full development. I was also taken by the overall musical nature of the structure. There is a kind of musical process

Luciano Berio. (Photo by Philippe Gras)

that goes from the relatively simple exposition of words to noise, that is to the moment where everything is saturated by sibilant sounds in a kind of cadenza on the white noise quality of the "s" sound.

Schrader: How did you go about interpreting the text for compositional purposes?

Berio: I made a selection of elements, preserving the important themes that will have a relevant development in this chapter of *Ulysses*. I created a hierarchy of importance among these elements, dictated by their acoustical and articulatory nature. I decided what things in the text could be discarded and what things were relevant and important. This procedure, of course, is nothing new; it is common to much older music. Composing with a text is always a problem of how to construct a musical form with words without destroying the text. What I emphasized and developed in *Thema* is the transition between a perceivable verbal message and music. And so, in the choice of words for a particular section of the piece, there was a close relationship between the meaning and the sound of the words. In *Thema*, I transposed to a different, and perhaps higher, level, that which already exists in the text. I didn't "set to music"—what a disgraceful expression!—a text by Joyce; rather I extracted music from it and developed it in a way congenial to the text itself.

Schrader: Why did you choose to do this work as a tape piece rather than as an acoustic work?

Berio: Because of the types of transformations I wanted to achieve. But, of course, I could think of these transformations only because there was an electronic music studio. At that time, techniques and procedures were quite time consuming. Everything was done by cutting and splicing tape, and there was a great deal of testing and trying out of ideas. The amount of transformation that I wanted was possible only through these means. In order to create certain effects, some sounds had to be copied sixty, seventy, and eighty times, and then spliced together. Then these tapes had to be copied further at different speeds in order to achieve new sound qualities more or less related to Cathy Berberian's original delivery of the text. I was interested in constant and controlled transformation from discontinuous to continuous patterns, from periodic to nonperiodic events, from sound to noise, from perceived words to perceived musical structures, and from a syllabic to a phonetic view of the text.

Schrader: How do you feel that the particular technology of the time influenced the style of *Thema*?

Berio: Certainly I was bound and conditioned by what I had. The general idea of the work, however, was very clear to me, and I didn't surrender to the difficulties. At times, it was really a close fight between what I wanted and what was possible. It's surprising now to think that I spent several months of my life cutting tape while today I could achieve many of the same results in much less time by using a computer. In this case, the overall approach to the possibilities of shifting from poetry to music would be different.

              Of course, that brings up a different problem. Usually, a work of music is not perfectly conceived; in composing a piece, there is always a shift. The musical idea forces the meaning of the work to take a different direction as it is being composed. There was always some conflict between the reality of technical possibility and the desired musical idea.

Schrader: What determined the overall structure of *Thema*? Was it the text, or was it the structure you imposed on the text?

Berio: Both, but mainly the text. In fact, the structure of *Thema* can also be seen as a blowup of Joyce's original text, like looking at some of its parts through the microscope. But the structure of *Thema* is also made up of the many acoustical transformations touching upon different meanings relative to the text, resulting in the transition from poetry to music

[and] back again to poetry. The purpose of the structure was to provide a framework for an aural journey [that] would allow one to rediscover the words in a completely different light. The words generate their own context. They are the subject and the object of a process of transformation both at an acoustical and semantic level.

Schrader: Does the piece have any extramusical significance because of the use of words? Is it a dramatic work?

Berio: I'm never concerned with specific extramusical significance, although I know very well that music does not exist in a limbo and that we cannot perceive music without being involved with intellectual emotions and without making associations with sentiment and feelings. But I'm certainly not planning the representation of these emotions and feelings with sounds. *Thema* is dramatic simply because any musical experience is, in a deep sense, dramatic: it deals with meanings, of whatever nature, in time.

Schrader: Why did you choose not to include any electronically reproduced sound material in *Thema*?

Berio: I wanted to reach a degree of transformation where the transition to electronically produced sound would have been almost natural. This was part of the discipline of the work. But, at the same time, I must confess that in *Thema* the use of electronic sounds could have given me problems of structure that I was not then equipped to cope with.

Schrader: It has been over twenty years since you composed *Thema*. How do you now view it with regard to your current work, and also with regard to its place in the literature?

Berio: It was a fundamental experience that contained the seeds of many other developments. In fact, dealing with Joyce, dealing with this specific work, I became more involved with the miraculous relationships between sound and meaning. My next tape work, *Visage*, composed in 1961, further explores these meanings by connecting certain aspects of speech stereotypes, gestures, and nonverbal material with electronic music.

Schrader: What is your current interest in electro-acoustic music?

Berio: Right now I am involved in using a new system, a digital sound processor developed at IRCAM by Peppino Di Giugno. This also involves the use of computers. I'm not interested in the computer as a musical instrument, but rather as a processor of sound. In the musical use of a computer, it is the input that counts.

Schrader: Do you have any thoughts on the future of electronic music?

Berio: I think that the electronic tape piece is dead. It is useful only for personal research purposes and it should be kept either at home or, if it is soft enough, in a restaurant. The relevance of electronic music was in creating a bridge between the familiar and the unfamiliar, the known and the unknown. Electronic music certainly opened a new and important experience in music. This experience is still a very important one, as long as it allows for coherent connections between the macro-structure and the microstructure. The new sound processors are the answer to the future of electronic music. Electronic music on tape sounds to me, at best, like a soundtrack; at worst, it is a garbage-sound-collector.

17

INTERVIEW WITH PAULINE OLIVEROS
I of IV

Schrader: How did you become interested in composing electronic music?

Oliveros: I have to attribute the first motivations to my mother: She gave me my first tape recorder. This was in 1954, shortly after tape recorders became readily available. I recorded everything I could. Then I began to change speeds and play things backwards. I didn't know about tape music at the time, but I was fascinated by the possibilities. Eventually I heard some of Pierre Schaeffer's music, and I began to seriously explore the tape medium.

Schrader: What kinds of tape music interested you?

Oliveros: In the beginning, I was interested in just about everything I heard because it was all new to me. That changed, of course, as I became more involved in making electronic music. Eventually I got so involved in composing that I was most interested in my own work.

Schrader: Did your early experience with electronic music affect your musical style?

Pauline Oliveros.

Oliveros: I think my experience with electronic music greatly affected my style. In the first place, I became more and more liberated from traditional notation because it wasn't possible to notate the sounds that interested me. I was not working with things like pitch or rhythm, but rather with the overall quality of sound. I also adapted to working with long expanses of time. Working with sound and time, without reference to any notation, opened up new territory for me.

Schrader: Your composition *I of IV* deals with these long time spans, yet it is a real-time composition. Why did you choose to do *I of IV* as a real-time work?

Oliveros: Ever since I began composing, the most important thing for me has been to be in contact with the sound. I always listened very carefully in my mind to what I was writing. Often, I worked things out at the piano. In my studio work, I wanted to bypass editing, if I could, and work in a way that was similar to a performance. In this way, I could be close to what I was doing.

Schrader: *I of IV* was composed at the University of Toronto Electronic Music Studio, which is a classical electronic music studio. Did this present any problems or difficulties in composing *I of IV?*

Oliveros: At the time, 1966, the University of Toronto Studio was a blessing. It was beautiful, well kept, and it had excellent equipment. That studio was a great advance over what I had been working with at the San Francisco Tape Music Center, which has been put together with World War II surplus equipment; Don Buchla's system had not yet been installed. So, rather than causing difficulties, the Toronto studio made things easier. I had already developed ways of working in real time with classical studios.

Schrader: One of the interesting features of *I of IV* is the use of combination tones. Why did you decide to use them in this piece?

Oliveros: That was part of my invention. It was a way to work and also a way to get a lot of material from relatively few sources.

My original interest in combination tones came from my experiences as an accordion player. Combination tones are fairly easy to produce on an accordion, and they always fascinated me. I used to think how interesting it would be if one could hear the combination tones without having to hear the original generating tones. I tried it, and, lo and behold, I couldn't hear anything! I wondered why, and decided that the combination tones were there, but they needed more amplification. So I stuck another amplifier on the line, and bingo—I got my combination tones. Suddenly I had a huge range of things that I could do with amplitude and frequency modulation.

Schrader: One of the most noticeable features of *I of IV* is the repetition caused by the use of tape delay. What is the function of this repetition?

Oliveros: The repetitions are obvious; they are not the most important thing. More important is the function of the delay system and all of the delays and repetitions that you don't hear as such. They were masked by the way I sustained tones in *I of IV*. The sustained sounds are most important because they allowed me to create changes in the quality of the material. I was able to get different kinds of reverberation as well as an accumulated layering effect. Some of the delays were very long and afforded me long decay times, such as in the long ostinato at the beginning of the work.

Schrader: What would you like listeners to hear in *I of IV?*

Oliveros: I think the piece is very sensual.

As I was making *I of IV*, I was also listening to it. I was riding with it as it came out and I was enjoying it.

At one point in the piece there's a rather climactic scream-like melody that sweeps through most of the audible range. When that thing started coming out, I didn't expect it; it was incredible and very delightful. I was laughing and was amazed at that particular moment, and I still enjoy that part of the piece. I would hope that other people might experience something like that when they listen to *I of IV*.

Schrader: Are you still interested in electronic music?

Oliveros: I'm as interested in electronic music as I am in any other music, especially if it's good music. For some reason, however, I'm not interested in going into a studio anymore. I'm not sure why. During the last ten years, I've been interested in meditation techniques and in working directly with people. I guess I prefer the contact of nice warm bodies to the cold isolation of a studio.

Schrader: Do you have any thoughts on the future of electro-acoustic music?

Oliveros: I think that people who are now growing up are used to electronics. They relate more naturally to electronic instruments and they will probably design future electronic instruments that are more suitable to human beings than today's instruments are. There still exists a gap that has to be bridged. A Synclavier, for instance, is all right as a keyboard device, but you can't relate to it as intimately as you can to a saxaphone or a guitar. I would like to see the development of better human engineering in electro-acoustic music instruments.

18
INTERVIEW WITH MORTON SUBOTNICK
Until Spring

Schrader: How did you become interested in composing tape music, particularly electronic music?

Subotnick: My interest in tape music came through the theater. In 1958, I was living in San Francisco and writing music for the Actor's Workshop. I composed a musique concrète score for a production of *King Lear.* I thought that musique concrète would be good for the theater because it could come out of the play rather than being incidental music.

After that, I became addicted. I began to see the possibilities of tape music. Producing music with a tape recorder is a kind of studio art. This is similar to the studio art of the painter. One can produce a finished work in a studio environment. When the work leaves the studio, it is the completed work. No reinterpretation is necessary. I also liked being able to work directly with the sound. If one writes for instruments, it's necessary to imagine the sound; whereas with tape composition, one deals directly with the

Morton Subotnick. (Photo by Carlo Carnevali)

sound material. There is a kind of physicality in working with tape music.

Scrader: What were the important characteristics of your early electronic music?

Subotnick: The early records, *Silver Apples of the Moon* and *The Wild Bull*, were kind of imagined chamber music in the sense that chamber music would be played in people's homes. These works were conceived for records, and I had an image of the record as being a future chamber music. These records were not recordings of pieces that could exist in another format.

Silver Apples of the Moon and *The Wild Bull* are kinds of tone poems. They are like mythic dreams. I imagined *Silver Apples of the Moon* as a giant voyage. *The Wild Bull* clearly deals with a mythic theme in the sense that it goes back to beast-man qualities in which the language that gets developed is a preverbal language.

Schrader: *The Wild Bull* and *Touch* appear to be the first electronic music works in which you deal with timbre as a thematic and structural element. What were your procedures in creating and developing timbres in these works?

Subotnick: *The Wild Bull* was not solely a timbral piece. I dealt with timbre in *The Wild Bull* as a language. In *Touch* timbre was more integral to the composition. *Silver Apples of the*

Moon and *The Wild Bull* are almost orchestral works; they could have been realized with instruments. After *The Wild Bull*, I decided to move away from this approach. I wanted to create music that would be more particularly electronic and also more record-oriented.

In *Touch*, I used two main timbres. One is electronic and percussive. The other is the spoken sound of the word "touch." The word "touch" and its individual phonemes "t," "ou," and "ch" exist in the piece and also serve as models for the envelopes of the percussive electronic sounds. These sounds are almost thematic in the work. But it's not just timbre that creates these effects, it's an entire series of shapes derived from the "touch" sounds. Then I added the qualities of "touchness" and "not-touchness" as they generated themselves through the act of composition. These qualities develop almost programmatically and create a sense of structure. These were the main concepts of the piece.

Schrader: Is this approach to timbre still in evidence in *Until Spring*?

Subotnick: In all of my electronic works from *The Wild Bull* on, I used one or two primary timbres. I would create a kind of "instrument" and then look for a contrasting sound, just as an older piece would have contrasting themes or motives. There would be several variations, but they were always clearly related to the primary timbres.

Timbrally, *Until Spring* is probably the purest of all my electronic works. It's almost like a sonata allegro form. There are two main timbres: the percussive timbre, which is primary, and the other, nonpercussive timbre, which is derived from the first.

Schrader: Besides timbre, what other elements are important in *Until Spring*?

Subotnick: The timbres in *Until Spring* aren't really important to me; they're only there. I don't think that music is about sound. I think that sound is the carrier of music and, similarly, timbre is the carrier of what's important in *Until Spring*.

That, by the way, is why I worked with film and other mediums. I believe that music is the way you move things in time and also the way to change aspects of time. Other mediums, such as film, can be a kind of music.

Timbre is not the primary element in *Until Spring*. I found a timbre that would allow me to move things in time the way that I wanted. The most important thing in *Until Spring* is the quality of stretching: a quality of energy being expended. The particular sounds, which are usually short, are used to allow the movement to be easily perceived.

Until Spring is a stereo piece, and I imagined that the space between the two speakers was a kind of "space canvas," and that I was literally stretching things and pulling things from place to place across this canvas. *Until Spring* is like kinetic sculpture in sound. I found the right timbre that would allow me to do that. The most important element in *Until Spring* is the kind of energy that's being expended. and it manifests itself in what is ordinarily called rhythm, or durational qualities in time as they move in space.

Schrader: *Until Spring* is the fourth work in your *Butterfly* series, works dealing with the butterfly as a metaphor for composition. What is the meaning of this metaphor and how does it specifically apply to *Until Spring*?

Subotnick: I believe that music, as well as other things, is the result of powerful metaphors. The particular music of any given time exists because it resonates with a particular metaphor. In the eighteenth century, the metaphor was the machine: weights and balances. The nineteenth century used evolution as its metaphor, and music became transformational and developmental. In the twentieth century, the metaphor has been relativity, and as a result, there have been twelve-tone technique, chance music, open form, and various kinds of mathematical approaches. All of these approaches go away from the directionality that would come from structural balance or evolution.

I was concerned that, for me, relativity as a metaphor didn't provide sufficient depth. Since, "relatively speaking," one metaphor is as good as another, I decided to search for my own. I hit upon the metaphor of the butterfly. The butterfly became a very powerful metaphor in every part of my life, and I have even traced the metaphor back into my earlier life.

At the time that I was working on *Until Spring*, I was also writing an orchestra piece called *Before the Butterfly*. Both works dealt with the point of emergence of the butterly from the cocoon, and I felt that I was at that point in my life. *Until Spring* was kind of an elixir of my electronic music. I finally knew what my music and my life were about. I was about to become a butterfly, and so *Until Spring* became that moment of emergence, that moment of awareness of what things were all about.

Schrader: You speak about "becoming" as an aspect of *Until Spring*. In Part II, if one regards the changes in timbre from section to section, and the relationships of important pitches from one section to the next, a kind of linear hierarchial process seems to take place. The timbre is developing into its final state, and the pitches predict certain harmonic movements or resolutions. Are these things what you refer to as the "becoming" quality of the music?

Subotnick: Yes. The progress along the way is the becoming part of it.

The fact that you picked up on the timbral and pitch development has to do with the fact that our ears are trained to hear those parameters as primary, at least in Western music. But, as I said before, what I'm really dealing with is the movement of energy.

There are three kinds of energy in *Until Spring*. One is no energy, static energy. That takes the form of long notes, heard at the beginning of the piece, which are very beautiful but have no tension. You don't feel that they're going anywhere or that they've come from anywhere. Then there is the "becoming" energy, which manifests itself in moving from slow to fast, soft to loud, low to high, and so forth. It's a kind of energy that is moving from one point to another, sometimes only by implication. And then there's a third energy, which is the energy of "being." This almost doesn't exist in the piece because the whole idea of the work is to exist on the verge of being. Occasionally this state of energy does exist, as at the end of the piece when the whole thing emerges into a giant major triad. Also, the rhythmic activity, which has been becoming and moving towards something, finally "becomes" at the end of the piece. It's pulsating in such a way that it could not be moving anywhere.

This energy of "being" is different from the static energy at the beginning of the piece because the whole piece has been moving towards it. There is a constant decrease in the tempo from the beginning to the end of *Until Spring* of about ten percent. This creates a gradual motion towards something. As the piece progresses, I add various harmonic and rhythmic accents. These accents begin to produce what the butterfly will be, which in this case, is music, and moves, especially in the second part, from pure energy to an older form, which is music.

Schrader: Do you have any suggestions for the listener in approaching *Until Spring*?

Subotnick: Besides just listening to it, I would suggest that the listener try to feel the energy movement.

Schrader: You have been composing electronic music for twenty years. How do you feel that the technology you've dealt with has influenced your style?

Subotnick: Well, that's hard to say, because it's conceivable that my style has influenced the technology.

I worked with Don Buchla in the very early stages of synthesizer development. The first Buchla synthesizer was actually designed for me in order to do *Silver Apples of the Moon*. The Buchla synthesizer was tailor-made to suit my style, my concept of electronic music. But as I changed over the years, the synthesizer didn't change. The concept of the synthesizer hasn't changed radically, even with the newer digital systems. I'm not sure, but that may be one of the reasons I've gone back to instrumental music.

Schrader: What are your current interests in electro-acoustic music?

Subotnick: At the moment, I'm interested in using instruments as both sound sources and control devices. I've been working with location, frequency shifting, and gating, but using instrumental rather than electronic sounds. I've moved away from tape music as such.

Schrader: What are your thoughts on the future of electronic music?

Subotnick: I can answer that in two ways: I can say what I think is going to happen, and what I would like to see happen.

What I think will happen is that there will be a big increase in the amount of electronic music composed by using computers, analog synthesizers, and the like. These pieces will be played in auditoriums, people's homes, festivals, and other places where music is ordinarily heard. There will be a modest following for this music, just as there is for other specialized kinds of music.

Personally, I'm not fond of that notion. I think that, as a result, music will become more conservative stylistically. Music will become less dynamic and there will be less growth in the art of music because of the separation and specialization of electronic music.

What I would like to see happen is that composers become like artists in any other field. Sometimes composers would use electronics and sometimes they would use instruments. I would like to see electronic music as part of the whole of making music. Unfortunately, I don't see that as happening.

19

INTERVIEW WITH JEAN-CLAUDE RISSET
Mutations I

Schrader: How did you become interested in computer music?

Risset: My call to music occurred long before I heard of computers. I studied piano with a wonderful teacher, Robert Trimaille, who had learned from Cortot; later, I studied harmony, counterpoint, and composition with Suzanne Demarquez and André Jolivet.

I always had a vivid interest in timbre, and I was intrigued by the fact that certain timbres could or could not lend themselves to certain musical ideas. I am very attached to instruments, but I am very conscious of the limitations they introduce. And so, with my interest in timbre, as well as my extensive background in mathematics and physics, it seemed only natural to look to electronic music. However, I soon became disappointed because I felt it afforded less musical control than instrumental music. One could select from an ocean of sounds, but controlling them was difficult, even with computer-aided compositions. Now, when I heard about the process implemented by Max Mathews for synthesizing sounds by computer, I realized that only such a process could

Jean-Claude Risset. (Photo by Philippe Cocqueux)

afford the desired refinement of control over sound. I was fortunate to be able to work with Mathews in 1964-65 and again from 1967 to 1969. Since that time, I have been incurably infected with the virus of computer music.

Schrader: Do you feel there are any fundamental differences between electronic music composed with synthesizers and computer music?

Risset: Yes, I do; or rather, I should say that I am only interested in the kind of computer music that differs from electronic music composed with synthesizers. A number of composers use the computer simply as a more elaborate synthesizer. Most synthesizer music is a "turn-off" to my ears; the sound is too mechanical, too dull, too repetitive; "dead, embalmed," as Varèse put it. It does not convey much feeling. Much of computer music is the same; but the computer, as a tool, is more powerful, more precise, and, above all, more flexible than a synthesizer. A computer can be shaped so as to be sensitive and congenial to an aesthetic concern about the sound.

Of course, what I said about synthesizers is too general to be true. There are skilled and musical uses of synthesizers. Yet, to me, the analog synthesizer rather restricts the sonic possibilities, and biases them toward instrument-like performance, whereas the computer can open them toward composing, shaping, and sculpting the sound.

In principle, recent digital synthesizers are different from analog synthesizers in that they retain the precision and power of the computer while permitting real-time operation, which can be invaluable. However, the temptation of prolixity is great, and the pressure of real-time performance is not easy to cope with. For me, digital synthesizers are still in their infancy since their software, which really determines how you can use them, is not yet advanced enough.

Schrader: How does your composition *Mutations I* [see Figure 19-1] reflect these distances between analog synthesizers and computers?

Risset: *Mutations I*, composed in 1969 at Bell Labs with the computer, could not have been realized with analog synthesizers. Many sounds it contains are, I think, more lively, more complex than could be obtained with synthesizers. The sounds that seem to go up indefinitely could not have been produced by analog means, because the oscillators could not be tuned one octave apart with enough accuracy and stability. Also, there is not a mere collection of sounds, the sounds are related. The way they are shaped internally is part of the composition of the piece and this is exemplified by the relation between pitch and timbre. In a brief serial section, the amplitude envelopes determine the rhythmic, agogic, and amplitude aspects of the music; and such internal relationships can evolve gradually.

Schrader: How does the title *Mutations* refer to this work?

Risset: The title *Mutations* refers to the gradual transformations which occur throughout the piece, and to the passage from a discontinuous pitch scale, at the beginning, to the pitch continuum, in the last part. There is a transition between the scale and the continuum, in particular through a process of harmonic development, which causes the successive harmonics of the notes of a chord to come out. The higher the harmonic order, the finer the pitch step; hence the scale finally dissolves into the continuum. This process is reminiscent of the use of pipes tuned to harmonics of a given pitch to reinforce or modify its timbre, in the "mixtures" stops of the pipe organ. These stops are also called "jeux de mutations."

Schrader: What are some other examples of transformation in *Mutations*?

Risset: Another example of transformation in *Mutations*, related to the dissolution of quantized steps into a continuum, is the gradually increasing deviation from initially fixed pitch steps. This becomes a pitch inflection, then a strong erratic deviation, then, at the end, a narrow band of noise that is somewhat reminiscent of a distant chorus. Also, the initial chords unfold into twelve-tone rows that, so to say, proliferate into dissolution. And chords made up to harmonic tones are transformed into inharmonic gong-like spectra.

Schrader: What is the relationship between pitch and timbre in *Mutations*?

Risset: In the transformation of chords into inharmonic spectra, the relationship is very close. The timbre of the gong-like clang is a kind of shadow, a prolongation of the harmony of the chord. Although one cannot hear the components of the clang, the relationship of the components to the chord is immediately clear to the ear.

In the harmonic development of a chord, depending on how the successive harmonics develop and what their dynamic contour looks like, the harmonics can be heard as arpeggios or as continuous textures. The timbres of these textures are the result of the pitches of the chord. Therefore, the timbres are a consequence of the pitches. [See Figure 19-1.]

Schrader: One is struck by the wide variety of timbres that exist in *Mutations*. Why did you choose to create this variety?

Risset: The variety of timbres in *Mutations I* reflects my timbre interest and my desire to explore some of the possibilities of the computer. But *Mutations* was also intended as a demonstration piece, an attempt to show that the computer could be more than a powerful, stable synthesizer. In fact,

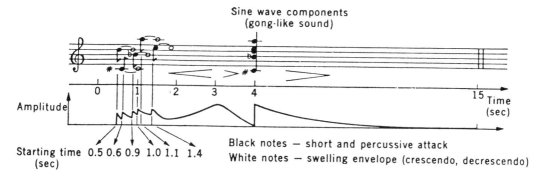

Figure 19-1 Musical excerpt from *Mutations I,* represented in quasi-conventional notation.

Mutations I was commissioned by the Group de Recherches Musicales of the French Radio. The aesthetics of the Groupe favors richness of sound, and tends to reject what has been called the "sequencer syndrome," "electronic note mill," or the "sewing machine music," which are all too common with synthesizers. I tried to show that one could avoid these traps with the computer.

Schrader: Besides pitch and timbre and their specific relationships, what other elements are important in *Mutations*?

Risset: The rhythms are not organized independently, but rather with relationship to the pitch and envelope structures. I extensively used rhythms made up of three or more different pulses with a common multiple so that the pulses would diverge and converge again. Actually, the synchrony is imperfect in order to create a feeling of bounce and multiplicity. I also worked hard at trying to convey a sense of varied dynamics.

Schrader: The general shape of *Mutations* and the type of changes that take place remind one of the theme and variations principle. Is this idea structurally relevant to the work?

Risset: Yes, definitely, although the piece includes continuous evolution and gradual transformation as well as separate variations. At the end of the work there is a kind of memory recapitulation of the initial elements and their transformations. This recapitulation does not happen separately but in superposition with the final glissando. Either of these events can be heard as background or foreground.

Schrader: What suggestions do you have for listening to *Mutations*?

Risset: The piece should be heard on a good playback system. Reproduction systems that are adequate for recordings of instrumental music can fail to do justice to works of computer music. It is difficult to mentally compensate for distortions introduced by mediocre playback systems in so far as one has no mental models of the timbres.

Apart from that, I have few specific suggestions for listening to *Mutations I*. The volume level should be loud enough, yet not too loud, so that the beginning is energetic but without brutality. I like the piece to be performed in a large, live hall, but a variety of conditions is possible. The piece is not difficult to listen to; some gestures are quite clear and one can easily be aware of certain sonic processes that take place.

Schrader: Has your compositional style changed greatly in the years since you composed *Mutations*?

Risset: I think my compositional style has evolved rather than drastically changed. Since composing *Mutations I*, I think I have continued to pursue similar goals but I have also tackled a domain that was an early concern of mine: the interaction between fixed tape and live performers. This is the main theme of my piece *Dialogues*, where the relation between the instruments and the tape is at first one of diaphony, echo, response; but it gradually evolves into one where the tape prolongates the instruments or emanates from their timbres. This close intertwining of instruments and tape is also pursued in my recent piece *Mirages*. In another work of mine, *Inharmonique*, there is a quasi-theatrical confrontation between the soprano and the computer tape. In *Inharmonique*, sounds emerge from noise, then the voice emerges from the tape sounds, flourishes, and is eventually sent far away and buried under the tape sounds. The title *"Inharmonique"* refers to the systematic use of synthetic tones made up of precisely controlled inharmonic partials. Such tones are composed like chords, and they can either fuse into single-pitched klangs or be diffracted into fluid textures. I believe that the control of inharmonic partials is a good example of the possibilities afforded by the computer to control sound structure in music.

Schrader: You have been involved with computer music for several years and you have experienced several technological changes. How do you think the technology of computer music has affected your compositional style?

Risset: In general, I think the computer has given a different perspective toward completely formalized processes that can be easily automated. This is similar to the way the camera gave a different meaning to the imitation of reality in painting.

One can now, to a large extent, design the constraints of one's sonic material. My compositional style is related to the implications of this situation.

Schrader: What are your specific interests at the moment?

Risset: My present concerns involve several continuing interests. For example, I am interested in the problems of the aural analysis of sound. How does hearing organize its perceptions? When are components fused into aural entities; when are they heard as magma; when does their interaction give rise to specific qualities?

Another problem is that of naturalness. How can one prevent a synthetic sound from being a "turn-off" to the ears? Natural sounds evolve and change during their duration.

Adequate programming structures that take such phenomena into account are necessary for the production of sounds with natural and sophisticated timbres.

With the advent of special digital processes, one will be able to control parameters of synthetic sounds in real-time via performance on a musical instrument. This raises the intriguing question of how to best "warp" instrumental gestures, how to use the elaborate and subtle musical skills of instrumentalists to control parameters different than those they are used to attending to.

The computer gives us access to the continuum of sound; does continuum imply indifferentiation? Are discrete categories, quantizing processes, scales, familiar prototypes essential to precise perception, hence to music, susceptible of elaborate listening? Is timbral space continuous and homogeneous, or does it contain sensitive areas, sharp edges, preferred dimensions? I am interested in the musical exploration of such issues.

Schrader: What are your thoughts on the future of electro-acoustic music in general, and of computer music in particular?

Risset: First, although one likes to think that ideas lead technology, things evolve in a more dialectic fashion. The explosion of digital microelectronics will no doubt influence strongly the nature of electro-acoustic music, but what this will imply musically depends upon many factors, including economic ones.

Electro-acoustic music has often developed as a separate branch of music where some amateurs have channeled their musical creativity. Yet I find this schism regrettable as I think that electro-acoustic means are often too rudimentary, especially those that the amateur can afford. The expansion of digital technology could help bridge the gap between electro-acoustic and instrumental music.

Digital systems should become more accessible to the extent that they will be private tools for the independent composer. Also, such digital systems will not by themselves work miracles. They will be demanding tools, especially if one wants to take full advantage of their possibilities.

In the long range, the expansion of digital techniques in music will probably have far-reaching consequences beyond the professional scene. It is possible to develop digital systems that can be used in a variety of ways from a record-player situation, where the "performer" has minimal control, to an instrumental situation where the performer has total control but is also subjected to considerable demands. Between these two extremes one may have many different types of control, like the situation of the conductor who does not produce all the notes but who, (it is to be hoped,) performs significant control. Such a system could offer genuine musical responsibilities to the user without necessarily demanding from him a professional technique. This is utopia, but making such systems available to the public might restore contemporary musical practice; it would help fill the gap between the amateur instrumentalist and this music, which they currently do not relate to their musical practice. In this case, the professional musicians could make proposals of pieces to be played as such, or to be completed or assembled in a variety of ways, and there would be a continuous gamut of degrees of initiative or responsibility that the listener-performer could take. Even if such systems do not become widespread among the public, they should offer to the musicians new and challenging situations. Needless to say, the design and implementation of such systems will take considerable ingenuity and know-how. In fact such development is dependent upon electronic, psychoacoustic, and musical research; but at the present pace of investigation, the prospect is promising.

20
INTERVIEW WITH GORDON MUMMA
Cybersonic Cantilevers

Schrader: How did you first become interested in electro-acoustic music?

Mumma: Several incidents occurred in the late 1940s. My father bought a record player for the newly introduced long-playing records. The 78-rpm device it replaced got into my youthful hands, where it became the victim of experimentation, resulting in my development of a primitive understanding of transducers, electronic amplification, and electrical shock. The local library supplied me with books of electrical projects for budding engineers. In the summer of 1949, while a high school student at a music camp in northern Michigan, I saw my first oscilloscope in action. A musical acoustician on the faculty there demonstrated it, and infected me further with his own enthusiasm for musical electronics. By his disciplined approach to the subject, he established the legitimacy of my pursuit of it. He introduced me to magnetic recording, then done on steel wire, paper, and plastic tape. Back home, near Detroit, a

Gordon Mumma. (Photo by Narrye Davis Caldwell)

few months later, I learned that a neighbor had a complete disc recording studio in his basement. He was a physician by profession, and a bassoonist by avocation. He introduced me to his X-ray machine and [to] the subject of radio-frequency electronics.

I began studying French horn and piano in junior high school, and was very active in amateur and semiprofessional orchestras during my high school and college years. I first studied composition formally with Homer Keller while I was still in high school.

By 1953, I was a university student in Ann Arbor, Michigan. There I composed music and sound effects for plays produced by the Theater Department. They had two tape recorders, which were ordinarily used to record conventional instruments, or sound effects records. I had soon modified them to interact with each other. My success at making electronically generated music with these tape recorders was probably due to a precarious balance between my knowledge of some aspects and ignorance of other aspects of electronic circuitry.

I don't recall when I learned that other people composed music with electronic means, and I don't recall when I first heard the term "electro-acoustic music." But, by 1956, I had disc recordings of musique concrète from the ORTF, of Les Paul, of electronic music from Cologne, and tapes of Ussachevsky's early works. By 1958 I had produced my first large scale electronic composition, music for an Ann Arbor production of Ionesco's *The Bald Soprano*, and had established an electronic music studio with Robert Ashley. We called it the Cooperative Studio for Electronic Music.

Schrader: A great deal of your work has been in the area of live/electronic music. What interests you in this medium?

Mumma: I may be best known for my work with live/electronic music, and certainly have spent much of my creative time involved with it. But, in terms of actual compositional output, it's possible that I have done more studio-composed electronic music and notated music for conventional instruments. Nonetheless, music for me has always been primarily a performance-oriented art.

What interests me particularly about live/electronic music is that it is an interactive art, either with other people or with electro-acoustic circuitry, or both. One of the hype claims for electronic music is that the composer can control everything. That's probably not true in any circumstances, and I'm uneasy with the political and philosophical implications of such an idea anyway. My personal interest is with matters of *influence* rather than *control*. In my live/electronic work I explore the influences and interactions among myself and other people and the electro-acoustic circuitry that is our "instrument." Quotation marks should be around "instrument" because it means environment as much as it refers to the object for making sound.

Music has a long history of being a means of influence. Early peoples used sound, if they didn't call it music, to influence the forces of their lives. In present day commodity-oriented cultures of mass communications, music-sound tends to be used to influence people to consume things: by things, I mean goods, gadgets, ideas, and my patience.

Returning to the question of live/electronic music, I still find myself excited by that precarious balance between what I know and don't know about the electronic components I use and circuits I design for my music. In that precarious state, I discover things to accomplish by electronic means that were not previously in my mind, nor probably in the minds of the designers of the components.

Schrader: How are these ideas represented in *Cybersonic Cantilevers*?

Mumma: My idea of *Cybersonic Cantilevers* was an interactive system, with electronic components and human participants having influence on each other. Thus, I thought of *Cyber-*

sonic Cantilevers as a process, rather than a composition or "product." And I made *Cybersonic Cantilevers* as an event for art galleries or places of relatively easier public access than concert halls.

My concern with easy public access was to make a situation where participants wouldn't be intimidated about the question of their performance skills, and yet they would really be live performers. Furthermore, I wanted the participants to be able to contribute the basic sounds of the piece. As much as possible, I wanted to be an equal participant with the public, and avoid the distinction of myself as composer or skilled performer.

In some respects, we weren't able to be equal, since I designed and built the electronic circuitry for *Cybersonic Cantilevers*, and that required experience and skills not common to the general public. It would have been a rather long event if we had all participated in building it from scratch! However, the way I design and build electronic circuitry is a special kind of participatory process of its own: we—the circuitry and my ideas about it—influence each other. Most of the circuits of *Cybersonic Cantilevers* involved analog rather than digital electronics. Here's a generalization: digital is a control technology, analog is an influence technology. As a designer-composer-performer with the mostly analog circuits of *Cybersonic Cantilevers*, I had more influence than control.

Performance skills develop mostly by participating in live performance. One of the things I intended with *Cybersonic Cantilevers* was to make a "composition" that would invite and encourage participants to develop performance skills and ensemble sensitivity.

Schrader: You have referred to *Cybersonic Cantilevers* as an "electronic system or process." What do you mean by this?

Mumma: The system had two parts: electronic and human. The electronic part was a configuration of electronic sound transforming and control circuits that I designed for *Cybersonic Cantilevers*. The human part was the public, which would bring sounds recorded on cassettes or live through microphones, and have access to the electronic part at monitor stations. Each of these stations had stereophonic headphones and an oscilloscope with which the participants could monitor the various transformations, and a panel of switches with which they could change or influence aspects of the transformations. This electronic system was spread over large tables in the gallery, visible and accessible to the public.

The sound transformations could be very simple, or develop such complexity that the original sounds became unrecognizable. Technically, there were four types of transformations: of the pitch, loudness, timbre, and combinations of sound. If the sounds were stereophonic, the modifications could maintain the stereo aspect. Some of the transformations were automatically derived from the sounds themselves, some were derived from the programmed control circuits, and some from the interaction of the participants with the electronic system. The entire system was really semiautomatic, since completely automatic aspects were derived from the interaction of the participants with the electronic circuits.

My invented term "cybersonic" originates with the Greek *kybernan*, meaning to steer or guide. It refers to the term *cybernetics*, the science of control and communication, and to the interactions between automatic control and living organisms.

The participants were free to remain passive spectators, using the monitor stations only to listen and look at the transformations. They could also listen over loudspeakers in the gallery. Or they could contribute original sounds, and use the monitor station switch-panel to influence the transformations and develop interactions with other participants. *Cybersonic Cantilevers* is related to other processes—games, communication, biofeedback, telemetry—in which people participate in discovery, development of perception and skills, intellectual challenge, and entertainment.

Schrader: What is the purpose of the use of indeterminacy in *Cybersonic Cantilevers*?

Mumma: There are certainly indeterminate aspects to *Cybersonic Cantilevers*. I designed the electronic control and modification circuits to do specific things, but made their configurations sufficiently complex to limit my ability to determine much of the results of the sound transformations. Further, my instructions to the public were limited to a simple introduction to the monitor station functions, and an invitation to explore the system and process on their own. The participants contributed the original sounds.

The musical structure of the event was not determined in musically traditional ways; it was a result of the process of interaction between the participants and the electronic system. The beginning and end of the event were determined by circumstances: It began as soon after the gallery opened as I could get the system operating, and ended when the gallery closed. At times during the event there might be no sound occurring, either because the transformation circuits made it inaudible, or because the participants hadn't put sound into the system; but the process and the event continued. So my main purpose in using indeterminacy was to maximize the participants ability to influence, and minimize their ability to control the event.

Schrader: How does the audience participation aspect of this work relate to this?

Mumma: Here are two examples. The *Cybersonic Cantilevers* excerpt recorded on Folkways has a brief introductory section. The sounds of that introduction are transformations of two young participants at the Everson Museum in Syracuse, New York. They are each at a monitor station, saying "hello" to each other into the live microphones, and laughing at the drastic transformations they hear on their headphones.

   The second example is more revealing. The last section of the Folkways excerpt is part of a "control signal chorale" from the late evening of a day-long *Cybersonic Cantilevers* production done at WBAI-FM in New York City. The several remaining participants, having exhausted their supply of cassette-recorded sounds and live sounds via microphones, explored the unforeseen possibilities of delicately adjusting the switches of their monitor stations to intermediate positions. By this means, they obtained access to control signals of the electronic system that I had not intended to be audible. They developed this "chorale" without my participation, and concluded it just before the end of the WBAI broadcast. I was very impressed that they had learned to interact with the *Cybersonic Cantilevers* system in a way I had not foreseen, and, with a collective intuition, had concluded the "chorale" at a convenient time for the end of the broadcast. Inquiring who they were, I learned that they did not know each other, had never previously spoken or made plans about their participation together. They had discovered and developed their "ensemble" entirely by participating in the *Cybersonic Cantilevers* process.

Schrader: What is the relationship between an actual "performance" of *Cybersonic Cantilevers* and the commercially released recording of the work?

Mumma: Remember that I didn't have in mind that *Cybersonic Cantilevers* would be a "performance," but rather an occasion in which performance activities might occur, depending on what the participants brought to it as sound materials, and how they interacted with the system or with one another.

   The commercially released recording on Folkways, then, is a "composition" made of materials recorded on two occasions where *Cybersonic Cantilevers* was presented. The New York State Council on the Arts, which gave me a grant to implement part of the original work, later became involved in a recording project and asked me to contribute some aspect of *Cybersonic Cantilevers* to it. I tried to give them something else, but, of course, the grant was for *Cybersonic Cantilevers* rather than for something else.

   I auditioned many hours of tapes that had been recorded directly from the *Cybersonic Cantilevers* system during the two occasions and chose three sequences that seemed to me to make compositional sense for a recording. I've described the first and last sections already. The middle section on the Folkways recording consists mostly of transformed sounds from contributed cassettes, including a vintage radio crime drama, popular music, and recycled transformations of previously processed sound. I developed the recycled material into a transition that evolves into the "chorale." The record producer told me they wanted music for an entire side of a long-playing record, so I made a composition of about nineteen minutes.

   This nineteen-minute composition is *not* what is on the Folkways recording. The nature of the recording project changed, without my knowing it, and the record company decided they needed about half as much as they had asked me to give them. So they cut off the last part of the piece. Simple as that. The ending "chorale," for which I have a special fondness, is very much abbreviated. Apparently they didn't listen very carefully to the tape I sent them. They seem to have assumed that the loudest part of the piece was the ending. They made a fanciful program note for the record jacket, which says "the end is followed by a few minutes of tape for use as 'Do It Yourself' participation." Well, that may have potential for some sort of autoerotic occasion, but it was not my idea. Indeterminacy strikes again.

Schrader: Much of the equipment used in *Cybersonic Cantilevers* was designed and built by you. Do you think these capabilities are generally important for the composer of electro-acoustic music?

Mumma: They were fundamental to me because I began composing with electro-acoustic means at a time when, except for tape recorders, microphones, amplifiers, loudspeakers, and clumsy oscillators, specialized equipment didn't exist. It was certainly fundamental to the development of my compositional aesthetics. It stimulated my experimentation with a syntax of electro-acoustical sounds that was minimally imitative of instrumental and vocal traditions. Further, my creative work with electronic circuitry was as rewarding to me as composing sounds, whether on recording tape or as notes on paper. This may account for my relatively early development of compositions that were process-oriented.

Since the development of relatively standard, commercial electronic music equipment, it isn't necessary for a composer to have much electronic background to compose with electro-acoustic means. But I find few composers or performers like this who are making interesting original work. I'm occasionally astonished by the virtuosity of a composer or performer who imitates another's work, sometimes with greater virtuosity even than the originator. But my astonishment with such surface virtuosity soon fades.

Large electronic arts systems are clumsy enough without clumsy human intervention. If for none other than humanistic reasons, I'd encourage creative artists to develop substantial technological background.

Schrader: What are your current compositional interests?

Mumma: During the past several years I've made electro-acoustic pieces for modern dance, theater, and live performance situations, and I'm now preparing them for recording. One of these was an evening long collaborative work with choreographer Jann McCauley and author Tom Robbins. The revisions necessary to make it musically sensible for a recording involve a substantial recomposition of the original piece. Another project was a collaboration of artists, actors, and dancers, in which Pauline Oliveros and I co-composed and performed the music. We're considering a re-creation of the work as a radio program. I've also been composing for solo harpsichord (a series of short pieces) and for clavichord. The clavichord work, *Los Desaparecidos*, is a single long composition that may have cybersonic aspects to it. I'm composing for clavichord and harpsichord because of the challenge of defined, limited resources for which there is a living tradition of virtuoso performers. Even in competition with extravagant electronic apparatus, the clavichord remains the most efficient of expressive keyboard instruments.

Schrader: What are your thoughts on the future of electro-acoustic music?

Mumma: The increasingly widespread availability of electronic music equipment, and particularly of computer technology, should attract more diverse creative artists to work with electro-acoustic media. Besides their artistic explorations, I hope those artists explore alternative ways of disseminating and sharing their work. Then, perhaps, the discouraging pressures of commercial and parochial academic interests will become less of an influence on creative imagination, and electro-acoustic music will develop greater cultural multiplicity.

BIBLIOGRAPHY

The following bibliography is intended to furnish the reader with additional and more detailed information on various topics in the field of electro-acoustic music. It is a limited and selective bibliography, consisting primarily of books and suggested periodicals. Readers who wish to do research in a given area are directed to the bibliographies listed below; they provide literally thousands of references on various aspects of electro-acoustic music.

I. BOOKS

A. General

Acero, Antonio. *Panorama de la Musica Conreta y Electrónica.* La Habana: Ediciones del Departmento de Musica de la Biblioteca Nacional José Marti, 1965.

Appleton, Jon H. and Ronald C. Perera, eds. *The Development and Practice of Electronic Music.* Englewood Cliffs, NJ: Prentice-Hall, Inc., 1975.

Berenguer, Jose. *Introduccion a la Musica Electroacustica*. Valencia: F. Torres, 1974.

Chion, Michel and Guy Reibel. *Le Musique Electroacoustique*. Aix-en-Provence: C.Y. Chaudoreille, 1976.

Deutsch, Herbert A. *Synthesis*. Port Washington, NY: Aflred Publishing Co., 1976.

Dolan, Robert Emmett. *Music in Modern Media*. New York: G. Schirmer, 1964.

Eimert, Herbert. *Das Lexikon der Elektronischen Musik*. Regensburg: Bosse, 1973.

Electronic Music. Washington, DC: Music Educators National Conference, 1968. (Originally published as the November 1968 issue of the *Music Educators Journal*.)

Ernst, David. *The Evolution of Electronic Music*. New York: Schirmer Books, 1977.

Gentilucci, Armando. *Introduztione alla Musica Elettronica*. Milano: Feltrinelli, 1972.

Judd, Frederick Charles. *Electronic Music and Musique Concrète*. London: Neville Spearman, Ltd., 1961.

Lorentzen, Bengt. *An Introduction to Electronic Music*. Rockville Center, N.Y.: Belwin Mills Co., 1970.

Schwartz, Elliott. *Electronic Music: A Listener's Guide* (rev. ed.). New York: Praeger Publishers, Inc., 1975.

Sear, Walter. *The New World of Electronic Music*. New York: Alfred Publishers, 1972.

B.   Acoustics and Physics of Sound

Backus, John. *The Acoustical Foundation of Music*. New York: W.W. Norton & Co., Inc., 1969.

Benade, Arthur H. *Strings, Horns, and Harmony*. Garden City, NY: Doubleday & Co., Inc., 1960.

Gulick, L. *Hearing, Physiology, and Psychophysics*. New York: Oxford University Press, 1971.

Hall, Donald E. *Musical Acoustics: An Introduction*. Belmont, CA: Wadsworth Publishing Co., Inc., 1980.

Helmholtz, Hermann. *On the Sensations of Tone*. Translated by A.J. Ellis. New York: Dover Publications, Inc., 1954.

Olsen, Harry F. *Music, Physics and Engineering*. (2nd ed.). New York: Dover Publications, Inc., 1967.

VanBergeijk, Wilhelm A. *et al. Waves and the Ear*. Garden City, NY: Doubleday, 1960.

Winckel, Fritz. *Music, Sound and Sensation.* Translated by T. Binkley. New York: Dover Publications, Inc., 1967.

C. Computer Music

Bateman, Wayne. *Introduction to Computer Music.* New York: John Wiley & Sons, Inc., 1980.

Beauchamp, James W. and Heinz von Foerster, eds. *Music by Computers.* New York: John Wiley & Sons, Inc., 1969.

Chowning, John M. *Computer Simulation of Music Instruments in Reverberant Environments.* Stanford, CA: Department of Music, Stanford University, 1974.

Hiller, Lejaren. *Music Composed with a Computer: An Historical Survey.* Urbana, IL: University of Illinois School of Music, 1969 (Illinois Technical Report No. 18).

Hiller, Lejaren, and L.M. Isaacson. *Experimental Music—Composition with an Electronic Computer.* New York: McGraw-Hill Book Company, 1959.

Howe, Hubert. *Electronic Music Synthesis.* New York: W.W. Norton and Co., Inc., 1975.

Lincoln, Harry, ed. *The Computer and Music.* Ithaca: Cornell University Press, 1970.

Mathews, Max V. *The Technology of Computer Music.* Cambridge, MA: MIT Press, 1969.

D. Electro-Acoustic Musical Instruments

Crowhurst, Norma. *Electronic Music Instruments.* Blue Ridge Summit, PA: TAB Books, 1971.

Douglas, Alan. *The Electronic Musical Instrument Manual: A Guide to Theory and Design,* (6th ed.). London: Pitman, 1976.

Dorf, Richard H. *Electronic Musical Instruments,* (3rd ed.). New York: Radiofile, 1968.

Engel, Georg. *Elektromechanische und Vallelektronische Musikinstrumente.* Berlin: Militarverlag der Deutschen Demokratischen Republik, 1975.

Juster, F. *Petits instruments électroniques de musique et leur réalisation.* Paris: Editions techniques et scientifiques Françaises; diffusion: Librairie Parisienne de la radio, 1973.

E. Electronic Music

Douglas, Alan. *Electronic Music Production.* New York: Pitman Publishing Corp., 1973.

Dwyer, Terence. *Making Electronic Music: A Course for Schools.* London: Oxford University Press, 1975.

Eaton, M.L. *Electronic Music—A Handbook of Sound Synthesis and Control.* Kansas City: Orcus Research, 1969.

Howe, Hubert S. *Electronic Music Synthesis.* New York: W.W. Norton & Co., Inc., 1975.

Jenkins, John. *Electric Music: A Practical Manual.* Bloomington, IN: Indiana University Press, 1976. *

Strange, Allen. *Electronic Music.* Dubuque: William C. Brown Co., Publishers, 1972.

Trythall, Gilbert. *Principles and Practice of Electronic Music.* New York: Grosset & Dunlap, Inc., 1973.

Wells, Thomas and Eric S. Vogel. *The Technique of Electronic Music.* Austin: University Stores, Inc., 1974. (Available from University Stores, Inc., P.O. Box 7756. Austin, TX 78712.)

F.   Electronics

Brown, Robert Michael and Mark Olsen. *Experimenting with Electronic Music.* Blue Ridge Summit, PA: TAB Books, 1974.

Buban, Peter and M.L. Schmitt. *Understanding Electricity and Electronics.* New York: McGraw-Hill Book Company, 1969.

Mims, Forrest M. *Electronic Music Projects.* Fort Worth, TX: Radio Shack, 1976.

Ward, Brice. *Electronic Music Circuit Guide Book.* Blue Ridge Summit, PA: TAB Books, 1975.

G.   History

Russcol, Herbert. *The Liberation of Sound.* Englewood Cliffs, NJ: Prentice-Hall, Inc., 1972.

H.   Live/Electronic Music

To date, no books have been written on live/electronic music. The reader is referred to the books listed in the *general* category of this bibliography.

I.   Musique Concrète

Dwyer, Terence. *Composing with Tape Recorders.* London: Oxford University Press, 1971.

Ernst, David. *Musique Concrète.* Boston: Crescendo, 1972.

Haynes, N.M. *Tape Editing and Splicing.* Flushing, NY: Robin Industries, 1957.

Schaeffer, Pierre. *A la recherche d'une musique concrète.* Paris: Editions du Seuil, 1952.

———. *La Musique Concrète.* Paris: Presses Universitaires de France, 1967.

———. *Traité des objects musicaux.* Paris: Editions de Seuil, 1966.

J. Notation

With the possible exception of part of an unpublished manuscript by Gardner Read, no one, as yet, has written extensively and systematically on the subject of electro-acoustic music notation. The reader is referred to the following bibliography which lists numerous references on isolated examples.

Warfield, Gerald. *Writings on Contemporary Music Notation: An Annotated Bibliography.* Ann Arbor, MI: Music Library Association, 1976.

K. Recording Techniques

Runstein, Robert E. *Modern Recording Techniques.* Indianapolis: Howard W. Sams & Co., Inc., 1974.

L. Twentieth-Century Music

Austin, William W. *Music in the 20th Century.* New York: W.W. Norton & Co., Inc., 1966.

Cope, David. *New Directions in Music.* (2nd ed.). Dubuque: William C. Brown Co., Publishers, 1974.

Martin, William and Julius Drossin. *Music of the Twentieth Century.* Englewood Cliffs, NJ: Prentice-Hall, Inc., 1980.

Saltzman, Eric. *Twentieth-Century Music: An Introduction.* Englewood Cliffs, NJ: Prentice-Hall, Inc., 1967.

Slonimsky, Nicolas. *Music Since 1900.* (4th ed.). New York: Charles Scribner's Sons, 1971.

II. PERIODICALS

Analog Sounds. New York (12 West 17th Street, NY, NY 10011).

Computer Music Journal. MIT Press.

Electronic Music Reports, Vol. 1-4 (1969-71). Utrecht: Institute of Sonology.

Electronic Music Review, Vol. 1-7. Trumansburg, NY: Independent Electronic Music Center. Publication ceased in 1969.

Gravesaner Blatter, Mainz, Germany.

Interface. Amsterdam: Swets and Zeitlinger.

The Journal of the Acoustical Society of America. New York: American Institute of Physics.

Journal of the Audio Engineering Society. New York: Audio Engineering Society.

Journal of Music Theory. New Haven, CN: Yale University Press.

Key Notes. Amsterdam: Donemus.

Perspectives of New Music. Annandale-on-Hudson, NY, 12504.

Die Reihe. Vienna: Universal Edition. English translations published by European-American Music, Clifton, NJ.

La Revue Musicale. Paris. Of special interest is *Music and Technology*, Stockholm meeting, June 8-12, 1970, organized by UNESCO, published by *La Revue Musicale*, Paris, 1971.

Source Magazine-Music of the Avant-Garde. Vol. 1-12. Sacramento, CA. Publication ceased in 1972.

Synapse. Los Angeles. (1052 W. Sixth St., 90017.) Publication ceased in 1979.

Synthesis. Minneapolis, MN: Scully-Cutter Publishing, Inc. Only one issue was published.

III. BIBLIOGRAPHIES

Bahler, Peter Benjamin.   *Electronic and Computer Music: An Annotated Bibliography of Writings in English*. Unpublished M.A. thesis. University of Rochester, 1966.

Bassart, Ann Phillips.   *Serial Music: A Classified Bibliography of Writings on Twelve-Tone and Electronic Music*. Toronto: University of Toronto Press, 1967.

Battier, Marc et Jacques Arveiller.   *Musique et Informatique: une bibliographie indexée*. Paris: Department Musique, Department Information Université Paris, 1976.

Buxton, William, ed.   *Computer Music 1976/77: A Directory to Current Work*. Ottowa: 1977.

Cross, Lowell M., ed.   *A Bibliography of Electronic Music*. Toronto:University of Toronto Press, 1967.

Davies, Hugh, ed.   *International Electronic Music Catalogue*. Cambridge, MA: MIT Press.

Edwards, J. Michele. *Literature for Voices in Combination with Electronic and Tape music: An Annotated Bibliography.* Ann Arbor, MI: Music Library Association, 1977.

Henry, Otto. *A Preliminary Checklist: Books and Articles on Electronic Music.* New Orleans, 1966.

Kostka, Stefan. *A Bibliography of Computer Applications in Music.* Hackensack, NJ: Joseph Boonin, Inc., 1974.

RILM Abstracts. New York. (International RILM Center, The City University of New York, 33 West 42nd St., New York, 10036.)

Tjepkema, Sandra L. *A Bibliography of Computer Music.* Iowa City, IA: The University of Iowa Press, 1981.

IV. DISCOGRAPHY

Kondracki, Miroslaw, Marta Stankiewicz, and Frits. C. Weiland. *International Electronic Music Discography.* Mainz: B. Schott, 1979.

V. SCORES

Arel, Bulent. *Stereo Electronic Music No. 1.* American Composers Alliance.

——. *Stereo Electronic Music No. 2.* American Composers Alliance.

Ashley, Robert. *The Wolfman. Source, music of the avant-garde,* 4 (1968), 5-6.

Badings, Henk. *Capriccio for Violin and Two Sound Tracks.* Donemus.

Brown, Earle. *Times Five.* Universal Editions 15285.

Cage, John. *Cartridge Music.* C.F. Peters 6703.

——. *Fontana Mix.* C.F. Peters 6712.

——. *Imaginary Landscape No. 1.* C.F. Peters 6709.

——. *Williams Mix.* C.F. Peters 6774.

Davidovsky, Mario. *Synchronism No. 2.* McGinnis and Marx.

——. *Synchronism No. 3.* McGinnis and Marx.

——. *Synchronism No. 5.* Belwin Mills.

——. *Synchronism No. 6.* E.B. Marks.

Druckman, Jacob. *Animus I.* Mercury Music.

Erb, Donald. *Reconnaissance.* Theodore Presser.

Hampton, Calvin. *Catch-Up.* C.F. Peters 66175a/b.

Ichyangi, Toshi. *Extended Voices.* C.F. Peters 66145.

Lora-Totino, Arrago. *English Phonemes 1970. Source, music of the avant-garde,* 9 (1971), 11-16.

Lucier, Alvin.   *I Am Sitting in a Room. Source, music of the avant-garde,*
    7 (1970), 60.

Luening, Otto.   *Low Speed.* American Composers Alliance.

Luening, Otto and Vladimir Ussachevsky.   *Concerted Piece for Tape
    Recorder and Orchestra.* C.F. Peters 66010.

———.   *Incantation.* American Composers Alliance.

Maderna, Bruno.   *Musica su Due Dimensioni.* S. Zerboni.

Messiaen, Oliver.   *Turanglia-Symphony.* Elkan-Vogel.

Moss, Lawrence.   *Auditions.* Carl Fischer.

Reich, Steve.   *Violin Phase.* Universal Editions.

Schäffer, Boguslaw.   *Symfonia.* PWP.

Stockhausen, Karlheinz.   *Hymnen.* Universal Editions.

———.   *Kontakte.* Universal Editions 13678.

———.   *Mixtur.* Universal Editions 14261.

———.   *Momente.* Universal Editions.

———.   *Study II.* Universal Editions 12466.

———.   *Telemusik.* Universal Editions 14807.

Subotnick, Morton.   *Laminations.* Belwin Mills.

Ussachevsky, Vladimir.   *A Piece for Tape Recorder.* American Composers
    Alliance.

———.   *Sonic Contours.* American Composers Alliance.

Powell, Mel.   *Events.* G. Schirmer.

———.   *Second Electronic Setting.* G. Schirmer.

Varèse, Edgard.   *Déserts.* Colombo.

Wourinen, Charles.   *Time's Encomium.* C. F. Peters 66455.

INDEX